GRAPHIC ART OF THE PRE-IMPRESSIONISTS

MICHEL MELOT

GRAPHIC ART OF THE

PRE-IMPRESSIONISTS

TRANSLATED FROM THE FRENCH BY ROBERT ERICH WOLF

HARRY N. ABRAMS, INC., PUBLISHERS, NEW YORK

to Jean Adhémar

Editor: Lory Frankel

Library of Congress Cataloging in Publication Data

Melot, Michel.
  Graphic art of the pre-impressionists.

  Translation of Les grands graveurs.
  Bibliography: p. 25
  Includes index.
  1. Prints, French. 2. Prints — 19th century — France.
  3. Printmakers — France. I. Title.
NE647.3.M4413 769′.92′2   79-26418
ISBN 0-8109-0975-8

©1978 Arts et Métiers Graphiques, Paris

English translation © 1980 Harry N. Abrams, Inc.

Published in 1981 by Harry N. Abrams, Incorporated,
New York. All rights reserved. No part of the contents of this
book may be reproduced without the written permission of
the publishers

Printed and bound in Switzerland

CONTENTS

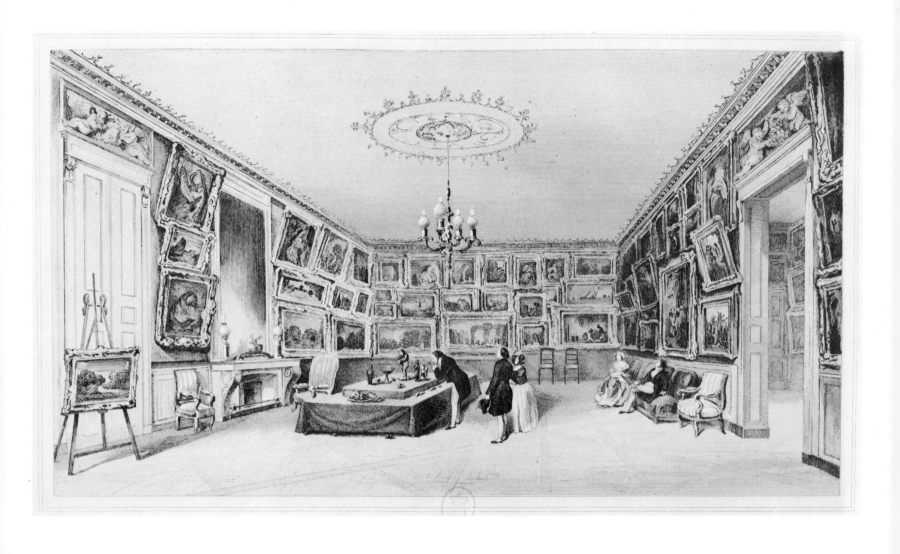

CHARLES-FRANÇOIS DAUBIGNY. *Main Salon of the Galerie Durand-Ruel*, frontispiece for *Spécimens les plus brillants de l'école moderne*, Paris, Durand-Ruel, 1845.

INTRODUCTION TO THE CATALOGUE

I

Nothing is so tendentious as a catalogue raisonné. More often than not such catalogues are unreasonable and in fact irrational, and this because they follow principles (often without even knowing them) that it never occurs to their authors might need justifying. The result is a good lot of conventions served up in blind obedience to what looks like, but is not, scientific rigor. And a good lot of contradictions that never even seem to bother the cataloguers.

Most often the body of works assembled in a catalogue looks homogeneous enough to give the impression that what you have in hand is reliably objective. Not so with the catalogues in this book. So different in nature and techniques are the prints studied here that some explanation is in order. The reasons for this, though, are not to be looked for within the period when the works were done but rather in the period when they were first catalogued, because such disparities can only come from a difference in the way those two periods appreciated them.

Here as elsewhere—though more than elsewhere—the catalogues appear to be selective, though with a choice marked by certain rules thought to be universal. They are, however, no more than the personal guidelines of the catalogue makers, of their time and particular situations, and are sometimes even in contradiction with the spirit of the works selected. This is particularly obvious in the present book. Between the earliest production—the lithograph by Corot of about 1820—and the latest—the etching by Boudin published in 1899—the role of the print and its appreciation by the public were radically altered by the industrial revolution and great social changes. Those two images have nothing in common: only the idea of the catalogue brings them together, giving the impression that there was a failure of communication between artists and cataloguer.

Take the most striking example of this. The reader should be forewarned that our catalogue of the engraved work of Daubigny, even after the monumental inventory of Loÿs Delteil, leaves aside the larger part of it: the vignettes he drew on wood to illustrate dozens of books, periodicals, and tourist guidebooks. Yet that same sort of work figures in the catalogue when engraved on steel. This is because when working on wood Daubigny did not really *engrave* in the strict sense of the word (from the German *graben*: to dig) but left that task to a mere worker, whereas with steel plates he himself took care of the biting. But since that technical difference affects neither the iconography, composition, nature of the print, nor, relatively, its style, why and how has it come to justify such a radical picking and choosing from the artist's overall output?

Whatever one's first impression might suggest, this is not a matter of keeping to *original* works exclusively, those in which the artist produced both the drawing and the engraving, since Daubigny's illustrations engraved on steel were often reproductions after works of which he was not himself the author. If one argues then that room should be made in catalogues only for engravings (in the strict sense) done by the artist himself, including even those of which he was the engraver but not the *inventor*, what is one to do about Corot who never, strictly speaking, engraved but left that to experienced practitioners and contented himself with drawing on copper plates—which was no more and no less than what Daubigny did on wood blocks? One can reply (but the argument barely holds water) that the drawing on wood may have been merely transferred or, as was surely the case at times, "mechanized," which means that the artist's hand never had to touch the block used for printing. Yet, when it comes to Corot, we do accept his "paper-transfers," the so-called autolithographs. And as for Millet, our catalogue of his engravings includes prints done from wood blocks on which he drew but which were incised by his brothers, in which case the definition of what is or is not an authentic art work seems to become a family matter or even—perhaps above all?—a matter of reputation.

Thus the reader will be startled to find, in one and the same catalogue, reproduction-prints, illustrations for documentary works, commercial posters (if executed in a certain manner), and original prints in the sense generally understood today. Nor do we intend to try to squirm out of it with the touching phrases resorted to by Étienne Moreau-Nélaton to "excuse" Daubigny for producing prints not really his: "Such a good soul, did he not accept without wincing, when there was no way of getting out of it, the duty of forgetting himself in order to serve the copper plate as interpreter of someone else? A job of that sort, inflicted on his modesty . . . " In the production of Daubigny the difference is clear between engravings done on order and others resulting from personal invention. In the catalogues, however, the distinction between the works he engraved and those engraved by others is rather less clear, and is not always the same as the former. In short, it is impossible to understand how these catalogues were arrived at without somewhat more explanation.

II

Each of the artists presented here has already been the object of more than one catalogue, and the first distinction to be made is between the generations to which their cataloguers belonged. The earliest were not necessarily professionals or collectors but merely friends eager to do their bit toward the glory of the artist. Frédéric Henriet was a functionary of the government Bureau of Fine Arts and may perhaps just squeeze into the professional camp as an occasional critic who turned out an article or so championing one artist or another. It was he who published in 1874, shortly before the painter's death, the catalogue of engravings by Daubigny, something he did for Léon Lhermitte as well. Alfred Sensier was also a functionary but in the Ministry of the Interior, and it was with rather less pretension in the cultural field that he collected everything to do with his friend Millet. However, when it came to putting together the first catalogue of that artist's engravings in 1861 it was the critic Philippe Burty who was asked to take it on, and his listings were very incomplete since he set aside everything that struck him as unfinished, perhaps seeing no urgent reason for including prints that ordinary collectors could not hope to acquire. Subsequently, his scarcely exhaustive list was given further circulation in a book devoted to Millet published in 1876 by the art lover Alexandre Piedagnel. Not until after Sensier died was his book brought out, thanks to Paul Mantz, and it contained the first complete catalogue of Millet's prints as compiled by the collector Alfred Lebrun from the material he had acquired from Sensier. As for Corot, it was in the family of his friend Dutilleux that he found his first hagiographer: Alfred Robaut, Dutilleux's son-in-law, like Sensier and Henriet played the ambiguous role of biographer-courtier.

After the reputation of those artists became established, due in part at least to the efforts of those first cataloguers, a second generation—specialists this time—took over the preparation of systematic repertories. The New York art dealer Frederick Keppel bought up the entire lot of Millet prints owned by Alfred Lebrun and in 1886 translated and completed that enthusiast's catalogue. Another art dealer, Loÿs Delteil, compiler of the great inventory published as the multivolume *Le Peintre-graveur illustré*, included Millet, Jongkind, Dupré, and Rousseau in his first volume in 1906, Corot in the fifth volume in 1910, Daubigny in the thirteenth volume in 1921. That was a period when the existence of a large number of collectors made such huge publications feasible. But cataloguing after 1900 art objects from before 1875, and doing it on the principles approved by those later collectors, led Delteil to commit anachronisms and made his entire task factitious for lack of a solid base of critical historical studies.

What then were the grounds for the choices—resulting in this volume—made by the cataloguers? To what conception of the art object did their choices respond? Such questions pose problems that are much more general than those concerning prints in particular. In this introduction to a volume of prints we certainly cannot cope with such vast matters as the rightness or wrongness of gathering works of art under the name of the individual who in fact produced them, or the reasons why this handful of artists should be singled out among the thousands who were their contemporaries and whose work has never been systematically catalogued. At the most we can say a few words about the specific aspects of those matters insofar as they concern us here. The idea that a work of art to begin with (and often to end with) must be explained as an individual creation does not date from the nineteenth century. However, this conception, born during the Renaissance, reached its peak at the precise time the prints catalogued here were being produced. One of the first French art magazines, founded in 1831 to champion the new Romantic school and which is often cited in our catalogue as the most faithful supporter of Daubigny, was given the name *L'Artiste*. In that period of profound changes in French society the personage of the artist was taking on a new stance. As late as 1910 Loÿs Delteil could begin the preface to his catalogue of the prints of Camille Corot with the exclamation "Corot!"—which is its own eloquent commentary. One does wonder, of course, why history, when it deals with art, immediately transforms itself into invocations. Corot is a perfect product of that mythified conception of the artist and, indeed, the one who most lends himself to being victimized by it. The almost piously worshipful literature by his self-appointed incense bearers Robaut and Étienne Moreau-Nélaton celebrates his every word, his every gesture. Even the scraps of paper to which the artist consigned quotidian banalities went through the transfiguration process and, with an extraordinary piety, were gathered in sumptuously bound volumes and enshrined in the Bibliothèque Nationale of France. All of which contrasts with the pompous personality of Corot, whose heart was bigger than his mind and whom the critic Pelletan could dub "the most inoffensive of artists."

But there you have the first rule of the catalogue raisonné: to gather every last crumb and hint of and about an individual who was born, lived, and died, which at first sight does seem to be some sort of objective criterion. But since one cannot really re-create the personage, among what he said and did there has to be a choice of certain of his inventions and these then become his "works," his oeuvre. And under that banner the merchandise is passed or ruled out by the cataloguer, who thereby becomes a sort of art-historical gendarme. This has grave consequences for prints, because it so happens that the very basis of selection, the status of printed images as works of art, is by no means clear. With Daubigny the weeding out and purging has been particularly severe, with Corot decidedly generous. Above all—advantage? drawback?—once the signature passes muster anything goes. It is clear, for example, that in the eyes of certain cataloguers who specialized in engravings, Corot was not an engraver of prime importance and that for them his fame as a painter largely underwrote what he did in the graphic arts. Delteil calls attention to the fact that his first catalogue of Corot's prints begins only at number 3,123 of his total works, and Beraldi makes no bones about it: "He left fourteen etchings, mostly of a summary and not very sure workmanship, but interesting *like everything that comes from such a painter*" (our italics). There you are: *all* Corot must be catalogued. That is a warranty for Corot. But nonetheless that necessity does seem rather less than necessary to anyone who seeks to appreciate in his work something other than the fruit of an isolated experiment. What gives support to the fundamental idea of the catalogue *by artist* is first and always the belief in the transcendental quality of one's man.

Be that as it may, that rule is anything but handy when it comes to cataloguing graphic works, works that demand the collaboration of a number of individuals and were in fact often collective before our present criteria were adopted. An example? The first two etchings listed here under the name of Daubigny have figures executed by Meissonier, and our catalogue entries have something to say of the rather special conditions (to modern eyes) in which those communal efforts were turned out. So too with the lithograph of Millet that is essentially the work of Karl Bodmer (M 24), and the etchings catalogued here under the name of Daubigny but which were exhibited in the Salons under the name of their co-author, Trimolet (D 8, 18). The fact is, the cataloguer cannot do much more than throw up his hands at these working cooperatives. After 1830 they tended to wither in the bud and were not very effective, but the dominant idea that a work of art should be executed by one man alone—an idea particularly propagated by the catalogues—threw obstacles in the way of all such enterprises. The "community" in which Daubigny worked was by no means an isolated case. Fourierism had inspired a number of such groups, and in any case the idea of joining forces came naturally to thousands of artists toiling in misery. But it had to be carried out without interfering with the entirely individual character of creativity, and that was not possible. "At the Château de Gruyères," Moreau-Nélaton tells us (*L'Histoire de Corot*, p. 183), "the Bovy family received [Corot] with open arms. Antoine Bovy, the engraver of medals, and his brother Daniel, the painter . . . smitten with Fourierism, lived in a phalanstery, and their house was the most hospitable you could imagine. Daubigny, Français, and Leleux met there." But in their Paris studio it was not only the living conditions but the work itself that Daubigny, Trimolet, Steinheil, and others shared. Still, the scope and character of those experiments and experiences should not be exaggerated, and they remained isolated and unfruitful for the reasons we have mentioned.

The individual nature of creation, when judged on the criterion of art for art's sake, was even more radically called into question by the practice of engraving. Only rarely was (or is) an engraving executed by one person alone, so if one insists on a single author a selection has to be made. Whence the inconsistencies in the catalogues that choose sometimes the man who drew the work (Corot), sometimes the engraver (Daubigny) when they were not the same, as was the rule before 1875.

Unlike Corot, who never, strictly speaking, engraved, Daubigny started out as an artisan-engraver to earn his living, with the idea of using a manual occupation as springboard to the higher and coveted position of artist. Corot, however, had a private income and from the outset could style himself an artist-painter and nothing else. Engraving for him was at the most a concession, a very secondary episode in his career, a means of relaxation. Besides, he had not an iota of interest in the technical and manual aspect of the medium, though that, for certain engravers, is the only thing interesting in it. For him it was enough to trace a drawing on the varnish of the plate, and what happened after that was no concern of his. In fact, he did not even bother to have his first plate acid-bitten and left it in the drawing state until a professional engraver, Félix Bracquemond, happened on it twenty years later. By that time the situation had changed: engravings were in fashion. An etching by Corot was a godsend. Bracquemond saw to the etching and printing of that plate, and subsequent works were taken care of by men of practical experience like Alfred Delauney or Jules Michelin. His lithographs likewise were those of a painter already celebrated, produced not because he had any specific interest in the medium but only as an act of goodwill in reply to the urging of his friend Robaut. The circumstances in which the album of autolithographs was turned out in 1871 are recounted in detail by Moreau-Nélaton, who leaves no room for illusions on that score. Corot felt himself so little involved in the technique of the print that even with transfer paper, which reduces to a minimum any constraints on the artist doing the drawing, he managed to mistake the correct surface and used the sheet on the unglued side, which caused no end of difficulties in the printing (see our entry for C 29). To say nothing of the etching turned over for printing without having been bitten by the acid (C 14) and which consists of no more than the trace left by the tool in scratching the plate through the varnish. Whence the question: To whom goes the credit for these prints since, by all rights of reason, Corot can scarcely be considered more than the author of the drawing?

III

The rule governing catalogues that calls for assembling the works produced by one artist and by himself alone in itself calls for a good deal of commentary. But collaborations have always existed and are not peculiar to either the mid-nineteenth century or engravings, so such reservations do not explain the very real ambiguity of the catalogues presented here. When Loÿs Delteil went back to the catalogues made by Henriet, Lebrun, and Robaut for his monumental *Le Peintre-graveur illustré*, it was with the idea of recording works of *artists,* not objects of craft, commerce, or industry, and he applied to them as a matter of course the criterion of the work of art executed entirely by a single individual. But that was after 1900. In 1874 Frédéric Henriet had already undertaken the same task of sifting through the printed images, and already his criteria and approach were unlike those that had governed the production of those images between 1838 and 1874. The fact is, the criteria applied after 1860 had grown up as a reaction against the new printing processes developed between 1830 and that date. The mid-century engravers had not yet made a clear choice between art and industry, and this for numerous reasons, the most obvious being that the problem had never before been posed so sharply and therefore they could not have suspected what and how much was at stake. Then too, a good segment of opinion, one with which Daubigny himself agreed, was convinced that art and industry were bound to get along together happily. And as time went on, because they were unable to know what path the art work would take in the future, many artists ventured into byways that seemed complementary but gradually proved antagonistic: art for art's sake (which expressed itself after 1860 in the movement for the original etching) and the industrial art that poured out thousands of images by first mechanical, later photomechanical means. Thus the criteria that determined which among the productions of the artists were to be recognized as works of art not only showed no awareness of the essential problem of their existence but even at times contradicted outright the very grounds for that existence. We shall see how within a mere half century, in the decisive period of the industrialization of France, such a considerable changeover could come about.

Aside from the lithographs Corot did in his youth, the earliest graphic works to be seen here were printed in 1835 (Dupré), 1836 (Rousseau), and 1838 (Daubigny), the last only a few months before the announcement made in January, 1839, of the invention of the daguerreotype. When Daubigny printed his last etching in 1874, Alphonse Poitevin had just come up with one of the most perfect processes of photographic reproduction. The history of the print during that period is explainable only by the difficult relationships that arose between drawing and industry, and with photography in particular. And we are not speaking only of reproductions of existing art works (which constituted the core of the initial work of Daubigny and all of Dupré's and disappeared in their work, it seems, after 1850) but in equal measure of the original prints by Millet or Jongkind, which the latter persisted obstinately in calling "drawings."

Photography made its influence felt in two ways. Positively insofar as the innovative artists became interested in what it could do and took from it what they could use, and so one finds Daubigny in 1843 engraving after a daguerreotype (D 86) and Corot preferring the glassplate medium to traditional engraving methods. Of rather more moment, however, was its negative effect. Very early, in 1850 and perhaps even earlier, the print began to justify its survival by redefining itself as an antiphotograph (as today still). If one asks why the print collectors who became more numerous after 1860, and especially after 1880, rejected photography (and the glassplate print along with it), we can reply that it was precisely because photography had come into existence that there were so many more collectors of engravings.

In 1838, when Daubigny had the idea of producing etchings he would exhibit in the Salon three years later as original creations, this was anything but a current practice and in fact had more of a future than a past, which is why we now find it difficult to grasp the idea itself without ambiguity. If we read his venture in the spirit of his time, it doubtless means that Daubigny was only concerned with putting out a personal work that would let people know his capabilities as the practical technician he aspired to become so as to earn his living. Viewed in the spirit of our day, those five etchings look like an end in themselves, a warning against the great advance in reproduction techniques, and therefore the work of a precursor. But that notion depends on knowledge of so many things to come that it is open to the charge of anachronism, of projecting our own prejudices onto the Daubigny of 1838.

Etching was the most fitting technique for a revival of the original art-print, but in 1838 it counted for less than nothing. That was the time when, thanks to the recently imported technique of steelplate engraving, the first progress was being made toward industrialization of the print, inexpensive production, and the democratization of the image. Two major steps forward had already been introduced: the steam press and machine-made paper, and these encouraged further development of the stereotypy process known since the eighteenth century and involving the transformation of an engraving into a stereotype plate to be printed by the usual typographic methods. At that time—1830 to 1839—the artisan-engravers had nothing to fear from the industrialization of the image; indeed, it could not do without them. On the other hand, the invention of photography came as a real threat because in the course of time it was to make it possible to go directly from the drawing to the stereotype plate without requiring the services of an engraver. Understandably, then, Daubigny threw himself heartily into this first phase of the industrialization of the image and like many engravers saw in it a handy new channel for his métier, be it craft or art. He even took part in the joint enterprise in photography and engraving published as *Excursions daguérriennes* (D 86). But soon after 1840 it became more and more probable that engraving by hand was under sentence of death because of the new needs and the inventions they inevitably gave rise to. Between 1855 and 1865 a number of works appeared in which the struggle between photographic and manual procedures was obvious: Nicolas-François Chifflart's album of 1859, *Dijon et ses monuments* in 1864, *Voyage au Soudan Occidental* in 1865, and the like. Characteristic of this transitional period is the engraving on wood done by hand after a photograph, something like the print of 1860, *The Jordan*, engraved on wood after a drawing by Daubigny that was itself executed after a daguerreotype, for the "Voyage en Palestine" published in *Le Tour du Monde* (in Fidell-Beaufort, vol. II, p. 101).

Still, the fate of these new techniques of photographic impression inaugurated in 1840 by Fizeau was anything but sure. Between 1850 and 1860 their application still appeared uncertain and costly, something perhaps for future times. By and large they were greeted with enthusiasm, and what objections were made were really a matter of principle. But it was in that period that the future of engravers like Daubigny was decided, and the control obviously was not in their hands.

France was in a phase of economic, social, and political transformation. To take an example that affected engraving, the French railways began to be laid down in 1844 in an initial stage that went on until 1857. The new means of travel gave rise to a great production of illustrated tourist guidebooks for which Daubigny, like many other engravers, drew numerous pictures for wood engraving. Such jobs were by no means thought of as alien to serious art: in his *Dictionnaire de poche des Artistes Contemporains* of 1858, Théodore Pelloquet praised Daubigny for the "vignettes only a few centimeters in size, drawn ten or twelve years ago for the railway guides, executed with more breadth and masterliness than many important and celebrated canvases."

A second and more direct example of that relationship is the rise of the cheap illustrated book after 1830, a development we know well through the history of publishers like Curmer, Delloye, Hachette, and others. In their catalogues we find a good many illustrations by Daubigny, specifically etchings on steel which he himself engraved. If this artisanal or indeed industrial type of work was granted a further lease on life, it was because the original art-print, when it came into being, followed the same criteria:

The post-1850 artist was the salvation of the pre-1850 artisan, though at the price of a confusion of genres. Likewise, if a catalogue of the lithographs of Jules Dupré exists, it should not be ignored that these works, from a time when he had not yet won his fame, are merely reproductions he himself made after his own works, doubtless for reasons of economy. They have more in common with the multiple reproductions of the same sort that he let others do, when he was at last able to drop such menial tasks, than they have with what a "painter-engraver" would do after 1880.

Take the case of Daubigny. After counting on engraving as a trade on which to live, he, like his friend Charles Jacque, found his livelihood threatened by the industrialization that had promised so much but whose technical progress was leaving the artists far behind. Whence their ambiguous positions, always a sure sign of a transitional period. Madeleine Fidell-Beaufort points out that in 1860, at the very moment when he was engraving a threshing machine (D 94) for *L'Art au XIXᵉ siècle,* a review advocating the alliance of art and industry, Daubigny wrote to Henriet that "wishing to do rustic landscapes with figures, I shall be really well placed there [in Auvers] in the midst of small farms where the plows are not steam-driven." That contradiction was the condition of his success, of his conversion from craftsman-engraver of reproductions and illustrations into "original" engraver of his own ideas, a change that came about remarkably early with the publication of his first album of original etchings in 1850, at a time when both Adolphe Hervier, who had already brought out an album in 1843, and Charles Jacque were in much the same position. Only from that date forward can one classify his output of engravings with the criteria applicable to original prints and not run the risk of anachronism.

Little by little, as the production of images became more industrialized and, in the opinion of art lovers and collectors, "degraded," the conception of the print as such changed. The manual techniques neither disappeared nor became absorbed into industry but instead, as time went on, came to constitute a reserved sector with the monopoly of producing engraved images that the contemporaries judged worthy of the dignity of art. One of the earliest signs of this was the success of the album Daubigny brought out: eleven printings have been identified for its title page (D 66). Not that Daubigny, torn as he was between his first métier as steelplate engraver and his ambition to be an artist-painter, had any other option once that ambition was satisfied and the situation permitted him to become an artist-painter-engraver and thereby rid his work of all contradictions. Certainly he was one of the first, with Charles Jacque, to campaign for that solution and to join with the art dealer Cadart in 1861 in planning the Société des Aquafortistes as the institutional organ for the movement that aimed to open the strait and ideal domain of art for art's sake to the engraving.

For Millet the contradictions began just when they had smoothed themselves out for Daubigny. An artist-painter induced very early on to turn out prints, he never did get into his mind just what sort of art object he was committing himself to produce. Certainly it was only to help him publicize his painting and earn a bit of money that his friend Sensier encouraged him to do etchings after the first few trials made on the corner of a table, so to speak, with his friends Jacque and Daubigny in the workshop of the printer Delâtre. Sensier was on the right track; there were indeed art lovers willing to buy the prints: "I have been seeing people again: two young enthusiasts. They want your etchings," but he adds, which confirms that engraving was no more than bait for a bigger catch, "I told you so, your name is going up, up" (May 16, 1863). That was the year when there was the embryonic start of those societies of print collectors which would become so numerous by the end of the century: ten friends clubbed together to commission a copper plate from Millet of which they would be the sole proprietors (see our entry for M 19). Still, for Millet an engraving was at best something auxiliary. He simply could not imagine that prints could be commercialized like other works of art. When Cadart wanted to commission engravings from him he was at a loss for a reply and had no idea how much to ask. One thing, though, was clear to him: the copper plate, the basis of his work, was of value in and of itself and was not to be parted with nor, even less, destroyed. Here we have the start of the movement in which engraving by hand, once and for all separated off from the industrial practice it had been not long before, set itself against that practice in all possible ways, even those most contrary to its own nature. The idea of destroying plates so as voluntarily to limit production and thereby keep up the price of the prints does not seem to have occurred to Cadart, nor was it done later even by the Société des Aquafortistes, which continued to distribute prints made from plates of Daubigny that were well and truly worn out from repeated editions. It did occur, however, to the amateurs at the close of the same decade, the 1860s, and in particular to the critic who was best informed in matters of modern prints, Philippe Burty. A first setback with Millet: Burty belonged to the Société des Dix organized by Sensier, but he posed conditions to the utter despair of the organizer. Sensier, who had shown him such goodwill, ended by writing him an annoyed and firm letter intended to make him back down from his pretensions: Burty was demanding to see the plate before the printing and, what is more, to have it brought to his home by Sensier in person. Worse, he was insisting that the plate be made unusable by scratching once the edition was printed—and, besides, there were signs that he was not willing to pay his due share. To the nine other members in 1863 the very idea of ruining a plate by Millet seemed at least outrageous: "I am obliged to inform you that nine of the subscribers hold an opinion entirely contrary to yours: they do not desire the destruction of the plate" (Sensier to Burty, December 2, 1863). Burty held his peace. But in 1869, when he was himself responsible for publishing an album titled *Sonnets et eaux-fortes* for which he had commissioned plates from the artists he was championing, Millet among them, he required that all plates be scrapped after the limited edition of 350 prints was completed.

Millet was indignant, refused, then gave in: "I find this destruction of plates absolutely and wholly brutal and barbarous. I am not well enough up in commercial manipulations to understand what is achieved thereby, but I do know that even if Rembrandt and Ostade had each made one of those plates they would have been destroyed. Enough said" (Millet to Sensier, January 24, 1869).

IV

While the new conception of the engraving as art for art's sake was giving birth to the Malthusian theory of the original print, the image industry throve even more. In one market, more and more differences in quality were being recognized and seen to be a matter of all-out concern; in the other, no one seemed even to be aware of them. This artificial separation into opposing camps could not help but give rise to further ambiguities. To the new notion of the artist-engraver the new industrial techniques acted rather as the bullfighter to the bull, forever leading the artist on only to sidestep him at the last moment. The development of reproduction-prints, still thriving as late as 1914, gives evidence of all these dubious combats. The way was laid in 1834 with the publication of *Le Musée* of Alexandre Decamps, who played on the ambiguity of the art object (defined simply as what an artist produced), asking the artists "themselves" to make reproductions of their works for him to publish so that he could assure his readers that what they were buying was not a reproduction but a "second version" of the work since it came from the artist who, by definition, can only create, not copy. Anyone reproaching his reproductions with being betrayals had the carpet pulled from under him: any "betrayal" was deliberate and controlled by the artist himself.

The production of Daubigny abounds in examples of this sort, which are excluded from catalogues raisonnés only because of the preconceived idea of art for art's sake behind most such repertories. Thus, along with a famous etching, *Tree with Crows* (D 120), he did a pen drawing for autolithographic reproduction in facsimile for the *Panthéon des illustrations françaises au XIXᵉ siècle:* one is in the catalogue, the other is not. *The Beach at Villerville* (D 88), an engraving published by the *Gazette des Beaux-Arts* in 1874, is catalogued. But "alongside this," says Moreau-Nélaton, "*Le Monde Illustré* had by force of zeal obtained a drawing after another canvas, *View from the Banks of the Cure,* which has become well known through a quite good rendering on wood by the engraver Étienne." Manual reproduction on wood blocks, which in the 1860s gave rise to the numerous albums of Ernest Boetzel reproducing the paintings in the Salons, was in its turn challenged by the Gillot process by which a stereotype plate could be made from a drawing without resorting to photography. Such a plate could fairly enough claim to be the drawing of the artist himself, and in fact the most celebrated painters of the 1860s were willing to make drawings specifically for reproduction by that process in *L'Autographe au Salon* and the *Album Autographique.* This was the approach also of the *Album contemporain,* which published such drawings by Corot (C 34) and Daubigny (D 132). These works, curiously enough, unlike those published in *L'Autographe au Salon,* were accepted by the cataloguers, though not without hesitation, Robaut classing them with the glass plates, Delteil with autolithographic prints. Since even the cataloguers were unsure, it must be admitted that the very obvious difference between mechanical and manual impressions was not always the indisputable criterion one would have liked it to be. Worse, with ever greater progress in the photomechanical industry, in photogravure retouched by hand, and in collotypy, it became more and more a ticklish matter to attempt such distinctions.

This is why the participation of Daubigny in publications of reproductions such as *Le Musée Universel* of É. Lièvre or *Panthéon des illustrations françaises au XIXᵉ siècle* of Victor Frond must be understood as perpetuating the artisanal approach as much as liberating and giving new value to the art-print. Madeleine Fidell-Beaufort attributes to Daubigny the engraving of the salon of Durand-Ruel (reproduced here at the start of this introduction), published in 1845 as the frontispiece of their first catalogue. Unsigned, that engraving was overlooked by the cataloguers, who no doubt would have qualified it as "modest." True, at that point Daubigny was only a jobbing workman doing documentary reproduction, and as such was of no interest to the cataloguers. But soon he was to become a well-known artist-painter, and then his works would appear in the catalogues of that same gallery—but reproduced by engravers whose names have remained obscure. All of which means that the cataloguer must simply once and for all decide between one or the other of those two types of production and say outright and without wavering just what to his mind deserves to be called a work of art.

V

What has been said so far permits a better understanding of the very special problem confronting print lovers when it comes to something like the glassplate print, the *cliché-verre,* which defies classification, and helps to explain the special nature of its technique, its scant success except in works by Corot, and the increasing regard in which it was held after 1900.

Its highly specific technique (for explanation and history see the "Note Concerning Glassplate Prints" following this introduction) was very much a result of the complex game that drawing played with photography between 1850 and 1875 and particularly in the 1860s. It is understandable that the glassplate print should reflect the concerns of certain artists who wished to keep alive the idea of individual and manual creation but were nonetheless attracted by the new technical means of reproduction. What is more, it offered a way of shaking off the contradiction between attachment to the traditional values of drawing and belief in a modernist future for art. To us today it seems highly characteristic of a certain mid-nineteenth-century taste, and the list of artists who practiced it coincides curiously with those that the liberal bourgeoisie, in the United States in particular, recognized as its own: Eugène Delacroix, Corot, Millet, Daubigny, Paul Huet, Antoine-Louis Barye, and their pupils or admirers. Such prints—the rough scribbles of Corot especially—are thought of today as prophetic, but there again it is our own eyes that complete and round them out through the catalogues where they figure.

How then did they manage to get accepted into the catalogues? Not easily, certainly, and what strikes the historian from the start is the almost total indifference that seems to have been accorded the birth of this process and which soon caused it to be abandoned. The letter of Delacroix politely excusing himself for dropping it after a first trial was certainly not that of an enthusiast. But Paul Huet, Daubigny, and Corot were rather more intrigued, and so too the group of Arras. The key, though, lies in the reaction of the public: glassplate prints simply made not the slightest impact on the art lovers of 1860. Consequently, even if certain artists did persist in turning them out they were destined to remain no more than a rainy day pastime, as they were for Corot according to Moreau-Nélaton. This makes it clear too why only Corot, who could get along very well without having to worry about publicizing his works and who made prints for relaxation or to gratify his friends, would continue to dabble in this medium up to 1874 while the others gave it up after a few trials in 1862, and also why his rough sketches in this technique display so much liberty—almost insolence—with regard to the academic landscape.

It should also be clear from what we have said why collectors should have rejected this sort of work at the very time when they were beginning to covet original prints. Print collectors were like sworn conspirators who had solemnly renounced photography, all its pomps and vanities and all its heinous works. The reason for this was explicitly stated in the first catalogue of prints by Corot, published by Beraldi in 1886 (*Les Graveurs du XIXe siècle,* vol. V, p. 54) with the aid of Robaut: "It should also be said that Corot made sixty-five drawings on bichromated glass from which photographic proofs were printed. This process was used often by painters several years ago. But photography is not engraving, and we mention the existence of these drawings only for the record." There we have it all: (1) glassplate prints are photographs, (2) they are drawings, (3) they are not engravings. Objectively Beraldi was right. But his objective judgment implicitly masked a value judgment that colored everything he was saying. For the print lover of 1880 a drawing was the unique, aristocratic work, an engraving had the advantage of being accessible to more collectors, a photograph was a mechanical product condemned to take second place to the engraving with its long tradition. The glassplate print was thus doubly suspect to the bourgeois clientele that favored a controlled democratization.

Thus, the negative judgment of Beraldi accurately reflected the dominant opinion. In 1912, in his *La Cote des estampes des différentes écoles,* a handbook of current prices for prints, Bourcard could still say of the glassplate prints by Corot: "Photography intervening here as a factor, we find ourselves in the presence of a mechanical process, the resultant products are of no interest to us" (p. 157). Nine years later, however, when the art dealer Maurice Le Garrec republished the glassplate prints in his possession, the reception was very different and was echoed in a number of articles, among them one by the dealer Osbert Barnard in the very serious *The Print Collector's Quarterly.* So much so that in one article Charles Tabarant could ask: "Why is it that this process was not given a better welcome by the artists, and how is it that they so completely abandoned it?" The shift in appreciation grew steadily and calls for some explanation.

The terrain had been prepared by an article Germain Hédiard published in the *Gazette des Beaux-Arts* in 1903. The following year his collection was put up for sale, and ninety glassplate prints appeared on the market. Their prices—often 6 to 13 francs and only exceptionally, for the *Young Mother at the Entrance to a Wood* (our C 59), as much as 110 francs—were in no way comparable with those of etchings, which at that time almost never went for less than 50 francs and often for more than 100 francs (in particular the first states at the Giacomelli sale of 1905, which reached 165, 175, and 210 francs). In 1902–3 likewise there had been a special number of *The Studio* devoted to the prints of Corot and Millet. The result was that in his catalogue of 1905 Robaut could include the glassplate prints following the others and with no particular comment of the sort Beraldi had had to append to them almost twenty years earlier.

The sales of the Giacomelli, Robaut, and Gerbeau collections in, respectively, 1905, 1907, and 1908 showed that print lovers were now willing to accept glassplate prints. Dealers like Delteil, Sagot, and then Maurice Le Garrec took to collecting them, and their exhibitions and sales brought a slow but steady increase in prices. Some were shown in 1907 by Durand-Ruel, Delteil included them in his catalogue in 1910, in 1912 Albert Bouasse-Lebel ordered the first reprintings from Paul Desavary, in 1921 Le Garrec arranged a major showing in his gallery on the Rue de Châteaudun and stated in his preface that "some of the proofs we are now presenting have been in our portfolios for twenty-three years." Since then glassplate prints have been in regular circulation though they are still quite rare in print collections. Still, that is what has saved them and explains too why whatever misgivings the collectors still had have been dispelled. Only the taint of "industry" clinging to the photograph had banned them in the first place from serious collections, but by 1921 the original print made up a very solid sector of the art market and industrial reproduction of images could no longer conflict with it. Besides, the glassplate process had been virtually crushed in its cradle and had never caught on, with the result that its products had found a place on the curio market before the catalogues finally consecrated their entry into the art market. The most recently sold early proofs of Corot were listed in France at 4,000 francs (Delteil no. 95, formerly Somary Collection); at the same date (October, 1977), a comparable proof of the same plate (formerly Desavary-Dutilleux Collection) fetched a comparable price, $1,200, in the United States.

VI

To catalogue glassplate prints with the same rules that serve collectors in appreciating engravings was a ticklish task. Beraldi had already realized that when it merely came to describing them, which in his time was the first obligation of the cataloguer: "This description will be of the utmost difficulty, since they are mere rough sketches, and to analyze their subjects one would have to speak in such a way as to remain vague and say only: *indication* of a personage, seated on the *indication* of a terrain, at the foot of the *indication* of a tree, beneath the *indication* of a sky." Further, the notion of "states" is simply unmanageable with works so often subject to constant and progressive alterations that radically affect their appearance. The sensitive, living surface of the plate itself may become modified on its own, and the cataloguer can do nothing about it any more than the artist could have anticipated and desired it. Even the dimensions of the sensitive surface on which the plate was printed may involve purely subjective appreciation: supposing, as is the case, that the existence of margins has a capital importance in estimating the sale value of a printing, the responsibility of the cataloguer extends even to gauging millimeters when it comes to deciding just where the print leaves off and the blank paper surround begins.

If today we are tempted to judge uncharitably the ironies of Beraldi, we should keep in mind that any catalogue, however *raisonné* it be, is open to criticisms of the system imposed by the values reigning during the time it was compiled. And the judgment of posterity, which is the only thing that justifies our having combined here such very different artists and very contradictory works, is by no means a universal judgment. Judging the work of an artist with the sole aid of a catalogue obliges one to judge that judgment even before judging the particular body of work.

This is evident in the very idea of making a catalogue—which can only be symbolic—for the three sole engravings done by Eugène Boudin: a reproduction lithograph which was purely an artisan's task for a poster at the start of his career; then a lithographed illustration for a collection of images by prominent artists; finally, unexpectedly, directly after his death, a small etching exhumed, mounted on rice paper, so rare as to be an object of veneration. If they are assembled here, it is for the simple reason that the last lends dignity to the first. But the hand that assembles them and the eye that compares them, who can believe that they are only those of the Artist?

NOTE CONCERNING GLASSPLATE PRINTS

The history and technique of this uncommon medium were well set forth by Germain Hédiard in his article in the *Gazette des Beaux-Arts* of 1903. The idea of the process is simple and struck a number of people at the same time. The artist draws on a glass plate which is then printed like a photographic negative. This is similar to what is done nowadays in retouching, in some photomontages, in the famous "rayograms" of Man Ray and Moholy-Nagy, and even in certain films of Walt Disney and Norman McLaren.

The *glass plate* can be of any thickness. To make it opaque it is treated chiefly in one of two ways, most often by coating it with collodion to make a surface which can then be scratched with a point or dabbed with a metal brush or tampon to make a drawing that can be printed in positive on sensitive paper. Because collodion tends to tear under the point and also to undergo numerous alterations with time, the plate is sometimes given instead a layer of printer's ink or some other opaque and fatty substance laid on with a roller and then worked by the artist with various types of brushes and other tools. This latter offers rather more resources for modeling, as Paul Desavary stressed in a lecture: "Another effect is obtained by a variant of that process [collodion coating] because it was found that it gave a slightly too dry effect. The glass was covered with oil paint (a mixture of white and yellow). By means of scumbling with rags and strokes made with a stick sharpened to a point, where the paint was more or less removed one obtained transparencies which on the photographic paper rendered the blacks and halftones of the image with a much more artistic effect." This second procedure, however, was much more rarely used, and glass plates have generally been treated as surfaces for line drawings.

To facilitate the work of the artist the coating of the plate was sprinkled with white lead and the plate placed over a piece of black velvet so that the drawing could be read straight off as black on white.

Printing involves the use of sensitized paper. In the earliest prints a "salted" paper was preferred to an "albuminized" paper. But the thicker and more brilliant albuminized paper came into general use. The prints are sepia or purplish blue in tint. Although printing is done by contact and allows little leeway for interpretation, between one print and another there are considerable variations—more pronounced than between different printings of an engraving—due to the duration of exposure, the products utilized, and the particular way the glass plate is handled.

In one, the direct print, the coated face on which the artist has drawn is laid directly against the sensitized paper. This gives a very faithful print because the lines are reproduced dryly. Although these prints are the most usual, the drawing and signature in them are reversed with respect to the original.

In the other method, which gives a *counterproof,* the glass is placed face upward over the sensitized paper so that the light is diffused through the entire thickness of the glass and with an intensity proportionate to that thickness. These counterproofs differ radically from direct prints. The line is unsharp, hazy, and shimmering, and there is a feeling of modeling but less contrast, effects that can be accentuated by interposing another glass between the plate and the paper. In these the drawing and signature are not reversed.

As for *states,* only two glassplate prints by Corot exist in two states as a result of additional work done on the plate after the initial printing. Leaving aside the addition of the signature, the other "states" catalogued by Robaut and Delteil cannot claim that name and are simply due to involuntary *alterations* of the plate. The plates are fragile, the collodion is easily scratched or stained, and halations, crackles, and pinholes appear in time. True, such alterations may be corrected or attenuated in certain printings, as in *The Festival of Pan* (C 79), of which we reproduce two "versions." Printings may also differ so considerably in intensity, with lines brought out or effaced, as to suggest different states, which is the case with *Corot: Self-Portrait* (C 69), of which we reproduce two prints as well as the plate itself.

There is no point therefore in comparing these differences with the different states of engravings. At the most they can serve to distinguish different printings, though there too there is a decisive difference from metal-plate engravings since the glass plate is not subject to being worn away mechanically through repeated editions, which means that there is no limit to the number of printings possible and the quality is not affected by extensive use. On the other hand the plate itself is fragile, easily scratched or broken, and susceptible to undesired alterations, for which reason it became the practice quite early to replace the original plate with a countertype.

Countertypes are copies of the original plate and can be fairly faithful or very crude. Charles Desavary almost systematically made them for the plates in his possession, and these are indicated in the catalogue. Useful as the procedure is, the result is inevitably hazier and less sharp than the original (though less so than a counterproof), and the most intricate and complex parts of the drawing generally end by being blocked up and the finest lines disappear.

A countertype can be established by either direct contact or reduction on a standard-size plate measuring 9 × 12 or 13 × 18 centimeters (roughly 3 1/2 × 4 3/4" or 5 1/8 × 7 1/8"). In the latter case enlargements must be made in printing so as to return to the original dimensions, and this opens the way to further interpretations and changes by the photographer who carries out this operation. For this substitute plate either glass is used (with, of course, all the drawbacks of the fragile original) or, more often, paper. It can be established from either the original glass plate or a proof printed on paper. The paper print can in its turn be simply rephotographed with a camera or else used to make a new negative by contact, in which case it is rendered translucent by impregnation with petroleum jelly or liquid paraffin.

With such a diversity of possible procedures in countertyping, it becomes impossible to judge the quality of reproduction of the original plate from prints obtained in this manner.

Reproductions: One may wonder why the glassplate process was not systematically transformed into true engraving so as to obtain an easy and original impression of artists' drawings. This was in fact done several times, and quite early, for example with *The Woodcutter of Rembrandt* (C 35), which was transposed onto metal and photogravured by Charles Nègre. Such prints are very faithful to the original drawing but are printed like etchings, and in fact look exactly like them. Though these processes have been little used, Desavary produced photolithographic reproductions, sometimes in the original format, but they are very different from the originals and are mere line reproductions without nuances.

COROT AND THE GLASSPLATE TECHNIQUE

Turning now to the history of the medium, it was around the painter and lithographer Constant Dutilleux (1807–1865) in Arras that there grew up a team of artists passionately enthusiastic about the applications of photography to drawing and to the reproduction of paintings. Responsible for devising the glassplate technique were L. Grandguillaume, professor of drawing in the engineer corps school in Arras, Adalbert Cuvelier, an oil manufacturer and amateur photographer, and the painter and photographer Charles Desavary, who married one of Dutilleux's daughters.

Dutilleux was an admirer of Corot and in 1847, without knowing him personally, had bought one of his pictures, this at a time when a sale was truly exceptional for the painter. Corot, who led the life of a nomadic bachelor, went to visit him in Arras on June 2, 1851, and they promptly became intimate friends. In February of that year Corot had lost his mother, to whom he was deeply attached, and in Dutilleux, his wife, and their nine children he seems to have found a new family. On his second visit to Arras on April 20, 1852, he made the acquaintance of Cuvelier and Grandguillaume, who photographed his paintings. There was a third visit beginning on February 14, 1853, and he returned soon afterward, on April 16, for the marriage of Élisa, the Dutilleuxs' oldest girl, to Alfred Robaut. It was during this last visit that he made his first glassplate prints whereupon, as Moreau-Nélaton tells it, "he developed a taste for them, had glass plates sent to him in Paris the following winter and, delighted with the result, did not fail on each visit to the north to enlist the services of his ingenious collaborators." His visits became more and more frequent: in the winter of 1853–54, in August of 1854, in 1855, 1856, 1857, and at least once each year. In 1858 he was working on a painting, *Hide-and-Seek*, and "between times amused himself by dashing off a few drawings on the photographic plates that Colin [Gustave Colin, a painter and pupil of Dutilleux] had brought him from Arras, and under the guidance of Jules Michelin tried his hand at etching" (Moreau-Nélaton, p. 186).

It was over a span of twenty-two years that Corot produced his glassplate prints, and in two periods of unequal length: from 1853 to 1860 and from 1871 to 1874. The last one was made in 1874 before old age and illness put an end to his traveling about. Only one such print was made in Paris, according to Desavary, and it is not known what became of it, but this contradicts the story we have from Moreau-Nélaton.

THE PRINTINGS OF THE COROT GLASS PLATES

Three series of glassplate prints by Corot can be distinguished.

1) The first, of 1853–54, were printed by Grandguillaume in Dutilleux's studio. Subsequently Charles Desavary got hold of these plates and did his own printings (except for C 37). From the notes

of Albert Bouasse-Lebel, who was a friend of Paul Desavary, it appears that "if they were returned to Monsieur Grandguillaume they have passed to the hands of a certain Guinet who later took over the little photographic studio. This Guinet is in the old people's home in Arras, his material has been destroyed and sold off piece by piece, the plates destroyed."

2) The next batch of plates, of 1854–57, was printed by Adalbert Cuvelier and remained the property of his son Eugène, who frequented the Barbizon group and married the daughter of Ganne, the famous innkeeper for those artists. It was there that Eugène Cuvelier approached the Barbizon painters with the idea of making glass-plate prints, and he obtained eighteen from Daubigny, two from Millet, two from Rousseau; Charles Jacque made at least two. Along with the fifteen plates by Corot that Cuvelier owned, this collection was sold in 1911 to the Parisian collector Albert Bouasse-Lebel.

a) This resulted in the *Bouasse-Lebel printing* (Fritz Lugt, *Les Marques de collections de dessins et d'estampes*, 2 vols., Amsterdam, 1921: no. Suppl. 67c). The son of Charles Desavary, Paul, who was a friend of Albert Bouasse-Lebel, had from his father a "notebook full of his formulas for printing, development baths, fixing, and artificial aging." Between 1911 and 1913 he reprinted the plates of Corot for Bouasse-Lebel, making ten to fifteen proofs of each on an old type of paper specially manufactured by Lumière in Lyons, and did this so well that when the margins are cropped it is scarcely possible to distinguish these prints from the first ones done, but ordinarily the entire surface of the plaque was printed so that the image is surrounded by a quite broad black margin.

b) This was followed by the *Le Garrec printing* (Lugt no. Suppl. 1766a). The collection of plates acquired by Bouasse-Lebel from the nephew of Eugène Cuvelier was sold again on December 30, 1919, to the Parisian art dealer Maurice Le Garrec, who in 1921 brought out a new edition of forty of them in a boxed portfolio entitled *Quarante clichés-glace de Corot, Daubigny, Delacroix, Millet, Th. Rousseau, tirés sur les plaques de la collection Cuvelier.* One hundred and fifty copies were printed plus five with double series (a second print in a different tint) or counterproofs, at the price of two thousand francs for the portfolio, each numbered on the back and bearing a stamp with the letters S.L. interlaced. In his preface Le Garrec stated: "Lengthy research has permitted us to find a paper with the same composition as that on which the old proofs were printed, and in order to avoid any confusion between those proofs and the modern ones we have applied to the back of each print a stamp in heavy black ink."

His prints, on a slightly thicker paper than the originals and always done in black, are in fact fairly easy to recognize and, in the judgment of critic Jean Cailac, are "too black, a little heavy, and all of equal intensity." They were done with very great care by M. Barry on a "salted" paper, presumably in great number since Le Garrec stated that "for certain plates we had to print at least 400 proofs to obtain 150 good ones." A limited edition was guaranteed by offering the plates to museums "on the express condition that no more proofs will be printed." Thus the Louvre was given the plates for *The Gardens of Horace* by Corot, *The Large Sheepfold* by Daubigny, *Tiger* by Delacroix, *The Maternal Precaution* by Millet, and *The Plain of La Plante-à-Biau* by Théodore Rousseau, and the Bibliothèque Nationale received *Souvenir of Ostia* by Corot, *The Ford* by Daubigny, *Woman Emptying a Bucket* by Millet, and *The Cherry Tree at La Plante-à-Biau* by Rousseau. Unfortunately, after publication the other plates were given away or sold off to persons or institutions unknown, and we have been able to track down only a few of them in the British Museum, London, the Metropolitan Museum of Art, New York, and the Boston Museum of Fine Arts.

3) The third and most important series of glass plates by Corot, those drawn between 1858 and 1874, were with few exceptions printed by Charles Desavary, the painter and photographer who married the second daughter of Dutilleux, Marie. Dutilleux had a deep affection for his son-in-law. When Dutilleux moved to Paris in 1860 he gave Desavary his lithograph workshop in Arras.

Desavary was a highly experienced photographer who did many reproductions of paintings, and he is the key figure in the history of the glass-plate medium since he made serious efforts to exploit the process commercially and to interest artists in it, though with no great success. Letters from his father-in-law encouraged him, among them one from the first days of 1861 which said: "Huet has just left, he looked at the glass plates of Corot with great pleasure and would like to have some. So send me a few proofs and also, at the first opportunity, a box of plates all prepared; he too will turn out some fine things for you. This is an encouragement to make good use of that kind of photograph. The first sunny day you would do well to get at it." A few days later, on January 16, he wrote again: "The prints were well received by Huet, but what really tempts him is the *Lioness* [the *Tiger*?] of Delacroix, in a large print if you have it."

From this came the *Robaut printing*. The glass plates owned by Charles Desavary passed to the first son-in-law of Dutilleux, Alfred Robaut, who had been quietly collecting everything to do with Corot and in 1905 published the first major catalogue of his works, *L'Oeuvre de Corot*. The book was produced in four hundred copies of which thirty were de luxe editions, printed on Japanese vellum and containing prints: one copy with two original etchings and twenty glassplate prints, four copies with twenty glassplate prints each, and twenty-five copies with ten glassplate prints each. But these prints cannot really be considered a new printing since it is probable that among them were

old proofs from the Desavary-Dutilleux holdings.

The glass plates then went to the collaborator of Robaut, the collector Moreau-Nélaton, who in 1936 donated them along with numerous engravings to the Bibliothèque Nationale.

OTHER ARTISTS AND THE GLASSPLATE PRINT

The idea of the glassplate process inevitably occurred to numerous precursors of photography. In his preface to the R. E. Lewis Collection catalogue, Sean H. Thackray recalls the experiments of Wedgwood and of Hercules Florence as well as the dispute between three English artists, William and Frederick J. Havell and James T. Willmore, and William Henry Fox Talbot, who claimed to have used the process (which he described in minute detail) as far back as 1834. Hédiard mentions the patents taken out by Barthélemy Pont for an *"autographie photographique"* on November 28, 1854, and for an *"héliotypie"* on November 24, 1855, which seem related to the glass plate. The name of Pont turns up again associated with those of Paul Salières, Beuvières, Berry, and Harville in a very similar process of *"gravure diaphane"* in 1847 and again in 1853. In the United States an album was published in 1859, *Autograph Etchings by American Artists,* New York, W. A. Townsend & Company, with a preface by John W. Ehninger, while in England, according to Osbert Barnard, something described as "electrophotography or etching on glass" was invented in 1864 by Charles Hancock and used in preparing electrotypes.

Cuvelier succeeded in obtaining plates not only from Daubigny, Corot, Millet, Rousseau, and Delacroix (who bowed out politely after his first and only try at it: see his letter of March 7, 1854, in his published correspondence) but from others as well, so the Le Garrec Collection also included prints by other Barbizon School artists: by A.-H. Brendel, *Large Sheepfold, Small Sheepfold* (1861), *Harnessed Horse,* and *Three Plow Horses* (1862); by Adolphe-André Wacquez, *Grove in the Bas-Bréau, Pond* (1860), and *The Bodelu Farm* (1860); by Charles Jacque, *Horses at the Watering Place* and *Entrance into the Woods;* by Desavary senior, *The Canal Barges, Souvenir of La Scarpe,* and *Horseman in Clearing;* by Cuvelier himself, *Forest Lane;* by Victor Lainé, *Shepherd Watching His Flock;* by Julius Bakof, *Rustic Hut;* by J.-E. Brandon, *Young Mother Giving Her Child a Drink;* by N. E. Trouvé, *Rustic Hut Among Trees;* by A. Collette, *Allegory;* by La Grosillière, *Marine View;* by C. Dutilleux, *The Edge of the Forest* and *Landscape;* and by Paul Huet, *Marshland.*

It can be supposed that Desavary and Cuvelier did others. Dutilleux did at least a dozen (shown in the exhibition of 1965 in Arras), and to him can be attributed *Women at the Edge of a Forest,* which along with its plate passed from the Frumkin Collection to the Art Institute of Chicago under the name of Corot (no. 223 in the Corot exhibition, 1960). Brendel did six, according to Hédiard, and Huet at least seven, some with the process of Barthélemy Pont. Among others who turned their hand to glass plates can be cited Antoine-Louis Barye (one example), Horace Vernet (two), Félix Bracquemond (a few sketches). The Bernard Lévy Collection includes an Antoine Chintreuil signed and dated 1854 and an anonymous *Country Road,* and the Cuvelier Collection had also an anonymous plate with three sketches.

Around 1895 Chincholle wrote to Adolphe Appian: "For your photographs without lens and aperture, here is how you can go about it: You smear a plaque of glass with bitumen or lampblack using a candle. With a match, a pen point, and the tip of a finger you remove some black, you clean off or film over the glass, you draw. Then you print on paper" (document from the archives of Jacques Gruyer, kindly communicated by Janine Bailly-Herzberg).

Nevertheless, the technique very soon fell into disuse. In 1921 Charles Tabarant wrote: "As for the artists of our day, we know scarcely anyone other than Charles Guérin, a relative of Hédiard, who has tried the process, though only in passing." Mention must be made, though, of the curious drawings by Henri Fantin-Latour (of which André Jammes possesses an entire collection), which Hédiard probably reproduced by direct countertyping on a sensitive plate. Pierre Gusman made a few tries at it to illustrate his article on the process. Four examples by Augustus John can be cited for 1900 along with some by Georges Le Meilleur. The École des Beaux-Arts in Lyons continues to list the glassplate technique among the graphic mediums taught, and the Italian engraver Lucio Saffaro quite recently exhibited an album of them, *Trattato dell'elongazione* (see *G7 Studio,* no. 9, February, 1977, p. 15, and *Nouvelles de l'estampe,* nos. 34–35, 1977, p. 53).

BIBLIOGRAPHY

GENERAL WORKS

Beraldi, Henri. *Les Graveurs du XIXe siècle.* 12 vols. Paris, 1885–92: vol. V, 1886, *Corot,* pp. 48–54, and *Daubigny,* pp. 91–98; vol. VI, 1887, *Dupré,* pp. 74–75; vol. VIII, 1889, *Jongkind,* pp. 278–79; vol. X, 1890, *Millet,* pp. 63–71; vol. XI, 1891, *Rousseau,* pp. 268–70.

Delteil, Loÿs. *Le Peintre-graveur illustré; XIXe et XXe siècles.* 31 vols. Paris, 1906–30: vol. I, 1906, *Millet, Rousseau, Jongkind, Dupré;* vol. V, 1910, *Corot;* vol. XIII, 1921, *Daubigny;* reprint, 32 vols., New York, 1969–70.

Bibliothèque Nationale, Département des Estampes. *Inventaire du fonds français après 1800:* vol. III, 1942, *Boudin,* p. 203; vol. V, 1949 (ed. Jean Adhémar), *Corot,* pp. 184–96, and *Daubigny,* pp. 411–24; vol. VII, 1954, *Dupré,* pp. 218–19; vol. XI, 1960, *Jongkind,* pp. 477–79.

Bailly-Herzberg, Janine. *L'Eau-forte de peintre au dix-neuvième siècle: La Société des Aquafortistes (1862–1867).* 2 vols. Paris, L. Laget, 1972.

Von Delacroix bis Munch: Künstlergraphik im 19ten Jahrhundert. Edited by Eckhard Schaar. Exhibition catalogue. Hamburger Kunsthalle, Hamburg, January 28–March 27, 1977 (despite the misleading title this exhibition involved precisely the problems posed by the works catalogued here).

It is in English and American publications that one finds the most revealing discussions of the graphic works of Daubigny, Corot, and Millet in particular:

Maberly, J. *The Print Collector: An Introduction.* Edited, with notes, an account of contemporary etching and etchers, and a bibliography of engraving by Robert Hoe, Jr. New York, Dodd, Mead & Co. and Frederick Keppel, 1880.

Hayden, Arthur. *Chats on Old Prints.* London, T. Fisher, 1906; 2nd ed., 1909.

Keppel, Frederick. *The Golden Age of Engraving: A Specialist's Story about Fine Prints.* New York, Baker & Taylor, 1910.

Whitman's Print-Collector's Handbook. 6th ed., revised and enlarged with additional chapters by Malcolm C. Salaman. London, G. Bell & Sons, 1912 (1st ed., c. 1900).

Leipnik, F. L. *History of French Etching.* London and New York, 1922.

GLASSPLATE PRINTS (CLICHÉS-VERRE)

Hédiard, Germain. "Les Procédés sur verre." *Gazette des Beaux-Arts,* vol. XXX (November, 1903), pp. 408–26.

Le Garrec, Maurice. Preface to the album *Quarante clichés-glace de Corot, Daubigny, Delacroix, Millet, Th. Rousseau.* Paris, Le Garrec, 1921.

Tabarant, Charles. "Les Procédés sur verre." *Bulletin de la Vie artistique,* November 15, 1921, pp. 577–81.

Barnard, Osbert H. "The Cliché-verre of the Barbizon School." *The Print Collector's Quarterly,* vol. IX, no. 2 (April, 1922), pp. 149–71.

Gusman, Pierre. "Le Dessin sur verre ou cristallographie." *Byblis,* no. 5 (1923), p. 22.

Heintzelman, Arthur W. "The Cliché-verre." *Boston Public Library Quarterly,* July, 1953, pp. 159–63.

Cailac, Jean. "Le Cliché-verre, tirages, contretypes, conclusion." *L'Information artistique,* no. 11 (May, 1954), pp. 78–81.

Edwards, Hugh. "Cliché-verre and Corot." *Art Institute of Chicago Quarterly,* vol. LIV, no. 3 (September, 1960), pp. 4–5.

Major Exhibition Catalogues Including Glassplate Prints:

Catalogue of a Corot exhibition, Galerie Durand-Ruel, Paris, 1876 (including seven etchings and five "original drawings on glass printed photographically"). Reproduced in its entirety in Alfred Robaut, *L'Oeuvre de Corot,* vol. IV, p. 277.

Catalogue d'une exposition de l'oeuvre gravé et lithographié de J. B. C. Corot. Preface by Maurice Le Garrec. Le Garrec, Paris, November 15–30, 1921. 12 pp.

Corot, son oeuvre gravé et dessins. Preface by Loÿs Delteil. Galerie Marcel Guiot, Paris, October 26–November 13, 1925.

Estampes et dessins de Corot. With a study by Jean Laran, "Corot dessinateur et graveur." Bibliothèque Nationale, Paris, 1931. 88 pp.

Corot, Constant Dutilleux, leurs amis et leurs élèves. Musée d'Arras, June 20–October 24, 1954.

Corot, An Exhibition of His Paintings and Graphic Works. The Art Institute of Chicago, October 6–November 13, 1960.

Constant Dutilleux. Catalogue by Hervé Oursel. Musée d'Arras, August–November, 1965.

Corot, An Exhibition of Paintings, Drawings and Prints. Introduction, notes, and catalogue by Cecil Gould. Arts Council of Great Britain with the Edinburgh Festival Society, Edinburgh, 1965.

Hommage à Corot (with a very thorough listing of Corot exhibitions). Orangerie des Tuileries, Paris, June 6–September 29, 1975.

Malerei und Photographie im Dialog (with a full chapter, "Die Sonderleistung: das Cliché-verre," pp. 143 ff.). Kunsthaus, Zurich, May 13–July 24, 1977.

Major Sale Catalogues:

Vente Germain Hédiard. Paris, November 10 (first part), November 28–30 (second part), 1904.

Une Collection merveilleuse d'eaux-fortes, lithographies, clichés-verre des grands maîtres français du XIXᵉ siècle. Foreword by Dr. Simon Meller. H. Gilhofer & H. Ranschburg, Lucerne, June 8–9, 1926 (the Bouasse-Lebel Collection).

Modern Original Etchings, Engravings and Lithographs. Catalogue XXI. H. Gilhofer & H. Ranschburg, Lucerne, n.d.

Catalogue of important nineteenth-century and modern prints comprising the property of the late Dr. Felix Somary. Sotheby & Co., London, April 23, 1974.

The R. E. Lewis Collection of Prints in Cliché-verre. Thackray & Robertson, October 15–November 30, 1977.

Archive Material:

Various documents from Constant Dutilleux and Charles Desavary, in the possession of André Jammes, Paris.
Various documents from Albert Bouasse-Lebel, in the possession of Paule Cailac, Paris.

COROT

Robaut, Alfred. *L'Oeuvre de Corot: Catalogue raisonné et illustré. Précédé de l'Histoire de Corot et de ses oeuvres par E. Moreau-Nélaton.* 4 vols. Paris, Floury, 1905 (catalogue of prints in vol. IV).

Moreau-Nélaton, Étienne. *L'Histoire de Corot et de ses oeuvres.* Paris, Floury, 1905.

Dantan, P. "Corot graveur." *La Lithographie et la gravure,* August–September, 1913, p. 171.

Angoulvent, P.-J. "L'Oeuvre gravé de Corot." *Byblis,* no. 18 (1926), p. 39.

Vingt estampes de Corot, eaux-fortes, lithographies, clichés-verre, reproduits en fac-simile d'après les originaux de la Bibliothèque nationale avec des notes de Jean Laran . . . et une étude de Paul Valéry. Paris, Éditions des Bibliothèques nationales de France, 1932.

Bailly-Herzberg, Janine. "L'École de Barbizon: 1. Corot, les eaux-fortes." *Connaissance des Arts,* February, 1975.

Letters of Corot and documentary material assembled by Robaut and Moreau-Nélaton, now in the Cabinet des Estampes, Bibliothèque Nationale, Paris.

See also the exhibition catalogues listed above under GLASS-PLATE PRINTS.

DAUBIGNY

Henriet, Frédéric. "Les Paysagistes contemporains: Daubigny." *Gazette des Beaux-Arts,* vol. IX (May 1, 1874), pp. 464–75 (the first catalogue of the etchings).
———. *C. Daubigny et son oeuvre gravé.* Paris, A. Lévy, 1875.

Catalogue of an Exhibition of Drawings and Etchings by Daubigny. Introduction by Robert J. Wickenden. New York, F. Keppel & Co., 1907. 16 pp.

Wickenden, Robert J. "Charles-François Daubigny, Painter and Etcher." *The Print Collector's Quarterly,* vol. III (April, 1913), pp. 177–206.

Catalogue d'une exposition de l'oeuvre gravé de C. Daubigny. Preface by Maurice Le Garrec. Paris, Le Garrec, December 15–31, 1921.

Delteil, Loÿs. "Les Eaux-fortes de Daubigny, fonds de la Chalcographie du Louvre." *Byblis,* no. 5 (1923), p. 9.

Moreau-Nélaton, Étienne. *Daubigny raconté par lui-même.* Paris, H. Laurens, 1925.

Fidell-Beaufort, Madeleine. *The Graphic Art of Charles-François Daubigny.* New York University doctoral dissertation, 2 vols., 1974 (vol. I, text; vol. II, catalogue).

Bailly-Herzberg, Janine, and Fidell-Beaufort, Madeleine. *Daubigny.* Paris, Geoffroy-Dechaume, 1975 (in French and English; English text by Judith Schub).

See also under GLASSPLATE PRINTS.

DUPRÉ

Hédiard, Germain. *Les Maîtres de la lithographie.* n. p., n. d. 7 pp.

Aubrun, Marie-Madeleine. *Jules Dupré, 1811–1889, catalogue raisonné de l'oeuvre peint, dessiné et gravé.* Paris, L. Laget, 1974.

JONGKIND

Bailly-Herzberg, Janine. "Lettres inédites de J. B. Jongkind." *Nouvelles de l'estampe,* no. 18 (November–December, 1974), pp. 13–16.

Hefting, Victorine. *Jongkind, sa vie, son oeuvre, son époque.* Paris, Arts et Métiers Graphiques, 1975 (with catalogue of 820 representative works).

MILLET

Burty, Philippe. "Les Eaux-fortes de J.-F. Millet." *Gazette des Beaux-Arts,* vol. XI, (September, 1861), pp. 262–66.

Piedagnel, Alexandre. *Souvenirs de Barbizon, J.-F. Millet.* Paris, Librairie Fischbacher, 1876; 2nd ed., 1888 (with a catalogue of etchings based on the Giacomelli Collection, pp. 103–9).

Sensier, Alfred. *La Vie et l'oeuvre de J.-F. Millet, manuscrit publié par Paul Mantz.* Paris, 1881 (in appendix, the first complete catalogue of the graphic work of Millet, by Alfred Lebrun).

Lebrun, Alfred. *Alfred Lebrun's Catalogue of the Etchings, Heliographs, Lithographs and Woodcuts done by Jean François Millet, translated from the French by Frederick Keppel, with Additional Notes and Sketch of the Artist's Life.* New York, F. Keppel & Co., 1887.

Keppel, Frederick. "The Etchings of J. F. Millet," in *Corot and Millet, with Critical Essays by Gustave Geffroy and Arsène Alexandre.* Special number edited by Charles Holme. *The Studio,* 1902.

Major Exhibition Catalogues:

Catalogue of a Complete Collection of the Etchings and Other Prints Done by J.-F. Millet. F. Keppel, New York, 1887 (also a second exhibition, 1908).

Estampes de J.-F. Millet et Th. Rousseau. Galerie Le Garrec, Paris, 1922.

Jean-François Millet. Galeries Nationales du Grand Palais, Paris, 1975–76 (etchings, pp. 167–75).

Letters of A. Sensier and documents, Cabinet des Dessins, the Louvre, Paris.

See also under GLASSPLATE PRINTS.

ROUSSEAU

Sensier, Alfred. *Souvenirs sur Théodore Rousseau.* Paris, 1872 (especially pp. 258–59).

Estampes de J.-F. Millet et Th. Rousseau. Galerie Le Garrec, Paris, 1922.

Théodore Rousseau, 1812–1867. Exhibition catalogue. Edited by Hélène Toussaint. The Louvre, Paris, 1967–68.

See also under GLASSPLATE PRINTS.

BOUDIN
(1824-1898)

Dessiné par COUVELEY, Lith. par BOUDIN.

CAVALCADE HAVRAISE 1851.

Lith. DAVID r de la Communauté M Havre.

B.1

B.2

31

B. 3

COROT
(1796-1874)

C. 1

C. 1

35

C. 2

C. 3

C. 4

C. 5

C. 6

C. 7

C. 8

39

C. 9

C. 10

C. 12

C. 11

42

CORO†

C. 14

C. 15

Souvenir de la feste de Barcelone

par la route — à Promeny 26 mai 73

C. 16

Théâtre - Comte.

C'est l'Obélis de Sousquisor qui me tombe
sur la tête

M^{ELLE} ROSALIE, Rôle de Mère Boisseau,
dans la Caisse d'Épargne.

C. 18

C. 20

46

C. 21

C. 22

49

50

51

C. 26

C. 27

COROT

C. 29

C. 30

Corot autog: 1871.

C. 31

55

56

C. 34

C. 35

58

C. 36

C. 37

C. 38

C. 39

C. 40

C. 41

C. 43

C. 44

C. 47

C. 48

64

C. 46

C. 46

C. 49

Im. d. E. Ducasse. 2 9bre 1872

C. 51

C. 58

C. 52 C. 53 C. 54 C. 55 C. 56

C. 52

C. 53

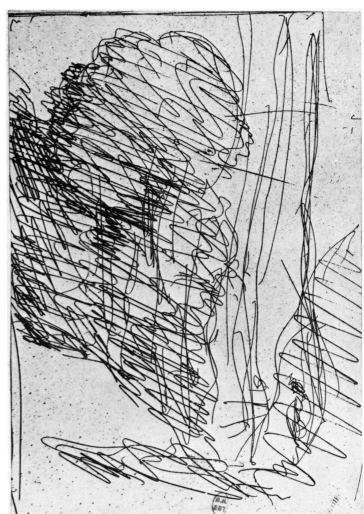

C. 54

C. 55

C. 56

73

C. 59

C. 60

C. 62

78

C. 66

C. 64

C. 67

C. 68

C. 69

82

C.69

C. 70

C. 71

C. 72

C. 73

87

C. 74

88

C. 75

89

C. 76

90

C. 77

C. 78

91

C. 79

C. 79

92

C. 80

93

C. 81

C. 82

C. 83

C. 86

95

C. 84

C. 85

C. 87

C. 88

C. 89

C. 90

C. 91

C. 92

C. 93

99

C. 94

C. 95

C. 96

C. 97

C. 98

C. 99

102

CORO*

C. 100

103

DAUBIGNY

(1817-1878)

D. 1

D. 2

D. 3

D. 4

D. 5

D. 6

D. 7

DÉDIÉ A LA GARDE NATIONALE

28 Juillet 1840.

Partout luira l'egalité féconde
Les vieilles lois errent sur des débris
Le monde ancien finit d'un nouveau monde
La France est reine et son louvre est Paris

A vous, enfans ce fruit des trois journées
Ceux qui sont là vous frayaient le chemin
Le sang français des grandes destinées
Trace en tout temps la route au genre humain.

D. 8

D. 9

D. 10

110

Peint et Gravé par Daubigny

Paysage Saint Jérôme

D. 11

D. 12

III

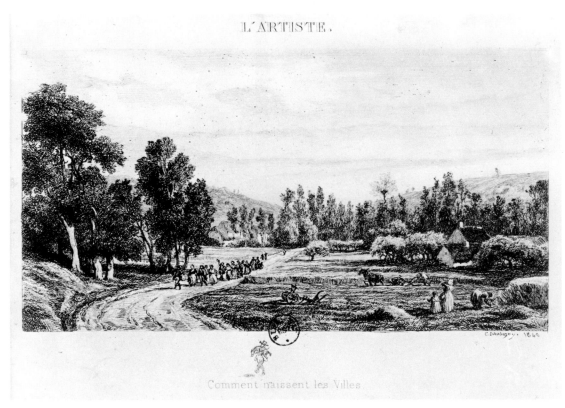

Comment naissent les Villes.

D. 13

LE CALEPIN D'UN ARTISTE

D. 14

D. 15

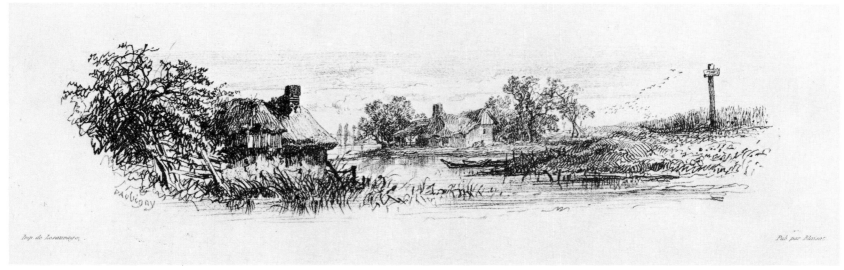

D. 14

113

D. 16

D. 17

D. 18

D. 19

Le Cèdre.

D. 20

L'Amphithéâtre.

D. 21

D. 22

Volière
des Passereaux.

D. 23

Pie.

D. 24

L'ORAGE.

Il pleut, il pleut, bergère,
Presse tes blancs moutons;
Allons sous ma chaumière,
Bergère, vite, allons:
J'entends sur le feuillage
L'eau qui tombe à grand bruit:
Voici, voici l'orage;
Voilà l'éclair qui luit.

Entends-tu le tonnerre?
Il roule en approchant;
Prends un abri, bergère,
A ma droite, en marchant;
Je vois notre cabane....
Et, tiens, voici venir
Ma mère et ma sœur anne
Qui vont l'étable ouvrir.

Bonsoir, bonsoir, ma mère;
Ma sœur anne, bonsoir;
J'amène ma bergère
Près de vous pour ce soir.
Va te sécher, ma mie,
Auprès de nos tisons;
Sœur, fais-lui compagnie,
Entrez, petits moutons.

LE ROSIER.

Je l'ai planté, je l'ai vu naître
Ce beau rosier où les oiseaux
Viennent chanter sous ma fenêtre,
Perchés sur ses jeunes rameaux.

Joyeux oiseaux, troupe amoureuse,
Ah ! par pitié ne chantez pas ;
L'amant qui me rendait heureuse
Est parti pour d'autres climats.

D. 27

Pour les trésors du nouveau monde
Il fuit l'amour, brave la mort.
Hélas! pourquoi chercher sur l'onde
Le bonheur qu'il trouvait au port.

Vous, passagères hirondelles
Qui revenez chaque printemps
Oiseaux voyageurs, mais fidelles
Ramenez-le moi tous les ans.

D. 28

D. 29

C'est l'amour, c'est sa flamme
Qui brille dans ses yeux :
Je croyais que son ame
Brûlait des mêmes feux.
Lisette à son aurore
Respirait le plaisir :
Hélas ! si jeune encore
Sait-on déjà trahir ?

Sa voix pour me séduire
Avait plus de douceur.
Jusques à son sourire,
Tout en elle est trompeur :
Tout en elle intéresse,
Et je voudrais, hélas !
Qu'elle eut plus de tendresse,
Ou qu'elle eut moins d'appas.

O ma tendre musette,
Console ma douleur :
Parle moi de lisette ;
Ce nom fait mon bonheur.
Je la revois plus belle,
Plus belle tous les jours :
Je me plains toujours d'elle,
Et je l'aime toujours.

D. 30

C. DAUBIGNY.

LES SOUHAITS.

Que ne suis-je la fougère
Où, sur la fin d'un beau jour,
Se repose ma bergère
Sous la garde de l'amour !
Que ne suis-je le zéphire
Qui rafraichit ses appas,
L'air que sa bouche respire,
La fleur qui nait sous ses pas.

Que ne suis-je l'onde pure
Qui la reçoit dans son sein !
Que ne suis-je la parure
Qui la couvre après le bain !
Que ne suis-je cette glace
Où son miroir répété
Offre à nos yeux une grace
Qui sourit à la beauté.

Que ne puis-je par un songe
Tenir son cœur enchanté !
Que ne puis-je du mensonge
Passer à la vérité !
Les dieux qui m'ont donné l'être
M'ont fait trop ambitieux,
Car enfin je voudrais être
Tout ce qui plait à ses yeux.

D. 31

D. 32

123

LA TENTATION DE St ANTOINE.

AIR : *Plus inconstant que l'onde.*

Ciel ! l'univers va-t-il donc se dissoudre ?
Quel bruit ! quels cris ! quel horrible fracas !
Devant moi je vois la foudre,
Elle tombe par éclats :
Tout est en poudre
Sur mon grabat.
Grand Dieu ! du haut des cieux,
Vois ma disgrâce,
Et par ta grâce,
Fais que je chasse
L'enfer de ces lieux.

AIR : *Du haut en bas.*

C'était ainsi
Qu'Antoine exprimait ses alarmes ;
C'était ainsi
Qu'Antoine exprimait son souci,
Lorsque le diable, par ses charmes,
Venait chez lui faire vacarmes.
C'était ainsi.

AIR : *Des folies d'Espagne.*

On vit sortir d'une grotte profonde
Mille démons, mille spectres divers ;
Des noirs esprits toute la troupe immonde,
Pour le tenter déserta les enfers.

D. 33

D. 34

AIR: *Turelure, lure, et flon flon flon*.

On vit des démons
De tous les cantons,
De la ville et de la campagne,
De la Cochinchine et d'Espagne;
    On vit des diables blondins,
Des bruns, des gris et des châtains;
Les bruns, surtout, méchans lutins,
Faisaient remuer des pantins,
        Turelure, lure,
        Et flon, flon, flon,
    Tous avaient leur ton,
        Leur allure.

AIR: *La faridondaine*.

Quelques-uns prirent le Cochon
    De ce bon Saint Antoine,
    Et, lui mettant un capuchon,
    Ils en firent un moine;
    Il n'en coutait que la façon,
        La faridondaine,
        La faridondon:
Peut-être en avait-il l'esprit,
        Biribi,
A la façon de barbari,
        Mon ami.

AIR: *Dans un détour*.

Sur un Sofa
Une diablesse en falbala,
    Aux regards fripons,
Découvrait deux jolis monts
        Ronds.

AIR: *Au fond de mon caveau*.

Ronflant comme un Cochon,
    On voyait sur un trône
Un des envoyés de Pluton;
    Il portait pour couronne
    Un vieux réchaud sans fond,
    Et pour sceptre un tison
Sous ses pieds un démon,
    En forme de dragon
    Vomissait du canon.
Le diable s'éveille, s'étonne,
    Et dit: garçon!

AIR: *La Pierre-Fitoise* (Contre danse)

Courez-vite, prenez le patron,
Et faites-le moi danser en rond ;
Courez-vite, prenez le patron,
Tirez-le par son cordon.
Bon !
Messieurs les démons, laissez moi donc !
Non, tu chanteras,
Tu sauteras.
Tu danseras.
Messieurs les démons, laissez moi donc !
Non, tu chanteras,
Tu sauteras.
Tu danseras.
Courez-vite, prenez le patron,
Tirez-le par son cordon.
Bon !

AIR: *Quand la mer rouge apparut*.

Le Saint, craignant de pécher
Dans cette aventure,
S'en fut vite se cacher
Sous sa couverture ;
Mais, montant sur son Châlit,
Il rencontra dans son lit
Un minois fripon,
Un joli tendron,
Sous des traits
Pleins d'attraits,
Une Concubine....
C'était Proserpine.

AIR: *Nous autres bons Villageois*.

Piqué, dans ce bacchanal,
D'avoir vu qu'on brisait sa cruche,
Et qu'un derrière infernal
Avait fait caca dans sa huche,
Crainte aussi de tentation,
Notre St prend un goupillon,
Et flanque aux démons étonnés
De l'eau bénite par le nez.

126

AIR: *Des folies d'Espagne.*

Tel qu'un voleur, sitôt qu'il voit main forte,
Tel qu'un soldat, à l'aspect des prevôts:
On vit s'enfuir l'infernale Cohorte,
Et s'abimer dans ses affreux cachots.

AIR: *Ah! maman, que je l'echappai belle!*

Ah! mon Dieu, que je l'echappe belle!
Dit le saint tremblant,
Tout en sortant
De sa ruelle.
Ah! mon Dieu, que je l'echappe belle!
Un moment plus tard,
Je faisais le diable Cornard.

AIR: *Le démon malicieux et fin.*

Le démon, quoiqu'il passe pour fin,
Ne fut pas lors assez malin;
Ah! s'il eut pris la forme de Toinette,
Son air charmant, sa taille et ses appas,
C'en était fait! la grâce était muette,
Et St Antoine eut volé dans ses bras.

Ma sœur, te souvient-il encore
    Du château que baignait la Dore ?
Et de cette tant vieille tour
    Du Maure,
Où l'airain sonnait le retour
    Du jour ?

Te souvient-il du lac tranquille
Qu'effleurait l'hirondelle agile,
Du vent qui courbait le roseau
    Mobile,
Et du soleil couchant sur l'eau,
    Si beau ?

128

D. 37

Te souvient-il de cette amie,   Oh! qui me rendra mon Héléne
Tendre compagne de ma vie?   Et ma montagne, et le grand chéne?
Dans les bois en cueillant la fleur   Leur souvenir fait tous les jours
           Jolie,   Ma peine:
Héléne appuyait sur mon cœur   Mon pays sera mes amours
           Son cœur.   Toujours!

DAUBIGNY

LEÇONS D'UNE MÈRE A SA FILLE

Cet étang,
Qui s'étend
dans la plaine,
Répète au sein de ses eaux
Ces verdoyans ormeaux
Où le pampre s'enchaîne ;
Un ciel pur,
Un azur
Sans nuages,
Vivement s'y réfléchit,
Le tableau s'enrichit
D'images.

Mais tandis que l'on admire
Cette onde où le ciel se mire,
Un zéphir
Vient ternir
Sa surface,
D'un souffle il confond les traits,
L'éclat de tant d'objets
S'efface.

Un désir,
Un soupir,
Oh ! ma fille !
Peut ainsi troubler un cœur
Où se peint la candeur,
Où la sagesse brille ;
Le repos
Sur ces eaux
Peut renaître ;
Mais il se perd sans retour
Dans un cœur dont l'amour
Est maître.

C. DAUBIGNY.

D. 39

130

LA CHANSON DE LISETTE.

Lise chantait dans la prairie,
En faisant paitre son troupeau ;
Blaise à sa voix bientot marie
Les accens de son chalumeau.
Le fripon suivit la coquette ;
Il la suivit jusqu'au hameau,
En essayant, sur sa musette,
La chanson que chantait Lisette.

En s'en retournant au village,
Elle lui jeta son bouquet ;
Il lui refusa mais je gage,
Pour le remettre à son corset.
Il le rendit à la coquette,
L'attacha d'un air satisfait,
Et répéta, sur sa musette,
La chanson que chantait Lisette.

Le soir on dansa sur l'herbette,
Blaise et moi nous dansions tous deux ;
Mais il me quitta pour Lisette
Qui vint se mêler à nos jeux.
Il s'en fut avec la coquette,
Le plaisir brillait dans ses yeux ;
En eut-il eu, si sa musette
N'eût jamais fait chanter Lisette ?

D. 41

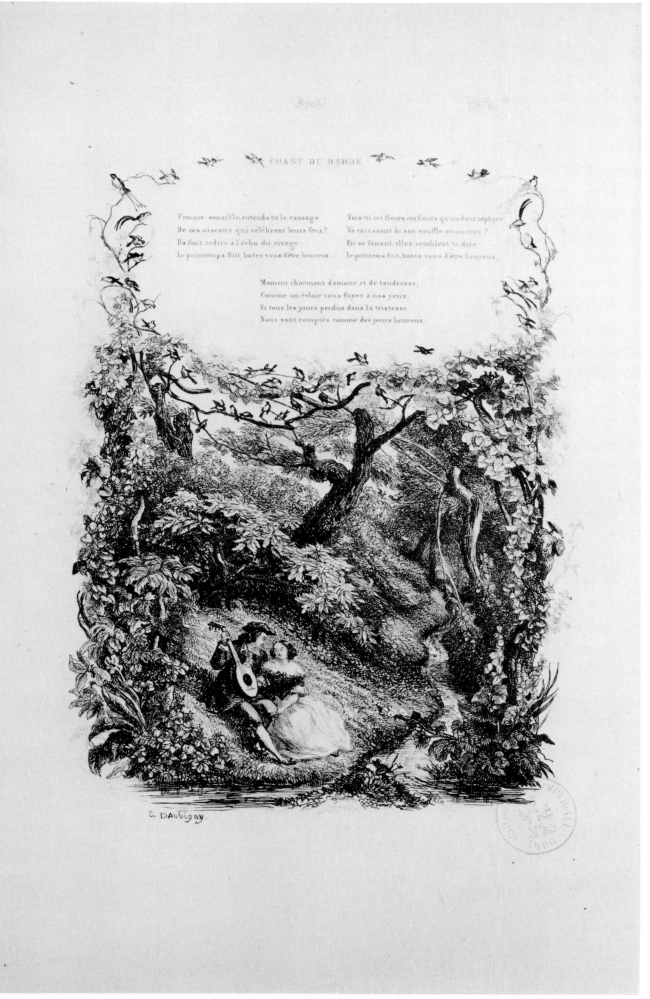

CHANT DU BARDE

Femme sensible, entends tu le ramage   Vois-tu ces fleurs, ces fleurs qu'un doux zéphyre
De ces oiseaux qui célèbrent leurs feux?   Va caressant de son souffle amoureux?
Ils font redire à l'écho du rivage: En se fanant, elles semblent te dire
Le printemps fuit, hatez vous d'être heureux   Le printems fuit, hatez vous d'être heureux.

Moment charmant d'amour et de tendresse,
Comme un éclair vous fuyez à nos yeux,
Et tous les jours perdus dans la tristesse
Nous sont comptés comme des jours heureux.

C. Daubigny.

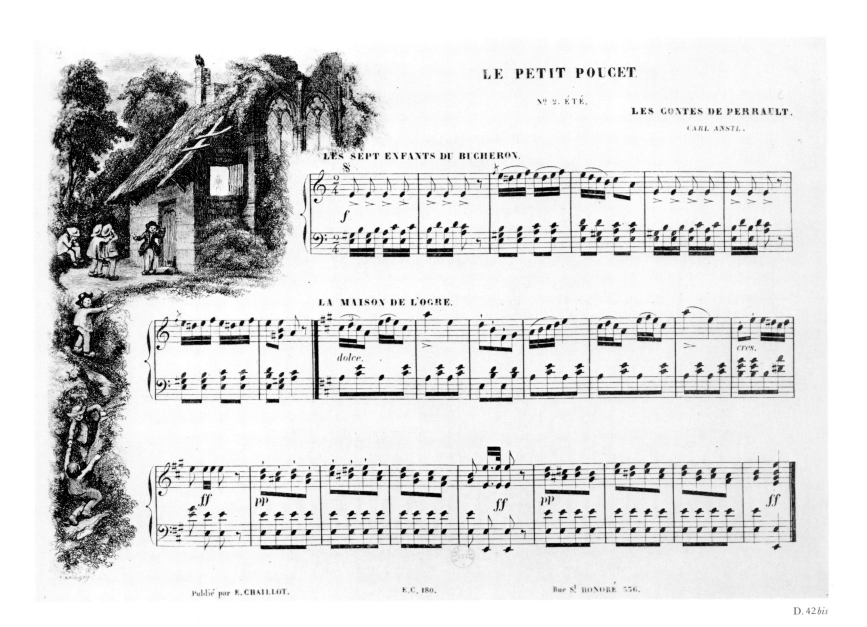

PEAU D'ANE.

N° 5. FINAL.

LES CONTES DE PERRAULT.
CARL ANSLT.

Publié par E. CHAILLIOT.   E. C. 180.   Rue St. HONORÉ 356.

D. 43

136

Le Marché du Temple

D. 45

Le Jardin d'Hiver

D. 46

ÉGLISE DE  Ste AMÉLIE.

Fondée en 1843 par Marie. Augustin. Xavier Feuillet.

Ancien Officier de Marine Militaire   Chevalier de la Légion d'Honneur.

au Places Commune de St Ham   *Département de la Nièvre.*

EXÉCUTÉE SUR LES PLANS DE Mr LENORMAND, ARCHITECTE.

D. 47

D. 48

D. 86

D. 86

L'ARTISTE

LE NID DE L'AIGLE,

dans la Forêt de Fontainebleau

D. 51

D. 52

141

D. 53

D. 54

142

D. 55

D. 56

D. 57

HABITATION DE M. A. THIERS

D. 58

CABINET DE TRAVAIL DE M. A. THIERS

D. 59

D. 60

D. 61

D. 61

145

D. 62

D. 62

Daubigny d'après Débas

D. 63

Claude Lorrain del.   musée du Louvre   Daubigny sculp.

D. 64

VALLÉE DE SAN JUAN DEL ORO.

D. 65

148

EAUX - FORTES,

PAR

DAUBIGNY

D. 66

D. 67

D. 71

D. 71

151

Dabigny. inv.

D. 72

152

D. 73

D. 74

D. 75

D. 76

D. 77

D. 78

D. 78

D. 78

D. 79

D. 80

D. 81

D. 82

D. 83

D. 84

D. 85

D. 87

D. 88

D. 89

D. 90

D. 91

D. 92

Daubigny

D. 93

D. 94

D. 95

un Cochon de propriétaire qui ne ferr de bien qu'après sa mort.

D. 96

163

Voyage
EN BATEAU
Croquis à l'Eau Forte
PAR
DAUBIGNY
1862.

D. 99

D. 99

D. 100

165

D. 101

D. 102

166

Le mousse tirant au Cordeau

D. 103

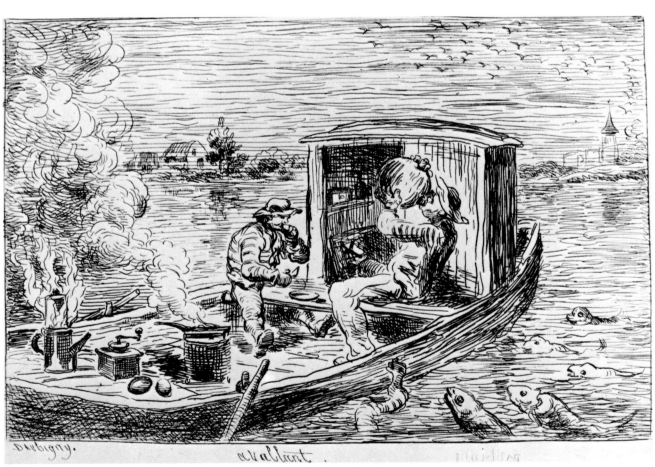

Vaillant

D. 104

Le mot de Cambronne

D. 105

La recherche d'une Auberge

D. 106

168

La recherche de l'auberge.

La recherche d'une auberge

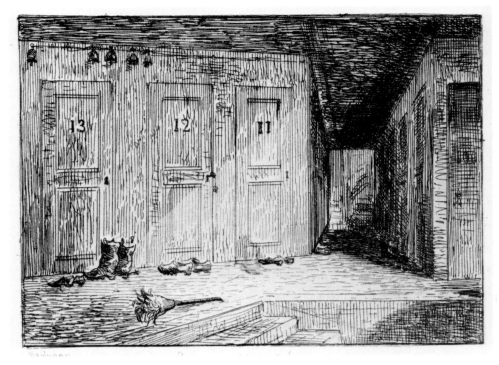

D. 107

D. 107

Voyage de nuit

D. 108

Daubigny.

D. 109

D. 110

Daubigny

D. 111

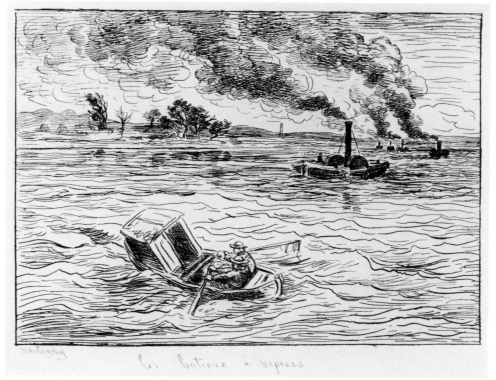

Les bateaux à vapeurs

D.112

coucher à bord du bottin

D.113

réjouissance des poissons du départ du bateau

D.114

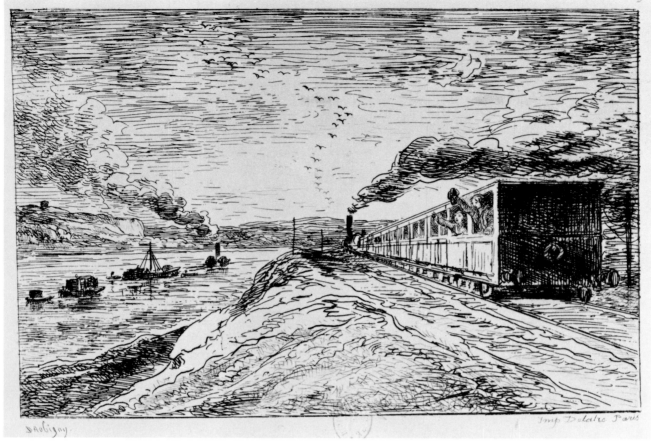

D. 115

173

D. 116

D. 117

D. 118

D. 119

D. 120

Daubigny. 1862.

D. 121

176

Daubigny 1874

D. 122

177

D. 123

D. 124

178

D. 125

D. 126

MAISON À ARGENTEUIL.
Rue des Ouches, N? 8.

Plusieurs grands et petits appartemens depuis 100ᶠ jusqu'à 500 et 600ᶠ à louer avec jouissance d'un beau jardin de deux hectares.

Départs pour Argenteuil toutes les heures depuis 7ʰ·1/2 du matin jusqu'à 9ʰ du soir par le Chemin de Fer de

St Germain. — Prix des places: 75 Centimes.

S'adresser sur les lieux au propriétaire.

LE PHALANSTÈRE (Village modèle) se compose d'environ 400 familles de fortunes inégales, **associées** en tous travaux exploitant 1500 hectares ou une lieue carrée de terrain comme la propriété d'un seul!!

Les économies résultant de la combinaison Sociétaire produiront un bien être considérable dont chaque associé profitera. Par exemple, les logements sont disposés suivant les goûts et les fortunes, dans une seule construction, ayant au 1er Étage une rue galerie, chauffée ou ventilée suivant les saisons, une seule Cuisine, une seule Cave, un seul Grenier, bien pourvus d'instruments et attirails; les four des Cuisines, Forges et Machines, font circuler partout le Calorique, chaque logement a des bouches de chaleur, des robinets d'eau chaude, bees de Gaz, &c &c

D'un côté sont les Ateliers bruyants, de l'autre sont ceux des savants et artistes, au centre sur le Jardin d'hiver et les Serres chaudes sont les appartements des **Vieillards**, à l'Entresol les Crèches et Logements des Enfants jusqu'à 18 ans, avec toutes les convenances appropriées aux âges et sexes.

La Société se charge de l'**Éducation de tous**, afin que chaque associé, Homme, Femme, Enfant, puissent développer les facultés qu'ils ont reçues de Dieu.

Les repas préparés en grand, n'emploient que 20 ou 30 personnes au lieu de 400 et sont servis aux consommateurs, soit en société choisie, soit séparément par chaque famille, ou chaque individu.

Par une combinaison toute nouvelle, les travaux deviennent plus **attrayants** que les Cartes, Billards, Bals et Spectacles, ce qui rendant la **Paresse** impossible

ramène à l'**Agriculture** les Ouvriers et les Agents **improductifs** qui encombrent les Villes, et permet de garantir à tous un minimum **copieux**, en Vêtements, Logements, Nourriture et Plaisirs.

En avant de la Cour principale sont les bâtiments ruraux, Étables, Bergeries, Granges, &c &c

Tous les éléments de bonheur qui sont aujourd'hui dans les mains du plus petit nombre, et souvent contraires à l'intérêt des masses, sont mis à la portée de tous, la mécanique loin de nuire aux travailleurs devient un auxiliaire dont ils profitent en donnant à la culture de leur esprit le temps pendant lequel les machines fonctionnent pour eux.

Chaque année les comptes sont réglés suivant le **Capital**, le **Travail** et le **Talent** que chacun a fournis pour le résultat général. Ce partage proportionnel fera cesser toutes les luttes que le salaire entraîne et rend inévitables.

Dans le Phalanstère enfin il y a association intégrale, la **Vérité**, la **Liberté** et la **Justice**, président à toutes les relations! L'emploi de l'activité humaine a pour base l'Agriculture, les travaux de Ménage, de Fabrique, de Sciences et d'Arts, lui viennent en aide. **Là, plus de Chômages**, plus de crises industrielles et Commerciales, plus de ces famines périodiques qui menacent à chaque instant l'ordre social, mais bien participation de tous aux jouissances légitimes auxquelles Dieu nous a destinés.

Voir le Nouveau Monde Industriel de Ch. Fourier) Librairie Phalanstérienne Quai Voltaire, 25

D. 129

PENSION DE Mᵐᵉ DAUTEL

33, Bourg-la Reine.

TENUE DES LIVRES

LITTÉRATURE

HISTᵣₑ NATURELLE.

ANGLAIS

MUSIQUE

DESSIN

D. 130

C. Daubigny.

D. 131

D. 132

D. 133

D. 134

D. 135

D. 1350   D. 136

D. 136

Daubigny.

D. 1350

D. 137

D.138

D.139

D. 140

D. 141

D. 142

D. 143

D.144

D.145

D. 146

D. 147

D. 148

D. 149

195

D. 150

DUPRÉ
(1811-1889)

Jules Dupré.

Lith. de Frey.

PACAGES DU LIMOUSIN.

(Salon de 1835.)

Jules Dupré.

Lith. de Frey.

MOULIN

de la Sologne.

Du. 2

199

Jules Dupré

Lith. de Frey.

VUE PRISE EN NORMANDIE.

Du. 3

J.D

Jules Dupré del.

Lith. de Frey.

Vue prise dans le port de Plimouth.
(Devon.)

Du. 4

Jules Dupré

I. de Briard et Frey

Vue prise en Angleterre

Salon de 1836

Du. 5

Jules Dupré

Lith. de Briard et Frey

Bords de la Somme,

(Picardie)

Du. 6

J. Dupre del   Imp. de Lemercier Benard & C.

Vue prise à Alençon (Dep.t de l'Orne)

Du. 7

J.D

Du. 8

Du. 9

203

JONGKIND

(1819-1891)

J. 1

CHEZ L'AUTEUR RUE CHEVREUSE 9
CAHIER
D'EAUX FORTES
PAR
JONGKIND
IMP. DELÂTRE PARIS 1862
RUE St JAQUES 365

J. 1bis

J. 2

J. 4

J. 5

211

J. 6

212

J. 7

213

maastad Jongkind 1862

Paris Publié par A. CADART & F. CHEVALIER, Éditeurs, Rue Richelieu, 66.

VUE DE LA VILLE DE MAASLINS. (Hollande)

Imp. Delâtre, Rue des Feuillantines, 4, Paris.

J. 8

214

Jongkind 1863

Jongkind 1863

216

143

Jongkind 1864

Paris, Publié par CADART & LUQUET, Editeurs, 79, Rue Richelieu.

SORTIE DU PORT DE HONFLEUR.

Imp. Delâtre, Rue St Jacques, 303, Paris.

J.11

217

Jong Kind 1865

J. 12

Jongkind 1866

J.14

J.15

J. 16

J. 17

J. 18

J. 19

3 Aout 1878 Paris

Jongkind 1878

J. 20

MILLET

(1814-1875)

M. 1

M. 2

M. 2

M. 2

M. 2

M. 3

M. 4

M. 5

M. 7

M. 6

M. 8

227

M. 9

M. 10

228

M. 11

M. 12

M. 13

230

M. 14

232

M. 15

233

M. 16

J.F. Millet 1861.

M. 17

J.-F. Millet

M. 18

J. F. Millet

M. 19

M. 19 *bis*

M. 19 *ter*

M. 19 *quater*

M. 19 *quinter*

M. 19 *quinter*

J.F. Millet

M.21

Certifié, épreuve no. 4

21 février 1889   H Leymarie

M. 22

OLIVIER DE SERRES
Seigneur du Pradel
Né en 1539, mort le 2 Juillet 1619

M. 23

241

M. 24

M. 26

M. 26bis

245

J. F. Millet

D. 1350

M. 29   M. 29

M. 29

M. 29

M. 29 *bis*

M. 30

M. 31

M. 32

M. 34

M. 34

J.F. Millet

M. 33

ROUSSEAU
(1812-1867)

R. 1

R. 2

R. 3

TH. Rousseau Mai 1861.   R. 4

TH. Rousseau

R. 5

R. 6

254

GUIDE TO THE CATALOGUES

NUMBERING

For practical purposes, and also for the reasons indicated in our introduction, we have not modified the numbering given in *Le Peintre-graveur illustré* by Loÿs Delteil, who catalogued all the artists represented here except Boudin. Works added to his lists are identified by *bis, ter,* etc., following his number.

However, though retaining the continuous numbering of the states, we prefer to make the distinction that Delteil does not make between *states* and *printings*. The *state* presupposes that the artist has reworked the plate in some way, and this is the sole justification for using the term in art history, whereas *reprintings* may involve certain inessential modifications generally affecting only whatever text there may be or such items as printer's identification but not the image.

The numeration of Delteil is generally chronological except, often enough, for the glassplate prints. We have chosen to present our catalogue entries and illustrations in correct chronological sequence, and if it occasionally happens that, by keeping to the Delteil numbering, ours turns out to be not consecutive, the transpositions are not so great as to make it difficult to find the number sought. In any case, this affects only the glassplates of Corot; the single instance of an etching by Daubigny, no. 86, which here precedes his no. 49; and the lithographs of Millet.

DIMENSIONS

The dimensions are those of the frame line (the *"trait carré"* of the French catalogues) or, when that is absent, of the "motif" or image itself. For greater precision in dealing with objects as small as prints, and to facilitate comparisons with foreign listings, measurements are given here in millimeters rather than inches (as a rough guide, 25 mm. = 1 in.), with height preceding width.

It should be kept in mind that the dimensions of prints, and even more of those made from glassplate negatives, are never identical on different proofs of the same plate, sometimes varying by as much as 10 millimeters (3/8 inch).

PAPER

Some names and treatments of paper have been given in French since they are regularly used by printmakers, collectors, and cataloguers. A fine paper (usually China) that is *appliqué* (or *fixé* or *collé*) is one which has been slightly moistened and then, by being passed under the press, made to adhere to a stronger paper. The opposite of this is *volant,* the fine paper being printed without such backing.

ABBREVIATIONS

References to catalogues other than those of Delteil are given for each print following the dimensions. Full titles will be found in the bibliography and are abbreviated here as follows: for Corot, R. = Robaut; for Daubigny, H. = Henriet; for Dupré, A. = Aubrun, Hd. = Hédiard; for Jongkind, Hg. = Hefting; for Millet, L. = Lebrun. Other abbreviations are self-explanatory.

The collections most often referred to are indicated thus:
Baltimore = Baltimore Museum of Art (houses also the prints of the Lucas Collection, Maryland Institute, and of the Garrett Collection)
BN = Cabinet des Estampes, Bibliothèque Nationale, Paris
Boston = Boston Museum of Fine Arts
Bremen = Kunsthalle, Bremen
BrM = Print Room, British Museum, London
Brussels = Cabinet des Estampes, Bibliothèque Royale Albert Ier
Chicago = Art Institute of Chicago
Dresden = Kupferstich-Kabinett, Staatliche Kunstsammlungen, Dresden
NYPL = Print Room, New York Public Library
V & A = Victoria & Albert Museum, London
Yale = Yale University Art Gallery, New Haven, Connecticut

Where no source is given for prints reproduced, they are in the collection of the Bibliothèque Nationale, Paris.

EUGÈNE BOUDIN
(1824–1898)

Boudin, like his friend Claude Monet, was never really interested in the graphic arts. The inventory of the French holdings in the Bibliothèque Nationale lists two prints, to which must be added a lithograph which, like the single etching, was done only because he had become a celebrated painter in his late years and something of the sort was expected of him. True, he had been asked earlier, but apparently in vain, by the newly founded Société des Peintres-Graveurs in a letter preserved among the documents in the Cabinet des Estampes of the Bibliothèque Nationale:

March 11, 1891

Dear Master,

The Painter-Engravers, meeting in general assembly for the foundation of their society in the quarters of M. Durand-Ruel, have on my proposal elected you a member of the said society. Have you done any sketches on varnished copper? Since my arrival I have been worked to death with all sorts of matters, but I am planning to get back to driving away at engraving as of next Monday, and if you had something ready I could etch it for you during the week.

Yours sincerely,
Félix Buhot.

It was perfectly normal in that period to elect to the Society of Painter-Engravers a painter who had never engraved, since the original aim of the association was to bring together painters and graphic artists and to encourage them to engrave and to exhibit their prints alongside their paintings and drawings. The Société got along very well, but without Boudin.

1851

B 1. *Cavalcade havraise*
Lithograph, 300 × 460 mm.
There are two prints of this in the Bibliothèque Nationale, including the duty copy for copyright *(dépôt légal)* registered by the printer David of Le Havre. This is not an original work by Boudin but was done after a drawing by his first patron, A. Couveley, director of the Le Havre museum.

1897

B 2. *Mathurins (Jack Tars)*
Lithograph, 112 × 157 mm.
This small blue lithograph was commissioned from Boudin as part of the album titled *Art et Nature* of L. Roger-Milès published by G. Boudet in 1897 and containing graphic work by or after thirty contemporary artists. There were original engravings by Albert Besnard, J.-C. Cazin, Paul Renouard, and Camille Pissarro and reproduction-engravings by Desmoulins, Duvivier, Kratké, Letterrier, A. Masson, A. Mongin, Paul Rajon, J.-J. Veyrassat, and Henri Vion done after works by Corot, Daubigny, Decamp, Delacroix, Narcisse Diaz, Dupré, Meissonier, Millet, Gustave Moreau, Charles Jacque, Théodule Ribot, F. Roybet, Théodore Rousseau, Constant Troyon, and Félix Ziem. The nature of the lithographs, however, is less clear. The table of contents lists "original" lithographs by Georges Callot, Boudin, Jean-Louis Forain, Albert Lebourg, Pierre Puvis de Chavannes, J.-F. Raffaëlli, and Alfred Sisley, and while the captions for the tipped-in plates of Lebourg, Raffaëlli, Alfred-Philippe Roll, and Sisley state *"lithographie originale,"* that of Puvis de Chavannes says only *"lithographie,"* and that of Boudin *"croquis lithographique"* (lithographic sketch). In a book intended for print lovers and collectors such a distinction could only be deliberate. The edition was limited to 525 copies, with 25 on Japan paper and 500 on wove paper *(vélin)*.

1898

B 3. *Marine View*
Etching, 117 × 159 mm.
This etching was published shortly after the death of Boudin in the December, 1899, issue of *L'Estampe et l'affiche*, a magazine put out by Clément-Janin and Mellerio which printed engravings as premiums on China paper with wide margins for the de luxe copies of the review and on laid paper *(vergé)* for ordinary copies. The commentary that went with this print gives little information:

The etching by Boudin that we give as premium in this issue is a unique piece in the work of the master. Boudin in fact confined himself to painting and only once attempted to transpose his faculties of vision into black and white, and the print we give you today was the result. Other works were in preparation. This master of harmonies ought to have felt himself at ease with the print, but of two copper plates on which he essayed his talent only one was subjected to acid-biting. This is the *Marine* that we publish today. We have preserved in this sketch all its character and its pungency as *first state*, with its holes and the smudges of the acid. Just as it is, it truly reveals a Boudin; it is therefore more than a curiosity, it is a work which it was interesting to make known. . . . It is to M. Georges Cahen that we owe access to this copper plate. Of this etching, besides our publication there will be put up for sale only fourteen proofs on China paper pulled before adding lettering [*avant la lettre*]: 10 francs.

1) Pre-lettering printing on China paper for the first 36 copies of *L'Estampe et l'affiche*, plus 14 copies, to a total of 50 *(reproduced)*.
2) Printing on laid paper for the ordinary edition of the review including as lettering on the plate at lower left: *Boudin inv. et sc.;* at lower right: *E & A,* and often with the uninked embossed stamp of the review in the margin.
3) Printing of 300 copies of which 25 on Japan paper for the book by Gustave Cahen, *Eugène Boudin : sa vie et son oeuvre,* Paris, H. Floury, 1900. On these the lettering was crudely scratched off.

CAMILLE COROT
(1796–1875)

ETCHINGS

c. 1845 and 1865
C 1. *Souvenir of Tuscany*
Etching, 122 × 178 mm.; Robaut cat. no. 3123.
This etching was executed in two stages, twenty years apart, according to Bracquemond, who claimed to have found the varnished and drawn but unbitten plate "in a box of nails" in Corot's home in 1865 and thereupon proposed to etch and print it for the aged master. The first, very summary drawing must have been done around 1845, though its eventual purpose is not known. What is certain is that Corot was sufficiently uninterested in this work to abandon it in its first state and uncompleted. Janine Bailly-Herzberg (1975) writes that "perhaps there was no particular reason [for his beginning it] outside of the fact that at that time etching was little by little gaining its autonomy," and recalls the publication of an album by Hervier in 1843 and Daubigny's showing of three etchings at the Salon of 1845 which Corot would

certainly have seen. Marcel Guiot (1925) wondered, rightly no doubt, if perhaps it was left unfinished because the artist was repelled at that time by the difficulties of acid-biting. The plain fact is, Corot simply had no interest in the technique of engraving, and the rare etchings he subsequently produced were generally undertaken at the insistence of friends and publishers and executed with the aid of technicians.

1) First state with apparently only three proofs printed by Bracquemond before Corot made considerable changes in the drawing. Of these Bracquemond kept one, Mouilleron had another which passed to Robaut, then to Moreau-Nélaton, and is today in the BN *(reproduced)*, and a third is in the NYPL.

2) Second state after definitive reworking by Corot but before lettering, including prints showing sharp corners on the plate and

3) others with rounded corners, some on Japan paper, some with very heavy inking *(reproduced)*.

4) Printing for the *Gazette des Beaux-Arts* (about 750 copies) in the issue of April 1, 1875, to illustrate the obituary article on Corot by Louis Gonse, director of the review, with lettering below the frame line, at the left: *Corot del. & sculp.*; lower: *Gazette des Beaux-Arts*; in the middle: *Souvenir de Toscane*; at the right: *Imp. A. Salmon, Paris.*

5) New printing to illustrate Roger Marx, *Études sur l'école française,* Paris, 1903.

A false pre-lettering state exists.

1857
C 2. *Ville d'Avray: Boat Under Willows (Morning Effect)*
Etching and drypoint, 72 × 121 mm.; R. 3124.
Entreated by his friend Edmond Roche to illustrate the book of poems he was planning, Corot executed this first project, which he then abandoned, plus a second not printed until 1862 (see C 3).

1) Etching only, before numerous reworkings, of which two proofs are known: one in Chicago (formerly Deering Coll.), the other in the BN (formerly Robaut Coll.: *reproduced*).

2) Completed. The proof in the BN came from Jules Michelin, the engraver who helped Corot to bite and print the trial proofs of the second plate (C 3), which makes it likely that he performed those services for this as well, although Bailly-Herzberg thinks that it was thanks to the Société des Aquafortistes, and therefore not before 1862, that collaboration was made possible. Other proofs in BrM, Chicago, and NYPL.

1862
C 3. *Ville d'Avray: Boatman on Pond (Evening Effect)*
Etching and drypoint, 72 × 121 mm.; R. 3125.
Done for the posthumous edition of the poems of Edmond Roche, which includes poems dedicated to various artists, among them one "À M. C. Corot" dated from Ville d'Avray, which begins (p. 99): "Nous regardions l'étang d'une eau morne et plombée" (We were gazing at the pond with its bleak and leaden water), and ends: "Cette idylle à nos yeux peut encor reparaître/ Si vous le voulez bien: N'êtes-vous pas le Maître/ Qui l'avez recréée après le Créateur?" (This idyll can appear once more before our eyes/ Should you so wish: Are you not the Master/ Who has created it again after the Creator?).

1) Before a few drypoint strokes and the signature at the upper right. The proof in the BN is annotated by Jules Michelin, who assisted Corot: "Corot, pour les poésies posthumes d'Ed. Roche, 1ʳᵉ épr. d'essai" (Corot, for the posthumous poems of Edmond Roche, first trial proof).

2) With drypoint work and signature *Corot* in upper right, "lightly re-bit" according to Robaut (in Beraldi). "State printed in thirty or so proofs by Jules Michelin who had seen to the biting of the plate in October, 1862" (Delteil) *(reproduced)*.

3) Printing for Edmond Roche, *Poésies posthumes,* Paris, Michel Lévy, 1863, of about 200 copies. A proof cited by Delteil bore the remark: "Avant l'aciérage 24 9bre 1862, une des 2 Ep. sur chine volant" (Before the steel coating [of the plate], September 24, 1862, one of the two proofs on unfixed China paper).

1863
C 4. *A Lake in the Tyrol*
Etching, 112 × 173 mm.; R. 3126.
This was done for the illustrated monthly of the Société des Artistes Réunis, *Le Monde des Arts,* an ephemeral publication that lasted only from October, 1864, to June, 1866.

1) A single state, and of that state a single known proof before lettering (Chicago).

2) With lettering at lower right: *Paris, Imp. Houiste r. Mignon 5* (Baltimore).

3) With printer's name as above plus at lower left: *Le Monde des Arts.* Edition of about two hundred prints published in the issue of September 1, 1865 *(reproduced)*.

False pre-lettering state in quite numerous copies, perhaps some twenty proofs on Japan, gray-blue, and other papers.

C 5. *Souvenir of Italy*
Etching, 294 × 220 mm.; R. 3127.
The dates of 1866 and 1865 given respectively by Delteil and Beraldi are to be corrected since this plate was the first contribution of Corot to the Société des Aquafortistes, who published it as no. 38 in their eighth selection, April 1, 1863.

1) For Corot himself there was a single state of this plate, but after the printing for the Société des Aquafortistes it underwent numerous alterations that were not properly speaking voluntary and usually not intentional. Rare prelettering proofs, one annotated by Jules Michelin, who no doubt aided Corot in biting the plate and pulling trial proofs (Delteil's attribution of that task to Bracquemond does not mean he alone did it).

2) Edition for the Société des Aquafortistes with the number *38* at the upper right plus the addresses of the publishers and printer: *A. Cadart & F. Chevalier, Éditeurs, Rue Richelieu, 66* and *Imp. Delâtre, Rue Sᵗ Jacques, 303, Paris (reproduced).*

3) New printings with alterations: a slight scratch beginning in the middle of the lines underscoring the large cloud in the upper left and continuing downward as far as the hill on the horizon to the left of the cathedral, also "some prickings in the sky and an acid spot to the right of the foliage on the left are more or less visible according to the particular prints and in some have completely disappeared because of the wearing down of the plate" (J. Cailac). P. Prouté (cited by Bailly-Herzberg, 1975) noted "retouchings in the backgrounds; a few strokes with the point have in part re-formed the monument whose steeple has become invisible; the left-hand hill has also been outlined by the needle."

In these last printings the plate has its upper corners rounded.

3-b) Edition in *L'Eau-forte depuis 10 ans,* Paris, Cadart, 1872, with the address of Cadart.

Printings with the lettering removed and which, according to Beraldi, are "heavy and excessively printed."

PLATE: Belonged to the New York art dealer Frederick Keppel, but its present whereabouts are not known.

1866
C 6. *Environs of Rome*
Etching, 284 × 210 mm.; R. 3128.
A second contribution to the Société des Aquafortistes, again with the technical assistance of Bracquemond.

1) As with the preceding work, Corot drew only one state, but after the very extensive printing by the Société retouchings became necessary, though nothing proves that they were from the hand of the artist himself. Rare prelettering proofs: NYPL, BN (print bought by Robaut from Cadart: *reproduced*).

2) Printing for the Société des Aquafortistes, 4th year, 7th selection, March, 1866, with the title, the number *211,* and the addresses: *Cadart & Luquet Editeurs, 79, Rue Richelieu* and *Imp. Delâtre, Rue Sᵗ Jacques, 303, Paris.* P. Prouté (cited by Bailly-Herzberg, 1975) divides the edition into two printings: "the first on Holland paper with the backgrounds very visible, the second generally printed on China paper *appliqué*, the backgrounds worn away."

2-b) With the title but not the address of Cadart (removed).
—New edition in *L'Eau-forte depuis 10 ans,* Paris, Cadart, 1872.
—New edition in *L'Eau-forte depuis 12 ans,* Paris, Cadart, 1874.

3) The lettering obliterated, the plate retouched on the monument in the background and the hill, a few lines added in the sky at the left and in the foliage; printed on Japan paper.

PLATE: Belonged to Keppel in New York, but its present whereabouts are not known.

C 7. *Italian Landscape*
Etching, 157 × 234 mm. (motif); 158 × 237 mm. (plate); R. 3129.
Third and last contribution of Corot to the Société des Aquafortistes, though it seems that Daubigny may have attempted to induce him to take part in the movement once again, according to a letter of 1868 (in Bailly-Herz-

berg, 1972, vol. II, p. 52) in which Daubigny invites Bracquemond to come to see him "at Auvers in June, in Paris during the winter months; among those invited will be Corot, Ribot, Vollon, Daumier, and M. Jacquemart, to discuss our Société des Aquafortistes." Bailly-Herzberg considers that

... if the late date of 1868 is correct, it was probably a matter of convincing Corot to take part in the new society, L'Illustration Nouvelle, in which however he did not appear. Did he really give up participating in the Cadart editions or did he rather hope to return to them some day as is suggested by the formula used on the first page of the announcement of Cadart and Luce: "I share the ideas expressed by my friend Daubigny who hopes to see the enterprise prosper, and approve the request of Messrs. Cadart and Luce."

1) A single state, a few proofs before addition of lettering and number, with needle lines going over the frame line into the lower margin (BN, print from Giacomelli and then P. Cosson: *reproduced*; Chicago, NYPL); biting and trial proofs done by F. Bracquemond.
2) Printing for the Société des Aquafortistes, 5th year, 2nd selection, October, 1866, with *Corot, sculp.* engraved at lower left, the number *246*, and the addresses of Cadart and Luquet, publishers, and Delâtre, printer.
—New edition for *L'Eau-forte depuis 10 ans*, 1872.
—New edition for *L'Eau-forte depuis 12 ans*, 1874.
3) Printing for *Musée des Deux-Mondes*, vols. III–IV, May, 1874–April, 1875, with the address of the Librairie Bachelin-Deflorenne and of Cadart as printer.
False pre-lettering state with the lettering obliterated and a random vertical line in the sky at the left but without needle lines going over into the lower margin.
A photographic reduction to 150 × 178 mm. is in existence.

C 8. *Wooded Countryside (Solitude, or The Cottage)*
Etching, 100 × 131 mm.; R. 3130.
Done at the request of F. Henriet to illustrate his book *Le Paysagiste aux champs*, published in 1866 (see Daubigny 119).
1) Of the first and definitive state, lacking only the signature, there are a few pre-lettering proofs (Chicago).
2) With the signature. Just before the book was published a pre-lettering printing of trial proofs was made and then an additional 40 prints (BN, print from Henriet: *reproduced*).
3) Printing for *Frédéric Henriet, Le Paysagiste aux champs, croquis d'après nature*, Paris, Achille Faure, 1866. Beneath the frame line at the left: *Corot inv. et sc.*; at the right: *Imp. Delâtre, Paris.* Total number printed unknown; 25 on Holland paper, numbered, with double series of engravings, of which one is pre-lettering. A few supplementary prints (on China paper, BN: formerly Curtis Coll. and copyright print of 1866).

4) Printing for second edition of the same book, Paris, Émile Lévy, 1876, 135 prints with the name of the printer Salmon replacing that of Delâtre. Pre-lettering proofs of this printing exist without the names of Corot and the printer.
PLATE: Belonged to Henriet, then to Bouasse-Lebel, who gave it to the BN.

1869
C 9. *In the Dunes: Souvenir of the Woods at The Hague*
Etching, 119 × 192 mm.; R. 3131.
This was the contribution of Corot to the volume of *Sonnets et eaux-fortes* for which the critic and print lover Philippe Burty solicited engravings from the artists he considered most representative (see also Daubigny 121, Jongkind 16, Millet 20). The dimensions were specified, and Burty matched the poems to the artists invited to illustrate them. Corot was assigned a sonnet by André Lemoyne, "Paysage normand," but this Dutch dune scene can scarcely pass as a landscape in Normandy. Bailly-Herzberg (1975) thinks it may be a recollection of the trip Corot made to Holland in 1854. Again it was Bracquemond who assisted Corot with the acid-bath and trial runs.
1) Definitive state, the sole subsequent modification being a slight scrawl in the form of a star or asterisk in the upper left. A few pre-lettering proofs: according to Le Garrec (1921) only four known, among them those now in Chicago (formerly Deering Coll.) and the BN (formerly Curtis Coll.: *reproduced*). Delteil claimed to own a signed proof, something exceptional with Corot.
2) Published in *Sonnets et eaux-fortes*, Paris, Alphonse Lemerre, 1869, printing of about 350 copies on *vergé*, page size 365 × 260 mm.; 2 or 3 copies on vellum paper, plus a few on China paper, *appliqué* or *volant,* in black or bistre.

c. 1869–70
C 10. *Venus Clipping the Wings of Cupid* (1st version)
Etching, without frame line, so print dimensions can vary according to the extent of erasure of ink in the margins, from 200 × 150 to 220 × 160 mm.; R. 3132.
A trial abandoned in favor of the following plate; only very rare proofs exist of which we can cite two: that of Giacomelli, purchased by Beurdeley, and that of Robaut, donated by Moreau-Nélaton to the BN (*reproduced*).
Delteil states that the copper plates of C 10 and 11 were sold to Edmond Sagot at the Robaut sale of December 2, 1907.
RELATED WORK: Black-lead sketch of the same motif, reproduced in Moreau-Nélaton, p. 261.
As with our C 1, with this and the next three plates Corot went no further than the drawing on the varnish, then abandoned them in that state and gave them just as they were to A. Robaut, who wrote in his notes:

June 6, '73, I am having a trial printing at Salmon's of this plate and the two that follow. Of each one I am having printed two proofs on handmade paper—Holland—and five on China paper *volant*. It is M. Delaunay, Alf., who has taken care of biting the plates; they were, especially the landscape that follows, in a frightful state. The varnish had flaked off and scratches are numerous because these plates had got rubbed in a drawer. It was last winter that the Master rediscovered them and offered them to me, having no interest in printing them himself.

C 11. *Venus Clipping the Wings of Cupid* (2nd version)
Etching, 240 × 160 mm. (copper plate), with dimensions of inked part varying from 200 × 150 to 230 × 155 mm.; R. 3133.
Same circumstances as C 10.

C 12. *Souvenir of the Fortifications at Douai*
Etching, 157 × 230 mm.; R. 3134.
Same circumstances as C 10 and 11. Various printings between 1873 and 1890 of the plate belonging to Robaut, with twenty or so proofs, among them those in Chicago (formerly Deering Coll.) and BN (formerly Curtis and Paul Cosson colls.: *reproduced*).
Printing of one hundred copies in 1908 after Strölin purchased the plate at the Robaut sale the year before.

C 13. *The Cathedral of Florence*
Etching, 230 × 160 mm.; R. 3135.
Same circumstances as C 10, 11, 12.
Printings between 1873 and 1890 of 20 or so proofs while the plate was in Robaut's possession (*reproduced*).
Printing of 100 in 1908 after Strölin acquired the plate at the Robaut sale of the year before.
Printing of 50 on Japan paper with *Corot inv. et sc.* in the lower right for the first copies of the catalogue of Corot engravings in Loÿs Delteil, *Le Peintre-graveur illustré*, vol. V, 1910.
Printing of 350 for the ordinary edition of the same work in that year with *Corot inv. et sc.* below at right, *Le Dôme florentin* in the middle, and *Le Peintre-graveur illustré T. V* above at right.
Printing by Leblanc in 1976 for the Bibliothèque Nationale to which Strölin had donated the plate. (The library can execute printings, but they are distinguished by a special dry embossing stamp.)

Date unknown (c. 1865?)
C 14. *The Bath*
"Involuntary" drypoint, 151 × 196 mm.; R. 3136.
Why and when Corot undertook to engrave this plate is not known. What we do know is that it was treated with no more consideration than the others that he simply threw into drawers without bothering to have them bitten. This one was even taken to the printer in that condition: "The worker responsible for doing the trial runs removed the varnish! There then no longer remained any trace of the drawing on the copper plate except where Corot had put more pressure on the point and cut into the plate. The proof that was nevertheless printed and is owned

by M. Moreau-Nélaton is not however without charm just as it is" (Robaut). In his catalogue Robaut adds: "This plate, cleaned off by the printer before it was bitten, has remained in the state of an unfinished sketch, and no editions were made of it; one or two trial proofs only."

Two proofs are in fact known, one in the NYPL, the other in the BN (once owned by Burty, bought by Robaut at the Burty sale: *reproduced*).

In his preface to the catalogue of the Galerie Marcel Guiot exhibition in 1925, Delteil wrote that this plate must have been made "at the same time" as *A Lake in the Tyrol* of 1863 (C 4) and the pieces done for Cadart between that year and 1866, but gave no reasons for this supposition. One can also cite the amusing and severe note by Beraldi: "A plate which has not been bitten! There you have a curiosity to be talked about among fanatics active in the cult of a master. One can add, without lacking in respect for the memory of Corot, that it is one of those prints whose absence from a collection never would be missed."

LITHOGRAPHS

1818–22
C 15. *The Guard Dies and Does Not Surrender*
Lithograph, dimensions unknown; R. 3139.
The young Corot is known to have drawn two lithographs, but the copies for copyright *(dépôt légal)* made sometime between 1818 and 1822 by the printer Collas, whose workshop was in the Passage Feydeau, cannot be located, and we know them only from the drawings Corot made from memory in 1873 (C 15, 16). These sketches were done so much later that they are doubtless very remote from the original lithographs. Of the circumstances under which the sketches were done, Robaut writes:

In May of 1873 at Brunoy I asked the master to give me an idea of the lithograph he did in 1818 representing *The Guard Dies and Does Not Surrender*. No sooner had he finished than he was overcome with emotion at the recollection of our recent disasters [the Franco-Prussian War]. On handing me the sheet he said: "A sad counterpart of this fine device should be made, turning the phrase around! . . . But let us think no more about it and return to Nature." While drawing, the beloved master's tongue ran on: "I remember that I had posed the grenadier against a tree. . . . In his arms he held his flag which he had resolved to abandon only with death . . . his great blue redingote . . . his black gaiters. In front of him, the English who threaten him with their bayonets."

Robaut adds: "The dimensions are likewise supposed to be correct according to Corot, but I myself think that the master was mistaken and that it was a quarto of square or demy *(co-quille)* format."
The drawing (BN: *reproduced*) done in 1873 measures 258 × 337 mm. On the sheet on which it is mounted Moreau-Nélaton wrote: "Sketch drawn by

Corot in May, 1873, at the request of Robaut, as recollection of a lithograph executed in 1822 and of which no print is now known."
Despite Robaut, we still know nothing of the circumstances in which Corot, at the age of twenty-two and four years later in 1822, having just entered the atelier of Michallon, was led to lithograph these two subjects.

C 16. *The Plague of Barcelona*
Lithograph, dimensions unknown; R. 3138.
As with C 15, here too we know the lithograph, done in unexplained circumstances sometime between 1818 and 1822, only through a drawing made a half century later.
On the sheet on which it is mounted: "Sketch done by Corot in May, 1873, at the request of Robaut as recollection of the lithograph executed around 1818–1822 and of which no print is now known."
On the back of the sheet:

This is the recollection that the master has preserved today of the lithograph he made 55 years ago (1818): "Look here," he said, "let me try to recall his costume . . . large cloak, the arms crossed . . . but then the legs are not. He is seated on some stones by the side of the sea . . . in the foreground some waves—the city of Barcelona to the rear. . . . But how naive and clumsy all that must have been, because at twenty-one I knew absolutely nothing."

Here again the dimensions of the drawing are said to be those of the lithograph (from manuscript notes by Robaut).
The drawing (BN: *reproduced*) measures 222 × 332 mm. The title is written across the top, and along the upper left margin we find: "By the master at Brunoy, May 26, '73."
In his catalogue (vol. IV, p. 114) Robaut quotes Corot in a somewhat different and rather more precise version: " '. . . because, you know, I knew absolutely nothing whatsoever of my trade, and I did not have the leisure to dally over it. I was still at M. Delalain's, and I sneaked out in secret to bring my stones to Engelmann's.' "

C 17. *A Village Fête*
Lithograph, dimensions unknown.
"Of this lithograph, whose existence has been affirmed by Corot, we have no indication whatever, not even summary as for the preceding. At a distance of over fifty years, Corot's memory failed him on this subject. He recalled only that the scene included a great number of figures" (Robaut, 1905, vol. IV, p. 114). In his notes Robaut adds that the piece was "in the genre of the Flemish kermesses" and "in at least quarto format." No further indications have been forthcoming.

1838
C 18. *Mlle. Rosalie, Role of La Mère Boisseau*
Lithograph, 100 × 66 mm. (figure); 145 × 93 mm. (page); R. 3137.
Corot recalled that in his youth he

had done lithographs for his friends, the Delalain family, and had taken up the lithograph crayon one last time in 1838 to illustrate the title page of a play that the two Delalain sons, Édouard and Henri, published under a pseudonym. Their father was the cloth merchant on the Rue Saint-Honoré with whom the young Corot had been placed by his father and for whom he appears to have worked from 1817 to 1822, when he entered the atelier of Michallon to study painting. Despite his lack of taste for commerce Corot seems to have been on the best of terms with his employer and frequented the family even after leaving his post.
The half title reads: *Bibliothèque dramatique de l'enfance et de la jeunesse | Théâtre de M. Comte | La Caisse d'Épargne | 3e série | Paris, J. Bréauté, éditeur, à la librairie des pensions, Passage Choiseul 39, 1838.*
The date of the booklet, of which, according to Delteil, few copies were published, is therefore 1838 and not 1836, when the play was first staged. The title page reads: *La Caisse d'Épargne | Comédie vaudeville en 1 acte | par | MM. Saint-Yves | représentée pour la première fois à Paris sur le théâtre des jeunes élèves de M. Comte, le 1er octobre 1836.*
The illustration reproduced here shows a comic character with a malaprop-studded line from the play.
The BN has two proofs printed separately from the book, one that belonged to Charles Asselineau, the other to Édouard Delalain, who wrote on it: "This proof was offered by Édouard Delalain, Jr., man of letters, patron of Corot, on October 17, 1873—fine proof—see the other UNIQUE and light-toned *(blonde)* one offered by the same M. Édouard Delalain, author of the booklet, who has declared that no proof was printed without lettering."

AUTOLITHOGRAPHS

May, 1871
C 19–30. Twelve sketches and original drawings on lithograph transfer paper, dimensions of the album 565 × 385 mm.; R. 3141–52.
Aside from the few casual essays of his youth, Corot had practically nothing to do with lithography, merely reproductive mediums being of no interest to him. The Dutilleux family owned a lithographic printshop, but only the earnest entreaties of Alfred Robaut succeeded in inducing the aged master to draw these few sketches on transfer paper in 1871, an undertaking that seems to have been motivated more by commercial interests than by a real inner desire on the artist's part. It is known that at the close of his life Corot gave in easily to all the least disinterested demands and requests of his friends and dealers, and this album is proof of that weakness.
During the war of 1870 Corot had remained in Paris, but with the advent of the Commune Robaut convinced him to flee from the capital. On April 1, 1871, he left for Arras and the home of his friends, the Desavary family, and later joined Robaut in Douai, where he painted his famous *Belfry of Douai*. It

was there that his host had the idea of getting him to make some autolithographs—the process involving no more than drawing on transfer paper in crayon or ink and transferring the result to the lithographic stone—and Moreau-Nélaton (*L'Histoire de Corot*, p. 280) is outspoken on the subject: "The lithographer who was giving him hospitality having put into his hand a greasy crayon, he drew on the transfer paper charming compositions which M. Robaut took good care to publish."

The cover of the album reads: *Douze croquis et dessins originaux sur papier autographique par Corot . . . tirés à Cinquante exemplaires . . . Numéro . . . signé de l'auteur. Paris Rue Lafayette nº 113, Rue Bonaparte nº 18, à la Librairie artistique et chez les principaux marchands d'estampes. Imp. Lemercier & Cie, rue de Seine, 57, Paris.*

In his catalogue Delteil modified the sequence of the plates in the Robaut album. Robaut's order corresponds to our nos. 25, 19, 20, 21, 22, 23, 27, 30, 28, 24, 29.

The album was accompanied by a *Notice* not without interest:

We offer to the enthusiasts for the talent of M. Corot, nowadays so highly appreciated, a hitherto entirely unpublished collection of twelve drawings & compositions drawn on autolithograph paper by himself and transferred by us directly to the stone.

One thus has beneath one's eyes the intimate work of the Master without its having been translated by any intermediary, & we insist on the interest of this process since there is always, in the work of an artist like M. COROT, an indefinable aspect of poetry that no alien pencil could render.

It was after having spent the entire duration of the siege in Paris that in April, 1871, M. COROT came to the North for a rest and to produce, sometimes in Arras, sometimes in Douai, studies & even important pictures; meanwhile, and to vary his occupations, with that fecundity of imagination for which he is known he drew the Compositions and the Drawings we have just gathered into an album & which we have had printed in only Fifty numbered copies.

We are confident that these sometimes extremely fleeting reflections of the very thought of the Master will be appreciated by the Amateurs & by the Artists; that is why we have wished to omit nothing, deeming that the admirers of the work of M. COROT will be grateful to us for supplying them with the slightest sketches of such a painter in their spontaneous and frank execution. Those who have been able to approach him & know him will find something like the echo of his always varied and engaging conversation.

Some of these drawings are moreover very finely executed; the great Artist lavished all care on them; they thus embody much of the charm of his incomparable paintings.

Paris, September, 1872

C 19. *The Belfry of St.-Nicolas-Lès-Arras.*
Autolithograph, 274 × 220 mm.; R. 3142.
1) Four or five trial proofs on light gray paper. There exists a proof slightly tinted with a light-colored wash by Corot himself. The definitive printing is in black on Manila paper *appliqué*. A few pre-lettering proofs.
2) Signed with a special stamp: *COROT (reproduced).*

C 20. *The Isolated Tower*
Autolithograph, 215 × 273 mm.; R. 3143.
One proof slightly tinted by Corot with a light-colored wash. Printing in black on China paper *appliqué*, signed in the drawing.

C 21. *The Meeting in the Grove*
Autolithograph, 275 × 224 mm.; R. 3144.
1) A proof annotated by Robaut: "On my advice Corot tinted this proof, he was thinking of Prud'hon" (Le Garrec exhibition catalogue, 1921). A few proofs without the stamp.
2) Definitive printing in black on Manila paper *appliqué*, with the name of Corot stamped in at the lower left *(reproduced).*

C 22. *The Rider in the Reeds*
Autolithograph, 215 × 268 mm.; R. 3145.
1) Proof annotated by Robaut: "In the dunes, near Boulogne-sur-Mer." A few proofs before the stamped signature *(reproduced).*
2) Definitive printing in black on light gray-violet paper, signed *COROT* with the stamp.

C 23. *The Sudden Squall*
Autolithograph, 223 × 276 mm.; R. 3146.
1) A proof retouched by Corot with red pencil to indicate the setting sun (BN); four or five proofs without stamped signature, printed in black on white or Manila paper *(reproduced).*
2) Definitive printing in brown on Manila paper *appliqué*, with *COROT* stamped in at the lower right.

C 24. *Sappho*
Autolithograph, 218 × 278 mm.; R. 3151.
1) A few proofs printed in black on gray-violet paper and in a somewhat orange bistre (Le Garrec exhibition, 1921) without the signature stamp *(reproduced).*
2) Definitive printing in reddish brown on Manila paper *appliqué*, with stamped signature in red.

C 25. *The Philosophers' Retreat*
Autolithograph, 216 × 144 mm.; R. 3141.
1) Ten trial proofs in bistre or black on different papers (white, China, or bluish) before addition of signature and address *(reproduced).*
2) A few proofs before the address but with *COROT* printed in the lower right of the drawing, some in brown on gray-blue paper.
3) Definitive printing in bistre with *Nº. 8* at the left above and *Imp. Lemercier et Cie, r. de Seine 57 Paris* below in middle.

C 26. *The Cows' Resting Place*
Autolithograph, 158 × 136 mm.; R. 3147.
1) Three trial proofs, before number and address, in black or bistre on yellowish paper, and five on China paper in various tints *(reproduced).*
2) Definitive printing in bistre on Manila paper *appliqué*, with *Nº. 9* at upper left and *Imp. Lemercier & Cie, r. de Seine 57 Paris* below in middle.

C 27. *Souvenir of Italy*
Autolithograph, 130 × 189 mm.; R. 3148.
1) Two or three trial proofs in black or dark bistre on China or ordinary paper, before number and address *(reproduced).*
2) Definitive printing in bistre on gray-blue paper *appliqué*, with *Nº. 10* at upper left and printer's address as in C 26 below in middle. A proof in the BN has the dedication, *"Offert à Madame Larochette, C. Corot, son ami."*

C 28. *The Mill at Cuincy, near Douai*
Autolithograph, 210 × 255 mm.; R. 3150.
1) A few proofs before number and address.
2) Definitive printing in bistre on China paper *appliqué*, with *Nº. 11* at upper left and printer's address as in C 26 below at right *(reproduced).*
PHOTOGRAPHIC COUNTERTYPE on glass plate, doubtless made by Desavary directly from the drawing.

C. 29. *A Family at Terracina*
Autolithograph, 261 × 405 mm.; R. 3152.
1) A dozen trial proofs in black or deep bistre on pink or otherwise tinted paper before the number and address *(reproduced).*
2) Definitive printing in bistre on Manila paper *appliqué*, with *Nº. 12* at upper left and printer's address as in C 26 below at right.
On the print in the BN Réserve (from P. Cosson) is written by hand:

Autolithograph made inadvertently on the reverse of the glued side (see the original drawing, thin paper, whose glue has quite naturally adhered to the spoiled second proof [*maculature*]. Absolutely first proof after different inkings during more than an hour, otherwise all of this superb piece would have been lost.

Delteil mentions the purchase of this spoiled proof for eighty francs at the Robaut sale.

C 30. *Willows and White Poplars*
Autolithograph, 258 × 393 mm.; R. 3149.
1) Two trial proofs in black before number and address (BN: *reproduced*).
2) Definitive printing in brown on gray-blue paper *appliqué*, with *No. 13* at upper left and printer's address as in C 26 below at right.
PHOTOGRAPHIC COUNTERTYPE on glass plate, doubtless made by Desavary directly from the drawing.

C 31. *Beneath the Trees*
Autolithograph, 222 × 168 mm.; R. 3153.
Besides the twelve autolithographs published in the album, Corot did three others at Arras. Two of them, done in 1874, were published independently in one hundred copies. This one, of 1871, should logically have preceded the

album prints in our catalogue because, according to Delteil, it was apparently "the first attempt of Corot on autographic transfer paper, of which a few proofs were printed, first in black and then in sanguine tone." It is curious that Robaut, who claimed that he wished to preserve everything done by Corot (see the *Notice* of the album given above), should have eliminated this piece. Was it for technical reasons or did he in fact judge it to be too summary and perhaps a mediocre scrawl?

A few proofs in black (Le Garrec exhibition, 1921, and BN: *reproduced*) or in sanguine on Manila paper *appliqué*.

July, 1874

C 32. *The Isolated Fort*
Autolithograph, 180 × 260 mm. (image); 192 × 280 mm. (mount sheet); R. 3154.
One hundred prints in black on various papers: yellow, gray, or white China *appliqué* or Manila *volant*.

C 33. *Reading Beneath the Trees*
Autolithograph, 267 × 184 mm.; R. 3155.
One hundred prints, as C 32. Catalogued by Beraldi (on the word of Robaut) under the title *Lecture attachante* (Interesting Reading).

C 34. *Souvenir of Sologne*
Lithographic transfer (?), 137 × 234 mm.; R. 3222.
The drawing for this must have been inspired by the single visit to the Sologne region that Corot made during June 15–26, 1855. For this print published in the *Album contemporain*, see our entry 132 for Daubigny. It is not known exactly what technique was used for this album. Printed lithographically, the drawings were probably transferred by a mechanical process. Robaut prudently catalogued this piece, without reproducing it, as a "glass plate transferred to stone." Nor is there more reason to think, as Delteil did, that the drawing was done on lithographic transfer paper and should therefore be included among the autolithographs. The question remains open.
1) Printed in *Album contemporain: Collection de dessins et croquis des meilleurs artistes de notre époque, ouvrage publié Sous le Patronage des principaux Maîtres contemporains, 1re Série de 25 Planches. Prix 15 francs, en vente au siège de la Société Iconographique, Boulevard Saint-Michel, 35, Paris,* a title which, as we shall see more fully in connection with no. 132 of Daubigny, gives certain clues to the nature of the print, thus: "The Contemporary Album: collection of drawings and sketches of the finest artists of our time, a work published under the patronage of the principal contemporary masters, first series of 25 plates. Price 15 francs, for sale at the headquarters of the Société Iconographique," etc. *(reproduced).*
If this print has become rare today it is not because, as Robaut thought, only a small number were printed but rather because it was not taken up by the collectors of the time. The Bibliothèque Nationale has a number of copies in this as well as another printing:
2) Printing with address, *Association*

d'ouvriers lithographes, Schmit et Cie, Quai Valmy, 21, Paris (copyright example, 1873).
To grasp the problem posed by this piece and that of Daubigny, one must keep in mind also the publisher's notice *(Avis des Éditeurs)* that went with it:

To offer to the Friends of the Arts and to preserve for the most remote Posterity the faithful Copy of the artistic Works of our epoch, such is the aim of the *Album Contemporain.* . . . Honor and thanks to the illustrious Masters, to the benevolent Artists who have been willing to aid us in this difficult undertaking; for, without their patronage and their equally priceless counsels, we would never have dared to take on such a task, despite the recognized advantages of our New Process of Printing.
Here, in fact, there are no longer those Photographs done with silver salts whose inevitable alteration, in portfolios especially, is the despair of Collectors and which, moreover, cannot give a true idea of the color of a Picture. (In Photography the red and the yellow are translated into black, the blue into white, etc.) The New Process, on the contrary, assures to our Copies an unlimited duration comparable to that of our oldest Manuscripts and of the old Prints whose high prices they will perhaps reach some day despite their present inexpensiveness. In addition, each drawing, executed by the Author of the Picture himself, recalls exactly the tone of the latter.

Among the artists whose works were reproduced were Corot, Daubigny, Auguste Feyen-Perrin, Maxime Lalanne, Albert Maignan, Charles-Henri Pille, Isodore Pils, Théodule Ribot, and J.-J. Veyrassat, and beneath the list of artists and their works was the identification: *Paris.—Lith. Schmit et Ce, 21, quai de Valmy. Typ. J. Rigal et Ce, 56, pass. du Caire.*

GLASSPLATE PRINTS (CLICHÉS-VERRE)
For a summary of the history and present whereabouts of the original plates, see the chart.

May, 1853

C 35. *The Woodcutter of Rembrandt (The Small Woodcutter)*
Glass plate drawn with engraving point, 99 × 62 mm.; R. 3158.
First prints by Grandguillaume *(reproduced).* On the mount of one that belonged to Dutilleux is the annotation: "C. Corot, first essay in drawing on glass for photography, May, 1853."
Other prints by C. Desavary, to whom Grandguillaume had given the plate.
Counterproof by Cuvelier, 1853.
Alterations: An oblique scratch in lower left corner. Subsequently the plate was cracked, the break traversing it toward the bottom and running just below the tree at the right, and this shows up in all later printings.
Countertype by C. Desavary, after the break.
Heliographic reproduction in the same format and resembling an etching, by Charles Nègre to whom the

plate was turned over around 1855 and who obtained from it a steel heliogravure plate. It was doubtless concerning this that Cuvelier wrote to him from Arras on November 12, 1861 (from the Archives of A. Jammes):

Monsieur C. Nègre, Grasse.
Before your departure from Paris you had promised me to engrave the glass plate of M. Corot either in Paris or at home. I should be very glad to know what you have done with it because M. Corot continually asks me for proofs of that plate and I am very much embarrassed at always replying the same thing; he will end up believing that I wish to offend him, so if you have not engraved it I should like to have the glass to print a few proofs, subject to giving it back to you upon your return. Please accept my sincere greetings.
A. Cuvelier

Plate destroyed.

C 36. *The Farm Children*
Point-drawn, 85 × 110 mm.; R. 3161.
First prints by C. Desavary *(reproduced).* On the mount of one which belonged to Dutilleux is the annotation: "C. Corot, second essay in drawing on glass for photography, May, 1853."
Alterations: Plate broken during printing after a very few proofs had been made. Desavary, who had the plate from Dutilleux, described it as "cracked," but Bouasse-Lebel stated that it had been repaired and could still be used. The break was vertical.
Countertype by C. Desavary.
Photolithograph by C. Desavary, 82 × 112 mm., with, in lower right: *C. Corot.*
Plate destroyed.

C 37. *The Cold Spring*
Point-drawn, 140 × 102 mm.; R. 3157.
First prints by Grandguillaume *(reproduced).*
Other prints by Dutilleux, one with note on mount: "C. Corot, May, 1853, third essay at drawing on glass for photography."
Countertype by C. Desavary, who apparently never printed the original.
Plate: J. Cailac believes that, contrary to what Delteil stated, the plate was not destroyed.

C 38. *Calling Card with Man on Horseback*
Point-drawn, 34 × 76 mm.; R. 3156.
First prints by Grandguillaume *(reproduced).*
Other prints by C. Desavary, who had the plate from Grandguillaume. These first printings are very diversified, with more or less heavy lines on brown, purplish blue, or purplish red paper, with or without margins, etc.
Plate in BN (formerly Moreau-Nélaton Coll.).

C 39. *Shepherd Bathing*
Point-drawn, 110 × 155 mm.; R. 3159.
First prints by Grandguillaume *(reproduced).*
Other prints by C. Desavary.
Counterproof exhibited at Arras, 1954.
Countertype on paper, printed after a proof, by C. Desavary.
Plate destroyed.

Glassplate no.	Grandguillaume	Cuvelier	Bouasse-Lebel	Le Garrec	Desavary	Robaut	Moreau-Nélaton	Present location
35	35				35			(destroyed)
36					36			(destroyed)
37	37							(destroyed?)
38	38						38	BN
39	39				39			(destroyed)
40	40							(destroyed)
41		41	41	41				unknown
42		42	42	42				unknown
43		43	43	43				Metropolitan Museum, NY
44		44						(destroyed)
45		45	45	45				unknown
46		46	46	46				British Museum
47	47							(destroyed?)
48	48							(destroyed)
49		49	49	49				unknown
50		50	50	50				Metropolitan Museum, NY
51		51						(destroyed)
52 to 56		52 to 56	52 to 56	52 to 56	on the same plate			unknown
57		57	57	57				BN
58		58	58	58				Louvre
59		59	59	59				priv. coll.
60		60	60	60				unknown
61								unknown
62		62						(destroyed)
63		63						A. Jammes Coll., Paris
64	64				64		64	BN
65		65	65	65				unknown
66		66	66	66				Boston
67					67	67	67	BN
68	(on same plate as 67)							BN
69					69	69	69	BN
70					70	70	70	BN
71					71	71	71	BN
72					72	72	72	BN
73		73	73	73				unknown
74					74		74?	(destroyed?)
75					75	75	75	BN
76					76	76	76	BN
77					77			unknown
78					78			(destroyed?)
79					79	79	79	BN
80					80	80	80	BN
81					81	81	81	BN
82					82		82	BN
83					83	83	83?	unknown
84					84	84	84	BN
85					85	85	85	BN
86					86	86		unknown
87					87	87	87	BN
88					88	88	88	BN
89					89	89	89	BN
90					90	90	90	BN
91					91	91	91	BN
92	(on same plate as 91)							BN
93					93	93	93	BN
94					94	94	94	BN
95					95	95	95	BN
96					96		96	BN
97					97	97	97	BN
98					98		98	unknown
99					99	99	99	BN
100					100			unknown

RELATED WORK: The painting *Le Bain du berger*, in the Salon of 1848 (R. 609). The title Robaut gave to the glassplate print was simply: "Souvenir of the Italian Landscape in the Douai Museum."

January, 1854
C 40. *Souvenir of Fampoux*
Point-drawn, 91 × 65 mm.; R. 3160.
FIRST PRINTS by Grandguillaume *(reproduced)*.
Another printing by C. Desavary.
COUNTERTYPE on paper by C. Desavary.
PLATE destroyed.

C 41. *The Little Sister*
With engraving point and tampon, 151 × 188 mm.; R. 3162.
FIRST PRINTS by Cuvelier *(reproduced)*.
ALTERATIONS: Glass plate broken vertically but so well remounted on another glass plate as support that the original again became serviceable and the crack scarcely visible.
COUNTERPROOFS with a very different effect, in purplish blue or sepia.
COUNTERTYPE on paper by C. Desavary.
PRINTING for Bouasse-Lebel.
PRINTING for Le Garrec.
PLATE: Whereabouts unknown after Le Garrec printing.

C 42. *The Rider Under the Trees* (small format)
With engraving point and tampon, 189 × 149 mm.; R. 3163.
FIRST PRINTS by Cuvelier *(reproduced)*.
ALTERATIONS: Plate broken after a very small printing and then remounted on a supporting glass plate. The break is horizontal but well restored and is scarcely visible on subsequent prints.
COUNTERTYPE on paper by C. Desavary.
PRINTING for Bouasse-Lebel.
PRINTING for Le Garrec.
PLATE: Whereabouts unknown after Le Garrec printing.
RELATED WORKS: A painting and glass plate C 46.

C 43. *The Daydreamer*
By impasto, 148 × 193 mm.; R. 3164.
FIRST PRINTS by Cuvelier *(reproduced)*.
Other prints by C. Desavary, who in a listing noted this down as " 'Soleil couchant,' couleur à l'huile, jaune" (Setting Sun, oil color, yellow).
REDUCTION by C. Desavary to 99 × 130 mm.
PRINTING for Bouasse-Lebel.
PRINTING for Le Garrec.
PLATE in the Metropolitan Museum of Art, New York.

C 44. *Souvenir of the Fortifications at Arras*
By impasto, 183 × 142 mm.; R. 3165.
FIRST PRINTS by Cuvelier *(reproduced)*, doubtless in very rare proofs of which two are in the BN.
PLATE: The plate was probably destroyed very early. Delteil and Cailac knew only one proof (in the Robaut Collection); two proofs in the BN come from Moreau-Nélaton.
As title Robaut gave *Fortifications de Douai* and Moreau-Nélaton *Fortifications d'Arras*. Bouasse-Lebel considered the latter more likely because the first proofs were printed by Cuvelier in that city.

C 47. *The Tomb of Semiramis*
Point-drawn, 132 × 185 mm.; R. 3168.
FIRST PRINTS by Grandguillaume *(reproduced)*.
COUNTERTYPE by Grandguillaume.
PHOTOLITHOGRAPH of the same dimensions but reversed, by Poitevin, in both pre-lettering state and with the lettering: *Photolithographie Poitevin Paris*.
ALTERATIONS: The plate was broken after a few proofs.
Despite the title, the print depicts a landscape with mill in the outlying quarter of St.-Nicolas-Lès-Arras.

C 48. *Horseman and Man on Foot in a Forest*
With engraving point and tampon, 150 × 186 mm.; R. 3169.
FIRST PRINTS by Grandguillaume.
This is one of the rare examples of a glassplate print with two genuine states:
1) a simple sketch, with the subject roughed in by large spots and with a few finer lines that would be used to make the shadows in the second state *(reproduced)*, and
2) finished state (reproduced by Delteil).
ALTERATIONS: Early prints with the glass cracked horizontally (formerly Charles Jacque Coll.).
COUNTERTYPE by Desavary on paper, with a large light area widthwise at about two-thirds of the height.
REDUCTION of second state by Desavary, 98 × 124 mm.
PHOTOLITHOGRAPH on yellow paper of same dimensions as original; done in 1875 by C. Desavary and titled *The Conversation*.
PLATE destroyed.

March, 1854
C 45. *Death and the Maiden*
By impasto, 202 × 153 mm.; R. 3166.
FIRST PRINTS by Cuvelier *(reproduced)*.
COUNTERTYPE by C. Desavary.
PRINTING for Bouasse-Lebel.
PRINTING for Le Garrec.
PLATE: Whereabouts unknown after Le Garrec printing.

Around 1854
C 46. *The Rider Under the Trees* (large format)
With engraving point and tampon, 283 × 225 mm.; R. 3167.
FIRST PRINTS by Cuvelier *(reproduced)*.
COUNTERPROOF in BN *(reproduced)*.
COUNTERTYPE by C. Desavary.
REDUCTION by C. Desavary, 155 × 122 mm.
PRINTING for Le Garrec.
PLATE in BrM.
RELATED WORKS: A painting and glass plate C 42.
In a letter from Corot to Dutilleux (BN, Cabinet des Estampes, Réserve) one reads: "I should like to ask you, if M. Cuvelier has not yet sent the box, to send me on that same occasion or later, if it has gone, three prints of the light etching with the man on horseback that I am so fond of." The letter is dated January 23, 1854, and according to the catalogue of the Corot exhibition, Paris, 1975, it may refer to this work, though in our opinion it applies rather to the small version of this subject (C 42).

1855
C 49. *The Little Shepherd* (1st version)
With engraving point and tampon, 325 × 250 mm. at frame line; R. 3170.
FIRST PRINTS by Cuvelier *(reproduced)*.
ALTERATIONS: The piece was considered a failure because certain parts of the foliage and the shepherd himself seem veiled over, and it was doubtless for that reason that Corot executed a second plate on the same subject (C 50).
PRINTING for Bouasse-Lebel.
PRINTING for Le Garrec.
PLATE: Whereabouts unknown after Le Garrec printing.
RELATED works: A painting of the same title shown at the Salon of 1840 and purchased by the French government, now in Musée Central, Metz, and a study identified by Robaut as the landscape drawing of *Volterra, Group of Trees Above Rocks* from around 1834 (R. 306). Another version, signed and dated 1850, was in the Corot exhibition, Chicago, 1960, cat. no. 67. See also the Corot exhibition, Edinburgh, 1965, cat. no. 37.

C 50. *The Little Shepherd* (2nd version)
With engraving point only, 340 × 260 mm.; R. 3172.
FIRST PRINTS by Cuvelier, without the tooled-in signature *(reproduced)*.
Printings with the name of Corot tooled in at the lower left.
PRINTING for Bouasse-Lebel.
PRINTING for Le Garrec.
REDUCTION by C. Desavary, 165 × 129 mm.
PLATE in the Metropolitan Museum of Art, New York.

C 51. *The Brook in the Woods*
Point-drawn, 184 × 150 mm.; R. 3171.
Dated 1854 by Robaut, 1855 (?) by Delteil.
FIRST PRINTS by Cuvelier *(reproduced)*.
PLATE disappeared immediately after these first printings.

C 57. *Souvenir of Ostia*
Point-drawn, 270 × 344 mm.; R. 3178.
FIRST PRINTS by Cuvelier, a few proofs before signature of Corot *(reproduced)*.
Printings with signature of Corot, reversed, in lower left.
COUNTERPROOFS, only slightly inked, with quite fine lines, signature not reversed.
COUNTERTYPE by C. Desavary, with black spot in lower left corner.
REDUCTION by C. Desavary, 129 × 167 mm.
PRINTING for Bouasse-Lebel.
PRINTING for Le Garrec.
PLATE in BN (gift of Le Garrec).

C 58. *The Gardens of Horace*
With engraving point and tampon, 356 × 273 mm.; R. 3179.
FIRST PRINTS by Cuvelier, a few proofs before signature of Corot *(reproduced)*.
Printing with signature of Corot, reversed, in lower left.
COUNTERPROOFS.
REDUCTION by C. Desavary, 170 × 134 mm.
PRINTING for Bouasse-Lebel.
PRINTING for Le Garrec.
PLATE in the Louvre, Paris (gift of Le Garrec).

1856

C 52–56. *Five Subjects*
Point-drawn, 293 × 365 mm.; R. 3173–77.
These five subjects catalogued and reproduced separately by Delteil exist also printed on a single sheet. Those prints are very rare and were unknown to Delteil. One was sold in the sale of possessions of Millet's widow in April, 1894 (as no. 310). The one in the BN *(reproduced)* was donated by Bouasse-Lebel and is a modern printing, as were those exhibited by Le Garrec in 1921 and by Guiot in 1925.
PLATE: Whereabouts unknown after Le Garrec printing.

C 52. *The Garden of Pericles*
Point-drawn, 149 × 157 mm.; R. 3173.
FIRST PRINTS by Cuvelier *(reproduced)*.
PRINTING for Bouasse-Lebel.
PRINTING for Le Garrec.

C 53. *The Painters' Lane*
Point-drawn, 121 × 173 mm.; R.3174.
FIRST PRINTS by Cuvelier *(reproduced)*.
PRINTING for Bouasse-Lebel.
PRINTING for Le Garrec.

C 54. *Scrawl (Griffonage)*
Point-drawn, 147 × 100 mm.; R. 3175.
FIRST PRINTS by Cuvelier *(reproduced)*.
PRINTING for Bouasse-Lebel.
PRINTING for Le Garrec.

C 55. *The Large Woodcutter*
Point-drawn, 148 × 84 mm.; R. 3176.
FIRST PRINTS by Cuvelier *(reproduced)*.
PRINTING for Bouasse-Lebel.
PRINTING for Le Garrec.
RELATED WORK: Glass plate C 35.

C 56. *The Tower of Henry VIII*
Point-drawn, 116 × 154 mm.; R. 3177.
FIRST PRINTS by Cuvelier *(reproduced)*.
PRINTING for Bouasse-Lebel.
PRINTING for Le Garrec.

C 59. *Young Mother at the Entrance to a Wood*
With engraving point and tampon, 355 × 264 mm.; R. 3180.
FIRST PRINTS by Cuvelier *(reproduced)*.
REDUCTION by C. Desavary, 164 × 125 mm.
PRINTING for Bouasse-Lebel.
PRINTING for Le Garrec.
PLATE in private collection, Paris.

C 60. *Trees on the Mountain*
Point-drawn, 187 × 152 mm.; R.3181.
According to Robaut's notes, the plate was prepared with printer's ink.
FIRST PRINTS by Cuvelier, a few proofs before signature of Corot *(reproduced)*.
PRINTING with signature of Corot in lower left, not listed by Delteil, but a proof exists in BN (from Moreau-Nélaton).
PRINTING for Bouasse-Lebel.
PRINTING for Le Garrec.
PLATE: Whereabouts unknown after Le Garrec printing.

c. 1856

C 61. *A Philosopher*
Technique unknown, presumed dimensions 100 × 120 mm.; R. 3182.

Neither we nor Delteil have found any trace of this plate described by Robaut (who did not own or reproduce it): "On a knoll at the left and in the shade one sees a man seated. On the other side, a large cluster of trees. This piece, *of which no prints exist in the collection of Alfred Robaut,* figured in a lot at the posthumous sale of Karl Daubigny" (our italics).

C 62. *The Little Shepherd* (3rd version)
By impasto, 354 × 272 mm.; R. 3183.
FIRST PRINTS by Cuvelier *(reproduced)*.
The proof in the BN (formerly Moreau-Nélaton Coll.) is perhaps the only one known. The plate disappeared very early.
RELATED WORKS: C 49, 50.

1857

C 63. *The Artist in Italy*
Point-drawn, 185 × 148 mm.; R. 3205.
FIRST PRINTS by Cuvelier, a few before signature.
Prints with signature, *Corot 57,* not reversed, in lower left *(reproduced)*.
COUNTERPROOFS exist with and without the signature (BN).
PLATE belonged to Bouasse-Lebel but was not among those he had printed and which later passed to Le Garrec. It now belongs to André Jammes, Paris, who has done printings on modern white paper.

C 65. *A Picnic in a Clearing*
Point-drawn, 160 × 187 mm.; R. 3185.
FIRST PRINTS by Cuvelier, with reversed signature, *Corot 1857,* below the frame line at the right *(reproduced)*.
Printings with a second signature in the plate, at lower left, and not reversed: *1857 Corot.*
COUNTERPROOFS with both signatures.
COUNTERTYPE on glass by C. Desavary after a proof on paper (see below).
PHOTOLITHOGRAPHIC REPRODUCTION on gray paper and without frame line, reduced to 143 × 183 mm.
PRINTING for Bouasse-Lebel.
PRINTING for Le Garrec.
PLATE: Whereabouts unknown after Le Garrec printing.
COUNTERTYPE GLASS PLATE in BN (Moreau-Nélaton Coll.): "The plate was the property of Cuvelier and came to me with his collection of plates. Desavary turned over to Moreau-Nélaton a plate which was only a reproduction on glass after a proof done by Cuvelier. That proof having been reversed, the reproduction was likewise. It is therefore by error that [in the Delteil catalogue] the subject is represented the wrong way around" (note by Bouasse-Lebel).

C 66. *The Gallic Round (La Ronde gauloise)*
Point-drawn, 183 × 142 mm.; R. 3186.
FIRST PRINTS by Cuvelier *(reproduced)*.
COUNTERTYPE by C. Desavary (plate in BN, formerly Moreau-Nélaton Coll.). See the entry for C 65, which explains why this plate also was reproduced the wrong way around in the book by Moreau-Nélaton.
REDUCTION by C. Desavary, 121 × 95 mm.

PHOTOLITHOGRAPHIC REPRODUCTION on gray paper, details very much clogged up, 180 × 142 mm.
PRINTING for Bouasse-Lebel.
PRINTING for Le Garrec.
PLATE in Boston.

1858

C 64. *The Ambush*
By impasto, 221 × 161 mm.; R. 3184.
FIRST PRINTS by Grandguillaume *(reproduced)*.
Prints by C. Desavary.
A state previous to the first state described by Delteil passed in the Bouasse-Lebel sale to the Somary Collection (sold in 1974 at Sotheby's, London, cat. no. 19) and reappeared in the Lewis Collection catalogue of 1977 (no. 9).
The crackles in the sky mentioned by Delteil cannot indicate a second state. Paul Desavary, who printed the plate in Arras for his father, advised Bouasse-Lebel that "the crackles in the sky at the right on the horizon had been intended by the artist and existed from the start of the plate. They were more or less apparent, depending on whether the photographic proof had been exposed more or less." In his notes Bouasse-Lebel adds: "In fact, I remarked the existence of those crackles on strong proofs from the start, while they were not to be seen on certain weak proofs printed thirty years later." This can be verified on the two early printings in the BN of which one, much more contrasty than the other, brings out much more the contours and reliefs.
PLATE in BN (formerly Moreau-Nélaton Coll.). Bouasse-Lebel thought that this plate, which had always been in Desavary's studio in Arras, must have been destroyed when the Maison Houbeu, photographers in Arras and successors to Desavary, moved their premises: "I looked over all of the plates of that concern without finding it. . . . No countertype was ever made of it."

C 67. *Magdalen Kneeling in Prayer*
Point-drawn, 170 × 121 mm.; R. 3187.
FIRST PRINTS by Desavary *(reproduced)*.
PRINTING for Robaut (this is actually an edition rather than a printing, but is traditionally referred to as a *tirage* or printing by collectors. See "Note Concerning Glassplate Prints").
PLATE: Considered lost by Bouasse-Lebel (along with C 64) and by Delteil, the plate turned up again when Robaut did his printing and is now in the BN; it includes also C 68.

C 68. *Magdalen in Meditation*
Point-drawn, 109 × 168 mm.; R. 3188.
FIRST PRINTS by C. Desavary *(reproduced)*.
PRINTING for Robaut.
PLATE in BN (see C 67).
RELATED WORK: Painting on same subject but with different composition (R. 1047), now in Cortland Collection, Los Angeles.

C 69. *Corot: Self-Portrait*
Point-drawn, 217 × 158 mm.; R. 3189.
FIRST PRINTS by C. Desavary with very different effects (two *reproduced,* as well

as the plate itself), in black or bistre.
PRINTING for Robaut.
PLATE in BN.

C 70. *Hide-and-Seek*
Point-drawn, 230 × 167 mm.; R. 3190.
FIRST PRINTS by C. Desavary, among them a proof once owned by Dutilleux (now BN) done before the plate alterations *(reproduced)*.
ALTERATIONS: Scratches in upper right corner and below on the terrain at 28 mm. (1 1/8″) from the figure.
PRINTING for Robaut.
PLATE in BN.

C 71. *The Clump of Trees at La Belle Forière* (or *Woods of La Serpentara*)
Point-drawn, 155 × 232 mm.; R. 3191.
FIRST PRINTS by C. Desavary *(reproduced)*.
ALTERATIONS: Spots have gradually formed on the plate, especially in the area of the sky.
PRINTING for Robaut.
PLATE in BN.

C 72. *The Woods of the Hermit* (or *Shores of Lake Trasimeno*)
With engraving point and tampon, 164 × 230 mm.; R. 3192.
FIRST PRINTS by C. Desavary.
ALTERATIONS: A vertical scratch in the upper left at 10 mm. (3/8″) from the margin, on the basis of which Delteil distinguished a second state, though the scratch is minimal and has practically no effect on the composition *(reproduced)*.
PRINTING for Robaut.
PLATE in BN.

C 73. *Souvenir of the Bas-Bréau*
Point-drawn, 190 × 157 mm.; R. 3196.
FIRST PRINTS by Cuvelier, without signature (proof in BN).
Printings with signature, not reversed, in lower right *(reproduced)*.
PRINTING for Bouasse-Lebel.
PRINTING for Le Garrec.
PLATE: Whereabouts unknown since Le Garrec printing.

C 74. *The Banks of the Po*
Point-drawn, 165 × 223 mm.; R. 3193.
FIRST PRINTS by C. Desavary *(reproduced)*.
ALTERATION: During first printings glass plate cracked horizontally at three-quarters of the height.
COUNTERPROOF with the break evident.
COUNTERTYPE on paper by C. Desavary.
PHOTOLITHOGRAPHIC reproduction by C. Desavary in 1875, titled *Le Lac* (The Lake), 155 × 223 mm. (height reduced).
PLATE mentioned as in possession of Moreau-Nélaton by both Delteil and Bouasse-Lebel, the latter pointing out that this could not be the countertype because that was on paper. However, it seems doubtful that the original plate has survived.

C 75. *Saltarello*
Point-drawn, 227 × 167 mm.; R. 3194.
FIRST PRINTS by C. Desavary *(reproduced)*.

ALTERATIONS: A vertical spot under the *R* of the signature of Corot in the lower right, two small parallel vertical scratches halfway between the dancer's feet and the signature.
PRINTING for Robaut.
PLATE in BN.

C 76. *Dante and Virgil*
Point-drawn, 218 × 165 mm.; R. 3195.
FIRST PRINTS by C. Desavary *(reproduced)*.
Print in BN annotated: "Single proof printed on the full sheet itself and without mounting, by Paul Desavary, 1891."
PRINTING for Robaut.
PLATE in BN.
RELATED WORK: Painting on this subject (R. 1099) exhibited in the Salon of 1859, now Museum of Fine Arts, Boston.

1860

C 77. *Orpheus Leading Eurydice*
Point-drawn, 105 × 151 mm.; R. 3197.
FIRST PRINTS by C. Desavary *(reproduced)*.
ALTERATIONS: Two parallel scratches between the trees at the left above the lyre of Orpheus; spots have gradually appeared in the foliage of the trees at the right.
COUNTERTYPE: Glass countertype plate in BN (formerly Moreau-Nélaton Coll.).
PLATE: Whereabouts unknown, was in possession of C. Desavary.
RELATED WORK: Painting on this subject in Salon of 1861, loaned by Mr. and Mrs. Edmund Stevenson Burke, Jr., to the Corot exhibition of 1946 held by the Philadelphia Museum of Art.

C 78. *Orpheus Charming the Savage Beasts*
Point-drawn, 136 × 101 mm.; R. 3198.
FIRST PRINTS by C. Desavary *(reproduced)*.
COUNTERTYPE: An inventory of C. Desavary, cited by Bouasse-Lebel, notes for this print "to be redone on paper," and it does seem that a countertype was made (a proof in the BN, also one reproduced by Delteil).
REDUCTION by C. Desavary.
PLATE: The original plate seems to have been destroyed, and if Moreau-Nélaton had a countertype it is not with his collection in the BN.

C 79. *The Festival of Pan*
Point-drawn, 110 × 160 mm.; R. 3199.
FIRST PRINTS by C. Desavary.
ALTERATIONS: The printings show spots in the right-hand corners and a cone-shaped one in the upper left *(reproduced)*. In the first printings the black cone is absent (proof in BN, formerly Moreau-Nélaton Coll.), and in some others the three spots show up blank *(reproduced)*.
COUNTERPROOF in the Hédiard Collection, according to Delteil.
PRINTING for Robaut.
PLATE in BN.
RELATED WORKS: Drawing (reversed) in the Robaut sale of December 2, 1907 (R. 2896), and a painting (R. 1111) with the same title.

C 80. *Environs of Genoa*
Point-drawn, 204 × 160 mm.; R. 3200.
FIRST PRINTS by C. Desavary, without spots *(reproduced)*.
ALTERATIONS: The plate became drastically altered, and this apparently very early, with the appearance of increasingly larger spots that finally invaded totally and extensively the right and lower borders and the upper left corner.
COUNTERPROOF before spots (BN, formerly Curtis Coll.).
PRINTING for Robaut.
PLATE in BN.

C 81. *Landscape with Tower* (sketch)
Point-drawn, 170 × 215 mm.; R. 3201.
Date uncertain, c. 1858–60.
FIRST PRINTS by C. Desavary *(reproduced)*.
ALTERATIONS: "This plate, barely sketched in, was marred by a faulty application of the opaque layer of paint. The subject has remained in the state of sketch" (Robaut cat., vol. IV, p. 154).
PRINTING for Robaut.
PLATE in BN.

C 82. *Souvenir of the Environs of Monaco*
Point-drawn, 97 × 160 mm.; R. 3202.
FIRST PRINTS by C. Desavary.
ALTERATIONS: A spot at the top of the foliage of the bending tree, just below the frame line at 52 mm. (2 1/16″) from the left margin *(reproduced)*.
PLATE in BN.

C 83. *Wagon Driving Toward a Town*
Point-drawn, 104 × 160 mm.; R. 3203.
FIRST PRINTS by C. Desavary *(reproduced)*.
ALTERATIONS: A vertical white streak through the clouds in the upper middle appeared with the first prints and was subsequently corrected, but can still be made out to some extent. Then the plate was broken, separating off the entire lower left corner as far as the wagon. Despite this, it was possible to print from it, though spots appeared more and more visibly in the corners.
PRINTING for Robaut.
PHOTOLITHOGRAPHIC reproduction by C. Desavary, 100 × 158 mm., with *C. Corot* in the margin at the lower right.
PLATE: The plate stated by Delteil to be in the Moreau-Nélaton Collection may have been a countertype, but in any case it is not in the BN.
RELATED WORK: Painting (R. 1153), *Le Chariot d'Arras* of 1853–54, loaned to the Corot exhibition, Edinburgh, 1965, by Mr. and Mrs. David Lloyd Kreeger of Washington, D.C.

C 86. *Cow and Cowherd*
Point-drawn, 103 × 137 mm.; R. 3206.
FIRST PRINTS by C. Desavary.
ALTERATIONS: A large black spot fills the upper right corner *(reproduced)*. In proofs without the spot the mark of a break can be seen in the lower left corner. The background has become marred by pitting and is dirty.
COUNTERTYPE on glass.
PRINTING for Robaut, no doubt from the countertype.

PLATE: The plate in the Moreau-Nélaton Collection mentioned by Delteil and now in the BN is in fact a countertype. The whereabouts of the original plate is not known.

1871

C 84. *Souvenir of the Villa Pamphili*
Point-drawn, 152 × 126 mm.; R. 3204.
FIRST PRINTS by C. Desavary *(reproduced)*.
PRINTING for Robaut.
PLATE in BN.

C 85. *Souvenir of Lake Maggiore*
Point-drawn, 168 × 225 mm.; R. 3208.
FIRST PRINTS by C. Desavary.
ALTERATIONS: Large spot in lower left corner *(reproduced)*.
PRINTING for Robaut.
PLATE in BN.

C 87. *Hagar and the Angel*
Point-drawn, 173 × 130 mm.; R. 3207.
FIRST PRINTS by C. Desavary *(reproduced)*.
PRINTING for Robaut.
PLATE in BN.
RELATED WORKS: Painting titled *Hagar in the Desert* (R. 362) in the Salon of 1835, now the Metropolitan Museum of Art, New York, and preparatory drawing in oils unknown to Robaut but published by Germain Bazin (pl. 44 in *Corot*, Paris, 1942).

C 88. *Souvenir of Salerno*
Point-drawn, 172 × 125 mm.; R. 3209.
FIRST PRINTS by C. Desavary *(reproduced)*.
PRINTING for Robaut.
PLATE in BN.
In the upper margin one finds the number *56*, and when the prints are not cropped close to the image it appears also below, in the middle. This may indicate the order in which it was done in the series of glass plates Corot produced. In the Delteil catalogue this number is incorrectly given as *53*.

C 89. *Souvenir of the Lake of Nemi*
Point-drawn, 125 × 166 mm.; R. 3210.
FIRST PRINTS by C. Desavary *(reproduced)*.
PRINTING for Robaut.
PLATE in BN.

C 90. *The Poet's Dwelling*
Point-drawn, 130 × 170 mm.; R. 3211.
FIRST PRINTS by C. Desavary *(reproduced)*.
PRINTING for Robaut.
PLATE in BN.

C 91. *Souvenir of the Valley of the Sole*
Point-drawn, 166 × 117 mm.; R. 3212.
FIRST PRINTS by C. Desavary *(reproduced)*.
PRINTING for Robaut.
PLATE in BN, with C 92 on same plate.

C 92. *The Paladins*
Point-drawn, 111 × 165 mm.; R. 3213.

FIRST PRINTS by C. Desavary *(reproduced)*.
PRINTING for Robaut.
PLATE in BN includes also C 91, but Delteil stated that "one scarcely ever now comes on prints containing the two subjects together."

C 93. *Tower on the Horizon of a Lake*
Point-drawn, 116 × 164 mm.; R. 3214.
FIRST PRINTS by C. Desavary *(reproduced)*.
PRINTING for Robaut.
PHOTOLITHOGRAPHIC REPRODUCTION by C. Desavary in exact format of original.
PLATE in BN, acquired with the Moreau-Nélaton donation, but broken.

C 94. *Poet and Muse*
Point-drawn, 188 × 153 mm.; R. 3215.
"This drawing was first begun breadthwise: turning it one discovers the trace of the earliest disposition" (Robaut, 1905, vol. IV, p. 160).
FIRST PRINTS by C. Desavary *(reproduced)*.
PRINTING for Robaut.
PLATE in BN.

1874

C 95. *Shepherd Struggling with His Goat*
Point-drawn, 176 × 130 mm.; R. 3216.
Dated precisely July, 1874.
FIRST PRINTS by C. Desavary.
ALTERATIONS: Three horizontal parallel scratches a few millimeters long on the right border near the top *(reproduced)*. A print without these in the Lewis catalogue, 1977.
PRINTING for Robaut.
PLATE in BN.
RELATED WORK: Drawing in pencil and graphite of 1852 (R. 2881).

C 96. *The Dreamer Beneath the Great Trees*
Point-drawn, 176 × 131 mm.; R. 3217.
FIRST PRINTS by C. Desavary *(reproduced)*.
PLATE in BN.

C 97. *Souvenir of Eza*
Point-drawn, 128 × 173 mm.; R. 3218.
FIRST PRINTS by C. Desavary *(reproduced)*.
PRINTING for Robaut.
PRINTING in 1906 for a book by André Marty, *L'Imprimerie et les procédés de gravure au XXe siècle* (one hundred copies); two prints in each copy: one normal, the other printed with a second glass interposed between plate and paper to show the effect of diffusion of the light.
PLATE in BN.

C 98. *Souvenir of Antibes*
Point-drawn, 121 × 150 mm.; R. 3219.
FIRST PRINTS by C. Desavary *(reproduced)*.
PLATE formerly in Moreau-Nélaton Collection, present whereabouts unknown.

C 99. *Horseman Pausing in the Countryside*
Point-drawn, 131 × 177 mm.; R. 3220.

FIRST PRINTS by C. Desavary, with an oblique scratch above the two trees at the right *(reproduced)*.
ALTERATIONS: Besides the scratch mentioned above another appears on new printings above the tall trees at the left. Then the first scratch was erased but the plate filled with dirty marks, especially at the upper border, with a black point above the horizon.
PRINTING for Robaut.
LITHOGRAPHIC TRANSFER of the same dimensions but surrounded by a frame line.
PLATE in BN.

C 100. *Boatman (Souvenir of Arleux-du-Nord)*
Point-drawn, 130 × 177 mm.; R. 3221.
FIRST PRINTS by C. Desavary *(reproduced)*.
PLATE: Whereabouts unknown since it was in the possession of Desavary.

CHARLES-FRANÇOIS DAUBIGNY (1817–1878)

ETCHINGS

1838

It was around 1839, on his return from his trip to Italy, that desiring no doubt to pin down his recollections he tried his hand at using the etching needle. Nor was he sorry to put himself in a position to satisfy the requests of the publishers who, at that time, were beginning to resort to steelplate etching as an engraving method which was at one and the same time economical, rapid and resistant.

(Henriet, 1874)

Interestingly enough, it was in 1839 that Daubigny's first wood-engraved illustrations were published, those done for the *Versailles ancien et moderne* of Laborde (see Fidell-Beaufort, 1974, vol. II, p. 74). That he thought of his graphic art as a means of earning his living is attested by the fact that very early in his career, in 1841, he exhibited a portfolio of six original etchings in the Salon, and these first attempts in the medium were evidently done both to train his hand and to provide a public demonstration of his skill that might bring him profitable jobs as an engraver. Indeed, even while preparing his first painting for the Salon, that of 1838 (see our D 5), he seems to have judged it prudent and necessary to assure himself a career as engraver-illustrator. He was then twenty-one and sharing quarters with his friends Joseph-Louis Trimolet and Louis Steinheil, the latter of whom he had met in the studio of David d'Angers. Meissonier was a friend of Steinheil and occasionally joined the group, and it was he in fact who engraved the figures in the first two etchings by Daubigny, who in those years was concentrating on landscape art.

D 1. *The Monk*
Etching, 100 × 145 mm.; Henriet cat. no. 1.
Delteil knew only three prints of this plate, one of which is now in the Avery Collection, New York, and another in the BN (formerly Giacomelli, Beurdeley, and finally Curtis colls.: *reproduced*). According to Henriet the copper plate was planed off after a few trial printings.
REPRODUCTION enlarged to 147 × 202 mm. by the Amand-Durand process; photogravure plate under the title *The Solitary Monk* now in the Louvre Chalcographie, the service that prints and sells engravings made from original plates.
RELATED WORK: Drawing in Baltimore.

D 2. *The Arbor*
Etching, 97 × 150 mm.; H. 2.
A few proofs printed, as with D 1, before planing off the plate.
1) A first state (formerly Giacomelli, Beurdeley, Curtis colls., now BN) described thus by Henriet: " . . . before the tone of aquatint that the artist had the unfortunate idea of using to cover his plate in places; a very fine proof of this state with roulette marks in the margin belongs to M. Coffetier" (*reproduced*).
2) Henriet describes the second state: "Plate dulled by the aquatint; discontented with the results, Daubigny had his copper plate planed off" (print in NYPL).
Concerning this and five other etchings shown in the Salon of 1841, the critic of *L'Artiste* wrote: "The etchings of M. Daubigny, Jr., recommend themselves by a *trait brisé* [the use of multiple short broken strokes] of an extreme fineness; the most energetic is the *Solitude of Saint Jerome* [our D 11]; the most seductive is that landscape where one sees a rustic hut at the left, peasants at table, a patch of water and a few trees in the background."
REPRODUCTION enlarged to 132 × 205 mm. by the Amand-Durand process; photogravure plate now in the Louvre Chalcographie.
RELATED WORKS: At least two drawings, one (reversed) in Baltimore, the other, formerly in the Giacomelli and Beurdeley collections, now in the BN, plus a third (or the same?) mentioned by Delteil as in the Geoffroy-Dechaume sale in 1893.

D 3. *View of Subiaco*
Etching, 96 × 153 mm.; H. 3.
Delteil distinguishes three states:
1) before the needled-in signature and various reworkings (BN, print from Burty: *reproduced*);
2) with signature and trials of a needle in the margins (BN, formerly Giacomelli and Beurdeley colls.);
3) with the trial needle marks removed.
REPRODUCTION in the same format by the Amand-Durand process; photogravure plate now in the Louvre Chalcographie. The reproduction has *3ᵉ eau-forte de Daubigny* at the lower left and *Vue de Subiaco* in the middle.
During his visit to Italy with his friend Mignan in 1836–37, Daubigny spent four months in Subiaco, where he made a great many drawings (see also D 6). This subject was used also for a

wood-engraved illustration in *La Vie des Saints* published by Delloye in 1846–47 (Fidell-Beaufort, vol. II, p. 75).

D 4. *View of Notre-Dame de Paris and the Île Saint-Louis* (study)
Etching, 97 × 166 mm.; not in H.
Of this essay unknown to Henriet, only one proof seems to exist (formerly Giacomelli, Beurdeley, Curtis colls., now BN: *reproduced*), and it confirms that the etchings of 1838 should be considered as experiments aimed at mastering the technique and at the same time at acquiring a reputation as an etcher. On the plate are also a "realistic" sketch of a man at a table, a study of a frog, two caricatures, a Madonna, and a rough reproduction of the picture Daubigny was preparing for the Salon (see D 5), as well as some trial needle marks as in D 3.

D 5. *View of Notre-Dame de Paris and the Île Saint-Louis*
Etching, 97 × 166 mm.; H. 4.
There is a single state of this small etching, Daubigny's first try at reproducing a painting (shown in the Salon of 1838). The young artist turned his hand to that genre in the hope of making his works known. Though *View of Notre Dame* was not published, this was not so with subsequent reproductions, and our catalogue makes clear how invaluable this art of reproduction was before photography came into general use.
Delteil lists only a proof on China paper, mounted, formerly in the Giacomelli, Beurdeley, and Curtis collections and now in the BN (*reproduced*), and two others now in Baltimore and the NYPL.
Henriet gives this interesting description:

Upriver from the Pont [bridge] de la Tournelle dominated by the great mass of Notre-Dame, on the Port [quai] Saint-Bernard rises a construction. This is the pier of the Passerelle [footbridge] de Constantine which was opened for use in January, 1838, and was soon replaced by the new Pont Saint-Germain. At the period to which this etching takes us back, the quais had not yet been constructed, and the bank of the Île Louviers was planted with poplars.

If the date of January, 1838, is correct, one must conclude that the etching was done after a drawing that dated from at least the year before.
RELATED WORK: A watercolor on the same subject (BN).

1840
D 6. *View from the Environs of Subiaco*
Etching, 116 × 186 mm.; H. 5.
This, the first etching Daubigny managed to publish, appeared in the review *L'Artiste*, which was then championing the Romantic movement. It seems unconnected with any painting, but the Italian subject may have sufficed to justify the magazine's publishing this landscape composed according to all the canons of the picturesque. Appended to the work was a commentary describing Daubigny as "an intelligent artist and one who handles finely and firmly this genre

of etching so much honored by our fathers."
Three states before lettering:
1) before the engraved signature and with some working of the sky (BN: *reproduced*);
2) with the signature etched in;
3) without the lines in the sky (BN, Brussels).
Two printings for *L'Artiste*, series 2, vol. VI, May 15, 1840, p. 164:
4) one with the legend engraved on the same plate; the signature has been removed and replaced by *Daubigny sculp.* below the frame line;
5) another with the legend engraved on a different plate.

D 7. *The Banks of the Furon near Sassenage (Isère)*
Etching with "*cravate*" process, 89 × 157 mm.; H. 6.
The painting *View of Notre-Dame* that Daubigny exhibited in the Salon of 1838 was followed in 1840 by his *Saint Jerome* (see D 11) and the next year by a painting (no. 460 in the Salon booklet) on the subject of this etching plus a portfolio of six etchings which marked his public debut as engraver. This etching was therefore made in the hope that the painting would be reproduced in *L'Artiste*, as *Saint Jerome* would later be. It should be noted, however, that Henriet dated it before the *Saint Jerome* and also stressed that it was done "*à la cravate*" (a process explained under D 54) and can therefore be considered a technical experiment. Like the other experiments of Daubigny, this engraving exists in only two or three copies, one in Baltimore, another in the BN (*reproduced*), and these are signed with the needle below the frame line at the lower left: *Daubigny inv. sculp.* The plate was destroyed.

D 8. *Ceremony of the Inauguration of the Column of July and the Translation of the Remains of the Victims of the Events of July, 1830, on the Place de la Bastille*
Etching, 164 × 300 mm.; H. 7.
This first large etching intended for publication was done together with Trimolet and shown under the latter's name in the Salon of 1841. It had a double purpose: one was political and clearly shows a certain commitment on the part of two young men deeming themselves heirs of the revolution of 1830, the other was financial since they were attempting to earn something through their engraving talents, publishing the print on their own and distributing it for sale through their own means in a fashion we would describe today as "militant." But Henriet reports: "The two young collaborators had not moreover had the advantage of getting in first. While they were working away at this plate with its hundreds of figures with a carefulness and conscience worthy of a better fate, a hastily crayoned lithograph beat them to it and was snatched up in thousands of copies. Nowadays these kinds of current-events pictures are done in advance. That, it appears, is the only way not to be left behind." Thus, an episode in the victory of the lithograph over the copperplate engraving which, in that field at least, was proving archaic. As for the com-

mercial side, the experiment was no more conclusive: "Trimolet and Daubigny had entrusted the drummers of the Garde Nationale with the sale of this print. The speculation was not lucrative because their agents regularly every evening drank up the whole of the day's takings." Madeleine Fidell-Beaufort (vol. I, pp. 35–36) cites from J. Claretie (*Peintres et sculpteurs contemporains*, Paris, 1873, p. 279) a letter of September 19, 1840, from Daubigny to M. de Rémusat, Minister of the Interior, requesting the French government to subscribe to the purchase of a few prints, an offer that seems to have had no reply. The piece has become rare.

Delteil distinguishes three pre-lettering states:
1) with the sky drawn with the needle;
2) with the sky reworked mechanically;
3) with the signature *Trimolet et Daubigny* [*sic*] *del. & sc.*
There are the following with letterpress:
4) with the date *28 Juillet 1840* but not the dedication;
4-b) with *Dédié à la Garde Nationale* but not the verses by Béranger;
5) with date, dedication, and verses (*reproduced*);
6) as above plus, in the middle below the verses: *À Paris chez les Mds d'Estampes.*
RELATED WORK: Preparatory drawing in the Louvre.

D 9. *Calling Card of the Molder Malzieux*
Etching, 69 × 94 mm.; H. 8.
Henriet and Delteil distinguish six states of this calling card which apparently correspond to that number of printings:
1) lettered *A^te Malzieux/Mouleur, 31 Quai de la Tournelle, 31*;
2) with the date *1840*;
3) inscribed *A^te Malzieux/Mouleur*;
4) with the address, *rue Neuve Saint-Paul*;
5) with the address, *Quai d'Anjou, 17 rue Poulletier, 12* (*reproduced*);
6) very much retouched and heavy and black in appearance.
This is a utilitarian engraving, in one of the rare sectors where copperplate engraving could survive, as indeed it still does in calling cards, wedding announcements, and the like. Auguste Malzieux must have been a neighbor and friend, and his profile appears with that of Daubigny in the upper left of the cartouche.

D 10. *Chamois Hunter in the Mountains of the Bourg d'Oisans (Isère)*
Etching, 195 × 285 mm.; H. 9.
It was in the summer of 1839 that Daubigny could permit himself a trip to Bourg d'Oisans to prepare his painting for the Salon of 1840: a mountainous landscape with a Saint Jerome (see D 11). This large etching is a souvenir of that expedition, but it was printed in only a few copies and its purpose is not known.
We are well informed about the voyage and the preparation of *Saint Jerome* from the many letters that Daubigny wrote to his friends Steinheil and Trimolet, with whom he had pooled his resources. One, dated October 27, may illustrate the scene recalled in this etching:

It is a god-awful wild spot, and it is quite an impressive thing to find oneself alone in these mountains. For the moment I look like a Robinson [Crusoe] because I have a jacket of chamois skin on my body, even a loaded double-barreled rifle alongside me. I am close to five miles from a village. I left Bourg with provisions for eating. You would have had a good laugh if you had seen the getup in which I took off.

This rather suggests it is not a hunter depicted here but the painter himself and that the etching was done as a memento for his friends.
A single state only is known (Baltimore: *reproduced*).
An almost effaced trace of the subject can be made out on the back of the plate of our D 72 preserved in the Louvre Chalcographie, so we know the plate was cut up and reused.

D 11. *Saint Jerome*
Etching, 129 × 162 mm.; H. 10.
In *Saint Jerome*, the second painting submitted to the Salon by Daubigny, the chief figure was originally intended to be a hermit parleying with the Devil, a more Romantic theme. But the fact that the artist was still undecided while at work on the picture tells us that this is purely a lay figure and that his real interest was in the landscape, for which he did not hesitate to undertake a long and difficult journey. The picture won the favor of the younger critics, and *L'Artiste* offered to publish it in reproduction. As Henriet commented, this was advantageous publicity for the young painter "invited to translate himself." The reproduction in its turn was exhibited in the Salon of 1841. A print (formerly Giacomelli Coll.) was offered to an engineer in the Department of Civil Engineering of the Isère, Héricaut de Thury, who had ordered a painting from Daubigny during his sojourn at Bourg d'Oisans. Doubtless invited by the painter to give his opinion, the engineer wrote in the margin: "Very good! Very good! I recognize perfectly the mountains of the Oisan. But in the interest of M. Daubigny I advise him to erase: 1st, his Saint Jerome with the cross; 2nd, the small trees from the hills of the environs of Paris [which are] not the trees of the Alps. But I repeat: it is good and very good, and I take my hat off to M. Daubigny."
1) Rare proofs before lettering, signed with the needle below the frame line (NYPL).
2) Printing by *L'Artiste*, series 2, vol. V, 1840, with *Peint et Gravé par Daubigny* below the frame line at the left (*reproduced*).

D 12. *The Orchard at Valmondois*
Etching with *"cravate"* (see D 54), 90 × 150 mm.; H. 11.
It is not known why this piece was made. Perhaps the first completed attempt at an original graphic work? There are three states:
1) with two little girls playing in the orchard;
2) with the girls replaced by chickens (NYPL, Baltimore: *reproduced*).
3) "The plate was tinted *à la cravate*

with the intention of accentuating the effect. It was only made heavier" (Henriet).

D 13. *How Towns Are Born (The Village Wedding)*
Etching on steel, 75 × 142 mm. (without the remarque or sketch in the margin); H. 12.
This was the third commission from *L'Artiste* in a single year (after D 6 and 11), a sure sign that Daubigny was amply backed by the review or even being outright launched by it. The subject here is rather curious and decidedly anecdotal for Daubigny, though since the anecdote was itself freely varied according to the needs of one edition and another it does not really seem to have had any particular importance for him. Henriet assures us that "this charming little village represents the hamlet of Valmondois with the house of Daubigny's nurse among the apple trees on the right." Perhaps. But it was retitled *A Wedding in Geneva* for a new printing in *La Nouvelle, Journal illustré de littérature et de mode*, a monthly founded in 1844 which published Alexandre Dumas, Eugène Sue, Lamartine, and so on in serial form and included in each issue a "genre engraving" (steel or wood) and a colored fashion plate. Daubigny himself made use of the motif for a vignette engraved on wood published in *Les Beaux-Arts* (vol. I, no. 16, 1843, p. 238) to go with a text titled "The Field of Cornflowers."
There are two pre-lettering states:
1) signed and dated, before numerous changes (BN, BrM);
2) reworked with the black horse hitched to the plow (BN).
Two printings signed *C. Daubigny. 1840* at the right below the frame line:
3) for *L'Artiste*, series 3, vol. I, 1842 (*reproduced*);
4) for *La Nouvelle*, with the title *Le Tour du Monde, une Noce à Genève* (BN).
REPRODUCTION enlarged to 105 × 200 mm. by the Amand-Durand process, with the village musician and the title *La Noce* (The Wedding), the photogravure here being retouched with the burin; plate in the Louvre Chalcographie.

D 14. *Thatched Cottages at the Waterside*
Etching on steel, 54 × 213 mm.; H. 13.
"This little Norman landscape was engraved with the soft-ground method by Daubigny at the bottom of a plate of sketches published in the *Album Blaisot*" (Henriet).
1) Rare pre-lettering prints (BN).
2) Printing in the *Album Blaisot* (*reproduced*): full plate and isolated print, which also included four sketches by Trimolet entitled *Lion, Duchesse, Croyant* (True Believer), and *Politique et Amour* on the same sheet measuring 214 × 273 mm. and headed *Le Calepin d'un artiste* (The Notebook of an Artist) and numbered *Pl. 34*, with at the bottom left: *Imp. de Lesauvage* and at the bottom right: *Pub. par Blaisot*.
The publisher was Antoine-Bara Blaisot (1794–1876), member of a dynasty of printsellers going back to the reign of Louis XV, who brought out the prints of Paul Gavarni, lithographed portraits, models for artists and artisans, designs for embroidery, etc., among

them the *Répertoire de l'Ornemaniste* in 1841 for which Meissonier worked. It may have been through his good offices that Trimolet and Daubigny received the order for these small etchings.

D 15. *The River in the Park*
Etching on steel, 150 × 110 mm.; H. 14.
From 1840 on, thanks to successes in the Salons, the prints published in *L'Artiste,* and the mutual aid of friends and acquaintances, Trimolet and Daubigny were able to make their living by doing illustrations, often working together. Beginning with this frontispiece for a new edition of *Fortunio* by Théophile Gautier brought out in 1840, the publisher H. L. Delloye became one of their most faithful employers. Like Curmer, he recognized in them artists who were sufficiently advanced in the modern style that he wished to give his publications, but not so much as to frighten off the general public, and this plate gives a good idea of what he was after.
The engraving was exhibited under the name of Trimolet in the Salon of 1841, but Henriet classes it among the works of Daubigny: "Often one can discern in the vignettes of Trimolet background landscapes executed by Daubigny, but the latter's body of work is rich enough that there is no need to credit him with all his minor services as friend and collaborator. If we have made an exception for this piece . . . it is because the landscape, so delicately treated, constitutes its most remarkable part."
Proofs without lettering or signature (BN: *reproduced*).

D 16. *The Tumbril of the Condemned Man on the Pont-au-Change*
Etching on steel, 113 × 84 mm. (motif); 178 × 110 mm. (full page); not in H.

D 17. *The Death of the Bricklayer*
Etching on steel, 107 × 83 mm. (motif); 178 × 110 mm. (full page); not in H.
This second commission from the publisher Delloye for the team of Trimolet and Daubigny was omitted by Henriet from his catalogue, not because he did not know these etchings but because the background by Daubigny, unlike that of our D 15, did not constitute "its most remarkable part," the important thing here being the realistic incidents that must be credited to Trimolet. For his part, however, Delteil did include them in his catalogue of Daubigny. He could just as well have added many others, as Henriet had realized earlier. Still, this does not mean that the works done in tandem were not as important as the individual efforts.
The second of these scenes was done as frontispiece for the first volume of *Le Maçon, moeurs populaires* (The Bricklayer, Ways of Life Among the People) by Michel Raymond (pen name of Michel Masson and Raymond Brucker), republished by Delloye in 1840 in a cheap edition, the Bibliothèque Choisie (1.75 francs the volume, pocketbook format), one of the numerous at-

tempts at illustrated editions for the masses during the July monarchy, reproducing either great classics or popular novels such as this one. In his advertisement for this novel the publisher expressed admiration for its "frank analysis of the popular classes" and showed himself enough of a progressive to write that "we scarcely understand a democracy in which such a large fraction would remain in the state of pariah with respect to the rest, unless there were frankness enough to admit that revolutions are only a pretext for the profit of some against all the others," a decidedly subversive idea in 1840. The realistic and progressivist content of the novel is not irrelevant to the style of the vignettes and the choice of the illustrators, who here again showed their devotion to the ideals of 1830 but also, being younger than the Romantics, their clear aspiration to a greater realism, on the part of Trimolet especially.
Delteil catalogued the two frontispieces in reversed order, since D 16 was done for the second volume, D 17 for the first.

1841
D 18. *The Good Pauper*
Etching on steel, 184 × 133 mm.; not in H.
Another collaboration of Trimolet and Daubigny, accepted for the latter by Delteil but not by Henriet because the essential element is not his very insignificant background but the figure by his partner. In any case, it was also under the name of Trimolet that this work was exhibited, in the Salon of 1841, and then printed in the magazine of the publisher Curmer, *Les Beaux-Arts* (vol. II, no. 45, 1844), with the title *Le Vieux Mendiant* (The Old Beggar). That magazine had a brief existence in 1843 and 1844. It published also an original engraving by Charles Jacque, *The Old Pauper* (vol. I, no. 5, 1843), as well as prints by Nicolas-Toussaint Charlet and Paul Gavarni, which indicates that its taste was modern but eclectic and at times realist. Daubigny gave it two original compositions (D 48 and 51) and several vignettes engraved on wood (see D 13).
Delteil cites two states before lettering:
1) before extensive work;
2) completed.
3) The printing for *Les Beaux-Arts* (*reproduced*) bears the signature *Trimolet* and the legend: "*Mon dieu: je vous rends grâce de ce qu'il vous a plu de me donner ce mur pour m'abriter; et cette natte pour me couvrir*" (My God, I render thanks unto You because it pleased You to give me this wall to shelter me and this mat to cover me). The subject is characteristic of Trimolet, who had shown a much-admired painting in the Salon of 1839, *The Poorhouse, or The Aid Given Poverty by the Sisters of Charity,* for which he took as models aged paupers and true blind men. One wonders if this print too was done after a "naturalistic" model and was therefore well in advance of the *Absinthe Drinker* in which, to the scandalized horror of his professor, Manet painted a bona fide drunkard.

1842
D 19. *Le Lai des deux aman[t]s*
Etching on steel, 126 × 97 mm.; H. 15.
Commissioned by Curmer from the two young illustrators who were beginning to make their reputation. It is not unlikely that they were brought to his attention by Meissonier, who had already illustrated certain major modern works, notably as one of the large group of illustrators of the celebrated *Paul et Virginie* and *La Chaumière indienne* of Bernardin de Saint-Pierre, brought out in 1838 by this publisher of the Romantics. Thanks to Curmer and Delloye, two of the major avant-garde publishers of the time, the young men would thenceforth not lack for work (see, for example, the next entry).
1) Proofs before lettering (Baltimore).
2) With the following printed in the center: *Marie de France/ Le Lai des deux aman[t]s.* Published in *La Pléiade: Recueil de ballades, fabliaux . . .* Paris, Curmer, 1842 (*reproduced*).

D 20–24. *Text illustrations for "Le Jardin des Plantes"*
In 1841 Curmer undertook to publish a large and well-illustrated work on the Paris botanical gardens, the Jardin des Plantes, which would be at one and the same time a scientific encyclopedia and a tourist guide, very much in the spirit of the popular educational books of the 1830s. It was to be sold at fifteen francs, and the writing was entrusted to Pierre Bernard, L. Couailhac, Gervais and Emmanuel Le Maout, and a "society of scholars." In 1841, obviously as advance publicity, Curmer brought out a booklet by Bernard and Couailhac, *Physiologie du Jardin des Plantes et guide des promeneurs* (32°, 93 pp.), illustrated with wood engravings, and this was followed in the next year by another small book by Bernard, *Les Aventures de M. Bric-à-brac, Roman zoologique, archéologique et paléontologique* (8°, 85 pp.). Finally the definitive work grew into two volumes, of which the first appeared in 1842 with the title *Le Jardin des Plantes, Description complète, historique et pittoresque du Museum d'histoire naturelle, de la ménagerie, des serres. . . .* When the second volume came out the following year it plunged Curmer into a court case brought by another publisher, Dubochet, who tried to publish a work with the same title before Curmer. Although Dubochet had registered his title with the appropriate public office before Curmer, the latter won because he was able to prove that his project was under way before that of his rival.
Like his other publications, Curmer's work is extensively illustrated with numerous wood engravings incorporated into the text and worked into a well-devised page layout. Daubigny furnished drawings for some of these. In addition, however, the work had a considerable number of tipped-in steel engravings which were mostly colored and glazed, a bit of one-upmanship doubtless intended to outdo the Dubochet project. The five engravings—in black and white—assigned to Daubigny involved to some extent his specialty, landscape. Among other attractions the book also contained a large fold-out panorama of the Gardens drawn

and engraved by Louis Marvy, as well as a handsome view of the kennels by Charles Jacque.

D 20. *The Cedar (of Lebanon)*
Etching on steel, 175 × 115 mm.; H. 16.
Published in *Le Jardin des Plantes,* vol. I, p. 238.
1) Pre-lettering proof with small test drawing in margin (remarque) of two cats fighting in an attic (NYPL).
2) Pre-lettering proof without the remarque, the plate having been cut down to fit the format of the book.
3) With title, *Le Cèdre,* and, below in the middle: *Daubigny del. & sculpt (reproduced).*

D 21. *The Amphitheatre (of the Jardin des Plantes)*
Etching on steel, 174 × 109 mm.; H. 17.
Published in *Le Jardin des Plantes,* vol. I, p. 19.
1) One state before lettering and some work.
2) One without printer's name but with the title, *L'Amphithéâtre,* and, below in the middle, *Daubigny del. & sculpt (reproduced).*
3) With lettering as above plus *Imp. de Drouart, r. du Fouarre, 11, Paris,* below the frame line.

D 22. *Interior of the Large Hothouse*
Etching on steel, 174 × 111 mm.; H. 18.
Published in *Le Jardin des Plantes,* vol. I, p. 243.
Two states before lettering:
1) with basic etching before the shadows and with the statue blank;
2) completed *(reproduced).*
Three printings with lettering:
3) with the title *Intérieur de la grande Serre;*
4) with the same title but the plate retouched and surrounded by a frame line;
5) with the title *Plantes tropicales.*

D 23. *The Aviary of the Passerines*
Etching on steel, 171 × 140 mm.; H. 19.
Published in *Le Jardin des Plantes,* vol. II, pp. 64–65.
1) Pre-lettering state with engraved signature.
2) State with title: *Volière des Passereaux (reproduced).*

D 24. *The Magpie*
Etching on steel, 170 × 120 mm.; H. 20.
Published in *Le Jardin des Plantes,* vol. II, pp. 112–13.
1) Unsigned pre-lettering state, before the plate was cut down to fit the format of the book.
2) With title: *Pie (reproduced).*
"Only the landscape is by Daubigny, the magpie was executed by an engraver using the burin" (Henriet).

D 25. *The Palm Tree*
Etching on steel, 150 × 100 mm.; H. 21.
Like Delteil, we have been unable to locate this plate indicated by Henriet as illustrating one of the numerous works of the botanist Jules Decaisne. We can add only that that scientist was the brother of a painter, Louis De-caisne, who with his toned-down Romantic style had won a good reputation for his portraits (one of Lamartine in a very Lamartinian style). It was not through the publisher but through Louis Steinheil, a friend of Jules Decaisne, that Daubigny may have entered into contact with him. Bailly-Herzberg and Fidell-Beaufort (1975, p. 91) advise that Steinheil "profited from his relations with the botanist Jules Decaisne to enter his brother's studio."

D 26–42. *Chants et Chansons Populaires de la France*
Etchings on steel, c. 190 × 130 mm. (engravings); 274 × 174 mm. (page size).
It was in February, 1842, that the fascicle installments of the folk-song collection, *Chants et Chansons Populaires de la France,* began to appear. The enterprise, which ran to three large volumes in octavo, gave work to a great many artists. The publisher H. L. Delloye, at that time associated with Garnier Frères, called on the team of Trimolet, Daubigny, and Steinheil among others, they having already worked for him. Daubigny collaborated in three different ways, which tells us a great deal about the modifications that the engraver's trade was going through at the time (see our introduction): as supplier of drawings for other engravers (in fascicle 67, *Le Point du jour* and *La Fin du jour* drawn by Daubigny, pls. 1 and 4 engraved by Mercier, pls. 2 and 3 by Ransonnette); as designer and engraver of his own drawings (in fascicle 4, *Le Rosier,* pls. 1 and 2, and *L'Orage,* pl. 1; in fascicle 13, *La Musette,* pls. 1 and 2, *Les Souhaits,* and *Les Hirondelles;* in fascicle 34, *Combien j'ai douce souvenance,* pls. 2 and 3, pls. 1 and 4 being engraved by Boilly after Steinheil; in fascicle 50, *Leçons d'une mère à sa fille, La Chanson de Lisette,* pls. 1 and 2, and *Le Chant du Barde);* and as engraver of reproductions after the drawings of others (in fascicle 25, *La Tentation de Saint Antoine,* 4 pls. after Trimolet). The catalogues of his engravings logically enough include only the plates he himself engraved, but this has the disadvantage of accepting reproduction-engravings while eliminating drawings he specifically made for reproduction but which were not engraved by him.
The enterprise of Delloye and Garnier is itself of some note. It was entirely consistent with the kind of popular and democratic educational publishing favored by Delloye, whose quite advanced opinions we have already noted (see D 16, 17), the rediscovery of popular folklore generally accompanying movements for the democratization of culture. Moreover, the work was sold at the lowest price possible, 60 centimes per fascicle in Paris, 70 in the provinces, with one appearing per week, as was the practice of the illustrated periodical encyclopedias so much in vogue since 1830 in France *(Magasin pittoresque, Musée des Familles)* and England *(Penny Magazine, Penny Encyclopedia).* Delloye's were much better produced, with delicate steel etchings replacing wood engravings, a choice he himself explained in his prospectus: "No collection really could better lend itself to the present taste in illustration and the custom of publication in installments. . . . In many books the illustration is an extraneous adjunct often out of place; here it is a felicitous complement and virtual necessity." In the introduction to the first volume he paid his respects to the engravers:

Messrs. Trimolet, Steinheil, and Daubigny, to whom we owe the drawings for this volume, not only gave all their care to reproducing the situations and epochs faithfully, but their clever and inventive pencil has often been able to add to the text details of a piquant oddity or an ingenious shrewdness. At the head of each installment we have cited the names of the engravers who lent us their aid. It is thanks to their talent and their devotion that it has been possible for us to resolve the problem of inexpensive production, satisfactory execution, and punctuality in the weekly publication of our installments.

Finally he pointed out one of the ambitions of the work which is quite revealing: "All classes of readers will find in our choice a stimulating attraction." With that in mind, says he, he has not neglected explanatory texts and has addressed himself to good authors and scholars (as did Curmer, with the same concern for a solid public education) such as Leroux de Lincy, the bibliophile Jacob, Du Mersan, and Ourry, men of some standing as serious commentators. Du Mersan, author of the preface to the third volume, expressed his satisfaction with the success of the first two and announced a fourth series to begin with nothing less than the "Marseillaise." As it worked out, though, the publication broke off at fascicle 84 in November of 1843 with this apologia: "Our artists, less pressed by the necessity of weekly publication, will await the inspiration they had been obliged to summon up. Their pencils will caress the subjects that their imagination will have time to embellish, and if they do not all attain to perfection they will strive to arrive at that point that distinguishes a work of commerce from a work of art." The problem in a nutshell: with their Romantic covers in chromolithography (by Engelmann and Graf at a remarkably early date) and their painstaking layout, printing (by F. Locquin, 16 rue Notre-Dame des Victoires), and illustrations that kept thirteen artists and some thirty engravers busy, the anthology remained a fine example of a contradiction: bibliophilism for the masses.
"Several prints of this series were engraved two by two on the same copper plate [*sic*]; we have met up with a few proofs with double-subject done before the copper plate was cut. There exist artist's proofs on China paper, mounted, without the verses, and others with the verses" (Henriet).

D 26. *L'Orage ("Il pleut, il pleut, bergère")*
1) Proofs before lettering and on the same plate as D 28 (NYPL).
2) Separate proofs.
Publication in *Chants et Chansons Populaires de la France,* vol. I, fasc. 4:
3) Printing without the name of the author of the poem and with the mis-

spelling "*éclaire*" in the last line of the first stanza *(reproduced)*;
4) Printing with correction, "*éclair*";
5) Printing with *Paroles de Fabre d'Églantine* added and with some retouching.
REPRODUCTION, 96 × 150 mm., of the upper portion by the Amand-Durand process. The photogravure plate, used to illustrate the book by Henriet, is now in the Louvre Chalcographie.
The figures are probably by Trimolet.

D 27. *Le Rosier* (first plate)
1) Proofs before lettering.
2) Publication in vol. I, fasc. 4 *(reproduced)*.
The figure is probably by Trimolet.

D 28. *Le Rosier* (second plate)
1) Proofs before lettering and on the same plate as D 26 (NYPL).
2) Separate proofs.
3) Publication in vol. I, fasc. 4 *(reproduced)*.

D 29. *La Musette* (first plate)
1) Proofs before lettering and on the same plate as D 32 (NYPL, BN from Giacomelli: *reproduced*).
2) Separate proofs.
3) Publication in vol. I, fasc. 13.

D 30. *La Musette* (second plate)
1) Proofs before lettering (reproduced by Delteil).
2) Publication in vol. I, fasc. 13 *(reproduced)*.

D 31. *Les Souhaits*
1) Proofs before lettering and with a few trials of needles in the margin.
2) Publication in vol. I, fasc. 13 *(reproduced)*.

D 32. *Les Hirondelles*
1) Proofs before lettering and on the same plate as D 29 (NYPL, BN from Giacomelli: *reproduced*).
2) Separate proofs (reproduced by Delteil).
3) Publication in vol. I, fasc. 13.
REPRODUCTION, 85 × 150 mm., of the upper portion by the Amand-Durand process. The photogravure plate is in the Louvre Chalcographie under the title *Le Départ des Hirondelles*. It is signed by Daubigny below the frame line at the left and does not bear the inscription "Chalcographie du Louvre."

D 33. *La Tentation de Saint Antoine* (first plate)
Reproduction-engraving after Trimolet.
1) Proofs before lettering.
2) Publication in vol. I, fasc. 25 *(reproduced)*.
3) Later printing with retouching and, below the title, *Paroles de Sedaine*.

D 34. *La Tentation de Saint Antoine* (second plate)
Reproduction-engraving after Trimolet.
1) Proofs before lettering.
2) Publication in vol. I, fasc. 25 *(reproduced)*.
3) A state reported by Delteil with oblique lines added to the music book and retouching of the image at the top.

D 35. *La Tentation de Saint Antoine* (third plate)
Reproduction-engraving after Trimolet.
1) Proofs before lettering.
2) Publication in vol. I, fasc. 25 *(reproduced)*.

D 36. *La Tentation de Saint Antoine* (fourth plate)
Reproduction-engraving after Trimolet.
1) Proofs before lettering.
2) Publication in vol. I, fasc. 25 *(reproduced)*.

D 37. *Combien j'ai douce souvenance* (second plate: "In the Woods")
1) Proofs before lettering.
2) Publication in vol. II, fasc. 34 *(reproduced)*.
Delteil distinguishes three different states after the publication:
3) with lines on the path removed;
4) with the path again shaded and cross-hatching in the sky;
5) the plate retouched, the sky extended as far as the top of the tall tree.

D 38. *Combien j'ai douce souvenance* (third plate: "The Moor's Tower")
1) Proofs before lettering (Brussels).
2) Publication in vol. II, fasc. 34 *(reproduced)*.
3) New printing with address: *Imp. de Chardon aîné et fils, 30, r. Hautefeuille, Paris.*

D 39. *Leçons d'une mère à sa fille*
1) Proofs before lettering.
2) Publication in vol. II, fasc. 50 *(reproduced)*.
3) Printing with *Paroles de Favart* beneath title.

D 40. *La Chanson de Lisette* (first plate: "The Return to the Village")
1) Proofs before lettering and on the same plate as D 41.
2) Separate proofs.
3) Publication in vol. II, fasc. 50 *(reproduced)*.
4) Printing with *Paroles de Monvel* beneath title.

D 41. *La Chanson de Lisette* (second plate: "The Village Dance")
1) Proofs before lettering and on the same plate as D 40.
2) Separate proofs.
3) Publication in vol. II, fasc. 50 *(reproduced)*.
4) Printing with the address of the printer Chardon.

D 42. *Le Chant du Barde*
1) Proofs before lettering.
2) Publication in vol. II, fasc. 50 *(reproduced)*.
3) Printing with *Poésies de Hoffmann* beneath title.

D 42 BIS–43. *Les Contes de Perrault mis en musique*
Among the works of Daubigny in the Cabinet des Estampes of the Bibliothèque Nationale are five storytelling illustrations which accompany musical settings of the fairy tales of Perrault. They were unknown to Henriet, and Delteil saw only these prints, which were acquired by the BN in 1918 and are still the only ones known.

D 42 BIS. *Le Petit Poucet: No. 2. Été* (Hop-o'-My-Thumb: Summer) 205 × 277 mm.

D 42 TER. *Le Petit Chaperon Rouge: No. 3. Poule* (Little Red Riding Hood: Hen) 205 × 285 mm.

D 42 QUATER. *La Barbe Bleue: No. 1. Pantalon* (Bluebeard: Pantaloon) 205 × 277 mm.

D 42 QUINTER. *Cendrillon: No. 4. Trénis* (Cinderella) 205 × 280 mm.

D 43. *Peau d'Âne: No. 5. Final* (The Ass's Skin) 205 × 280 mm.
1) Proofs before lettering and music, only two known (one in the collection of the BN).
2) Publication with lettering and music (BN: *reproduced*).

D 44. *Sailor Leading Away a Woman*
Reproduction-engraving after Trimolet. In the summary catalogue of Trimolet's works appended to his book on Daubigny (p. 205), Henriet mentions a composition by Trimolet engraved by Daubigny to illustrate a novel by Captain Marryat and depicting "a sailor who leads away a woman by orders of a corsair," but we have found no trace of it.

D 45. *The Market on the Square du Temple, Paris*
Etching and mechanical techniques on steel, 117 × 200 mm.; H. 40.
It was again thanks to Delloye that Daubigny was commissioned to do two engravings illustrating a new edition of *Les Mystères de Paris* of Eugène Sue, brought out in 1843–44 by Delloye-Gosselin. This very celebrated publication also has numerous wood-engraved illustrations on which Daubigny collaborated.
1) Proofs before lettering, some on China paper.
2) With the title *Le Marché du Temple* below in the middle *(reproduced)*.
3) The same state, published in the volume.

D 46. *The Winter Garden*
Etching on steel, 130 × 200 mm.; H. 41.
Two pre-lettering states:
1) etching only, before much additional work, with the signature *Daubigny* (Boston);
2) signed *Daubigny del. et sculp.*, all work completed.
With lettering:
3) with title in lower margin: *Le Jardin d'Hiver/ 1ʳᵉ Partie, Chap. 26 (reproduced)*;
3-b) the same state published in *Les Mystères de Paris*;
4) a later printing with title *La Huerta del Invierno*.

D 47. *Church of Sainte-Amélie-aux-Places* (*Nièvre*)
Etching, 233 × 338 mm.; not in H.
Delteil remarks on the rarity of this etching, found virtually only in Baltimore and the BN. The latter holds, however, besides the state reproduced by Delteil (the third), two others he did not describe.
1) Before any lettering, the medallion, or work with the mechanical tool.

2) Before any lettering but with the medallion in the lower margin, the entire plate worked with the mechanical tool.

3) With signature *Daubigny et Lavoignat* below the frame line at the right, together with an extensive text as seen here plus the address: *Paris, Imp. de A. Beillet, 10 rue de Pontoise (reproduced)*.

D 48. *Environs of Choisy-le-Roi*
Etching, 167 × 245 mm.; H. 22.
Following the lead of *L'Artiste*, the luxurious review *Les Beaux-Arts* that Curmer published in 1843–44 (see D 18) presented Daubigny's own reproduction of his Salon painting of 1843. Obviously the painter did not lack for support from the specialized press since all of his Salon pictures were reproduced in one review or the other: *Saint Jerome* of 1840, *Banks of the Furon* of 1841, then, after 1842 in which he submitted nothing, this *Environs of Choisy-le-Roi* in 1843; for 1844 see under that date.
Curmer, for whom Daubigny had already worked (D 20–24), published this reproduction, along with a lithograph by Charlet, in *Les Beaux-Arts* in 1843, and later brought out the engraving by Trimolet and Daubigny entitled *Le Bon Pauvre* (D 18) as well as numerous wood-engraved vignettes by Daubigny, followed in 1844 by his *The Threatening Storm* (D 51).
Delteil distinguishes two pre-lettering states and one final:
1) etching only, signed with the needle at the lower left: *Daubigny C. p. del. 1843;*
2) completed, signed *C. Daubigny pinx. & del.* (BrM, BN: *reproduced*);
3) printing in *Les Beaux-Arts*, vol. I, no. 10, May, 1843, p. 153, with the signature *Ch. Daubigny* in the center above, the title below the print, and the dry embossed stamp of Curmer in the margin.
REPRODUCTION in the same format by the Amand-Durand process. The photogravure plate, smaller than the original (190 × 266 mm.) is in the Louvre Chalcographie under the title *Le Joueur de cornemuse* (The Bagpipe Player).

D 86. *View from the Bas-Meudon*
Aquatint and etching on steel after a daguerreotype, 143 × 203 mm.; H. 59.
The date of 1852 given by Delteil must be corrected since he did not know that this engraving was done for the celebrated album titled *Excursions daguérriennes*, one of the very first attempts at collaboration between photography and printing. The first volume appeared in 1842 and contained sixty "views of the most remarkable monuments of the globe" done by engravers in aquatint on steel after daguerreotypes. A commentary explained: "After having obtained the transfer onto steel of a tracing using drypoint, by means of which the general disposition of the work is laid out, the special role of the artist in the execution is to complete the color, the expression of the sites, monuments, or objects depicted," and added that "the initial preparation, entirely mathematical as it is, and the rigorous exactness of the principal lines do not cast a chill over the work and in no way cramp it."

That is what Daubigny and several other engravers had to do for their contributions to the fifty-two plates of the second volume. The plate assigned to Daubigny, no. 17, did not, unlike the others, represent a monument. It was accompanied by a commentary signed by Challamel:

The magic wand of the daguerrian artist has made the old and mysterious basilicas surge forth before us . . . enough of old stones . . . give me greenery, water, shady banks and flowery valleys. . . . But let us return to our subject, for we have got very far from the Daguerreotype, and let us congratulate the artists who are turning their learned investigations toward the delicate and very difficult reproduction of landscape. We had been assured that it was impossible to obtain pure foliage because of the continual rustling of the trees, but the impossibilists have been reduced to silence; for it must be recognized that the *View from the Bas-Meudon* offers perfectly rendered foliage and effects of terrain, and that our predictions concerning the immense future of the daguerreotype tend with each new day to come true. Let us also address well-merited encomiums to the skillful and conscientious engraver whose beautiful etching so faithfully reproduces the photographic image. His foregrounds especially are treated with a freedom and boldness that do him honor, his tones are vigorous and handled with much truth and talent. There is air and freshness beneath his trees, and his greenswards would make one envy the fate of the rustic so nonchalantly stretched out near his flock. Let us hope that the *Daguerrian Excursions* will often lead us to the flowery banks of rivers or beneath the sweet-smelling bushes of the valleys, and that the engraving of M. d'Aubigny [*sic*] will be the prelude to a number of interesting works involving the reproduction of the landscape by the photographic apparatus.

A state not described in the literature and doubtless preceding the first state exists, with work done in aquatint and needle and with inking effects not carried over to the other states (Baltimore: *reproduced*).
Delteil lists three pre-lettering states:
1) before the sky and the shadow on the background (Baltimore: *reproduced*);
2) with a grainy ground of aquatint covering the plate (Baltimore);
3) with the aquatint removed and replaced by a mechanically engraved sky, still with the signature tooled in (BN); then
4) the printing for *Excursions daguérriennes* with *France* in the center above, *Daguerréotype Lerebours* below at the left, *Vue prise au Bas-Meudon* below in the center, *Daubigny sc.* below at the right, and *Goupil & Vibert, Bouievᵈ Montmartre, 15. Publié par N. P. Lerebours Place du Pont-Neuf 13. Hʳ Bossange, Quai Voltaire, 11* underneath the print.
5) Ten years later the plate was republished in *L'Artiste* (series 5, vol. IX, 1852–53) with, beneath the frame line at the left: *Daubigny Pinx. et Sculp.*; at the right: *Imp. de Pernel;* above the print: *L'Artiste;* below it: *Vue prise au Bas-Meudon.*

1844

D 49. *The Small Horsemen*
Soft-ground etching, 60 × 177 mm.; H. 42.
The year 1844 marked a turning point in Daubigny's career as engraver. For six years he had considered himself an illustrator and reproduction-engraver, but now he turned his hand to original essays that were to culminate in 1850 with his first album of etchings. Leaving aside the five attempts at the start of his career, meant only to make him known as an engraver pure and simple, and two plates (D 10, 12) that were not published, his engravings had always been done on order, either as illustrations or as reproductions publicizing his paintings. In 1844, however, he produced this small plate as an art work in itself, and printed so few proofs that the one owned by Giacomelli and cited by Henriet was long thought to be unique, according to Delteil. It can be considered his first venture as "painter-engraver," as "art-engraver" or what we would call "graphic artist," and was followed by the three plates of 1845 (D 52–54) which he exhibited in the Salon and deposited for copyright in the Bibliothèque Nationale.
Henriet explained that "Daubigny engraved this soft-ground piece after a sketch done from nature representing the Seine, the Île de Neuilly, and Mont-Valérien."
Three states:
1) before considerable work on the sky, trees, and water, signed *Daubigny* and *F. S.* or *F. V.* (NYPL);
2) completed, same signature (BN: *reproduced*);
3) signed *Daubigny* (BN).
4) In addition, the print dealer and publisher Laurent Dumont brought out a small number of prints on greenish paper, according to Delteil.
PLATE in BN, from Curtis Collection.

D 50. *The Eagle's Nest in the Forest of Fontainebleau*
Etching, 140 × 212 mm.; H. 43.
It was in 1843, the year of his marriage, that Daubigny began his sojourns in Fontainebleau. For the moment he could not seek inspiration in the great voyages he loved (Italy in 1836, Bourg d'Oisans in 1839) and instead joined the Barbizon group of landscapists to compose the picture he sent to the Salon of 1844 showing the crossroads known as the Nid de l'Aigle, the Eagle's Nest, in the forest of Fontainebleau. As had become his practice, he published a reproduction in *L'Artiste*.
1) Pre-lettering proofs with engraved signature, *Daubigny del. et sculp.* (NYPL, BN).
2) Printing in *L'Artiste*, series 4, vol. II, 1844 (*reproduced*).

D 51. *The Threatening Storm*
Etching, 110 × 170 mm.; H. 44.
Little by little, by training his hand through plates not done for publication and through reproductions, Daubigny developed a style of landscape in which Romanticism still had a large share (as in the storm and in the small figure at the left here) but which was more and more influenced by the Barbizon School (Théodore Rousseau, for one) and Paul Huet. In fact, Henriet states that "Daubigny told us that he con-

273

ceived this composition while pre-occupied with Paul Huet." Thus his graphic work became increasingly less descriptive and prepared the way for his album of 1850.

This *Approche de l'orage* is a composition that seems to have been done especially as an art-engraving intended for publication in *Les Beaux-Arts*. This was the third time that Daubigny published in that review but only the second time he had published in any periodical an etching unrelated to a painting (for the first, see D 6).

1) Pre-lettering proofs with engraved signature (BN: *reproduced*), some on China paper.
2) Printing in *Les Beaux-Arts,* vol. II, 1844, p. 288.

1845

The next series of three etchings executed by Daubigny anticipated the series he would publish in his albums of 1850–51 as works capable of standing on their own. Daubigny was beginning to wish to make himself known as a painter-engraver, a rare specialty at a time when the market for graphic art was almost nonexistent except for reproductions and old-master prints. To make his objective clear he presented these three etchings at the Salon of 1845, deposited duty copies in the Bibliothèque Nationale, and published one in *L'Artiste.* Their style is still very Romantic: the nicely composed group of animals in the *Pool with Stags,* the dramatic landscape of *Stormy Weather,* and the backlighting of the *Moonrise in the Valley of Audilly* were by then quite conventional. It is by no means certain that that sort of thing was to the pleasure of the rare clientele for original modern prints. They would more likely have looked for more novel effects, and in the print that followed this trio, *The Sheepfold* (D 55), Daubigny achieved just that, which is why that small etching, free as it is of all Romantic clichés, is considered his first masterwork in the graphic field. Its geometrical and rigorous composition is very different from the self-consciously picturesque compositions in which he strove for an all-pervading movement. Further, it was the first time that he did a merely domestic countryside view of the sort that by then was more appreciated than the untamed nature whose image had been handed down to Romanticism by the eighteenth century. Was he perhaps "preoccupied" with Millet as he had been with Huet?

D 52. *Pool with Stags*
Etching, 116 × 220 mm.; H. 45.
Three pre-lettering states:
1) "The signature had at first been engraved with the needle at the right, it was canceled and shifted to the left. Some proofs still show the trace of that first signature" (Henriet). Thus the first state is not only prior to considerable work but shows this double mark (BrM, proof from Burty);
2) the second state no longer shows the trace of the signature on the right, and branches have been added to the tree on that side (NYPL, Baltimore, BrM, BN: *reproduced*);
3) a third state with additional work

on the sky, which was reengraved (Baltimore).
4) The fourth state, without engraved signature, has the text: *Intérieur de la partie élevée de la forêt de Montmorency* (Interior of the high part of the forest of Montmorency) and, beneath the frame line at the left: *Ch. Daubigny del & sc.*

D 53. *Stormy Weather*
Etching, 122 × 215 mm.; H. 46.
Three pre-lettering states:
1) signed, before considerable work on the trees and water, and with the head of a greyhound sketched as a remarque in the right margin (Baltimore);
2) with additional work on the water but still without the branches standing out from the tree (BN, proof heightened with India ink: *reproduced*), some proofs on China paper *appliqué;*
3) completed, still with *C. Daubigny* engraved at the left (NYPL, BrM, BN: print deposited in 1845).
Two states printed in *L'Artiste,* series 6, vol. X, March, 1853:
4) with title *Temps d'orage* in the center below, *Daubigny, pinxt et Sculpt* at left, and *Paris, Imp. Pernel* at right;
5) with signature as in the previous states alone beneath the lower margin at left.
Commentary in *L'Artiste:* "Stormy Weather. What could we say that would be more eloquent than d'Aubigny [*sic*] himself? How Ruysdael would applaud!"

D 54. *Moonrise in the Valley of Andilly*
Etching with *"cravate,"* 93 × 143 mm.; H. 47.
In his quest for an original style of engraving Daubigny tried soft-ground (D 49) and aquatint (D 2) techniques, though for all their usefulness in rendering modeling neither seems to have satisfied him. Here, on the other hand, he mastered a procedure all his own, or, at any rate, one he was first to develop systematically (see D 7, 12) and which he dubbed *"la cravate,"* the necktie. This is a way of obtaining an effect like aquatint through the use of a soft varnish on which is laid a piece of silk. When peeled off, the cloth leaves the imprint of its weave on the soft ground, and if the operation is done delicately the weave will show up in the acid-biting and give a tint to the inking. Here we have one of the first tries at those homemade expedients so extensively indulged in by the painter-engravers of the second half of the century and which are very characteristic of the spirit in which original engraving as an independent graphic art developed: a concern with a new and revitalized technical language based on manual or artisanal means that are part and parcel of the artist's own language and are as expressive of him as his style of drawing.
Two states before lettering:
1) before extensive work (the moon is barely visible) and with trials of the woven texture in the lower margin (BN: *reproduced*);
2) terminated (NYPL, BrM).
3) State with lettering which has, below the frame line at the left: *Ch. Daubigny del. & sc.,* and the title in the center.

According to Henriet, this "pretty piece" was done for Curmer (no doubt for publication in *Les Beaux-Arts*) but "was never, we believe, published." The review in fact had ceased publication in 1844.

1846
D 55. *The Small Sheepfold*
Etching, 87 × 160 mm.; H. 48.
"This etching is executed with utmost care and charm. The sky and terrain are delicately modeled. This piece, which has become rare, is supple and colored like a painting" (Henriet). Here for the first time Daubigny abandoned the Romantic style, which was beginning to strike young art lovers like Henriet as all too pompous. This "realistic" and sober style, with restrained effects and undramatic subjects, corresponded to a new Second Empire taste already plain to read in this print of 1846. The success of Daubigny after 1848 can be explained by that evolution so characteristic of an entire youthful generation between the two revolutions.
1) Before extensive work, signed with the needle *Daubigny, Inv. 1846* (BN).
2) Completed, the plate still not beveled.
Delteil reproduced both the first and second states, and distinguished a third:
3) the print unchanged but the plate beveled (Baltimore: *reproduced,* NYPL, BN).
REPRODUCTION enlarged to 110 × 200 mm. by the Amand-Durand process, with signature but without the date; photogravure plate now in the Louvre Chalcographie.

D 56. *Women Bathing, Souvenir of the Stream at Valmondois*
Etching, 90 × 150 mm.; H. 49.
1) First state before extensive work and a re-biting (Baltimore, BN).
2) Second state, completed (NYPL, BN), signed at the left below the frame line *C. Daubigny inv. 18* (*reproduced*).
REPRODUCTION enlarged to 150 × 245 mm. by the Amand-Durand process; photogravure plate in the Louvre Chalcographie.

D 57. *Castel Gélos (Vallée d'Ossau)*
Etching on steel, 75 × 118 mm.; not in H.
This plate, not accepted for his catalogue by Henriet, was probably done on order as an illustration and is much like the numerous drawings Daubigny executed for wood engravings to be used in tourist and railway guides. It was engraved after a drawing by Laroche, and its date, given with a question mark by Delteil, is entirely subject to caution.
1) A pre-lettering state with the engraved signature *C. Daubigny sculp* at the left beneath the frame line (BN: *reproduced*).
2) State with the same signature and below, in the middle: *Castel Gélos Basses-Pyrénées / Vallée d'Ossau.*

D 58, 59. *The Home and Study of Monsieur Thiers*
These two prints, done on order, show the exterior and interior of the home of the historian, statesman, and future

president of the Republic Adolphe Thiers. (The site on the Place Saint-Georges in Paris is now occupied by a library dedicated to his memory.)

According to Henriet, "We do not know the intended purpose of this plate nor of the following plate done, we believe, around 1847 for the publisher Michel (?) now deceased. The Revolution of 1848 doubtless stopped the publication for which they were destined. M. Thiers, to whom we took the liberty of mentioning them, was not acquainted with them." Thanks, however, to the kindness of the late Mlle. Michaud, director of the Bibliothèque Thiers, we have been able to ascertain that both plates were published as frontispieces for two volumes by Alexandre Laya, *Études historiques sur M. Thiers*, Paris, Furne, 1846.

D 58. *The Home of Mʳ A. Thiers*
Etching on steel, 80 × 140 mm.; H. 50.
Two pre-lettering states:
1) before the sky and some additional work (Baltimore);
2) completed, with "tone laid on the sky and various other parts of the plate by mechanical means. There exist a few artist's proofs of this second state on mounted China paper" (Henriet); then
3) final state with title and signature at the left below the frame line, *Daubigny del. et Sc.*, published in the book by A. Laya (*reproduced*).
Henriet gives an interesting description of the site: "In front of the mansion at whose grille stands a carriage one sees the Fontaine Saint-Georges, the square with strolling passersby, and the start of the Rue Fontaine. We draw attention to the fact that the houses that form the left corner of the Rue La Bruyère were not yet in existence and that tall trees occupied the place where they were built."

D 59. *The Study of Mʳ A. Thiers*
Etching on steel, 80 × 140 mm.; H. 51.
1) Very rare pre-lettering proofs.
2) Printing with title and signature, published in the book by A. Laya (*reproduced*).
Henriet remarks that among the pictures decorating the sumptuous study can be made out *The Last Judgment* after Michelangelo between copies of *The Marriage of the Virgin* and *The Transfiguration* of Raphael. This *ne plus ultra* of academicism is significant not only of the personal taste of this man of letters and politics but also of the entire social category he represented, a bourgeoisie concerned with and for tradition.

1847
D 60. *Vintage at Champlay*
Etching with "*cravate*," 80 × 150 mm.; H. 52.
Another attempt at an original etching using the "*cravate*," this small piece was never published and remains very rare (both states in Baltimore but not in BN):
1) with etching only, before application of the cloth (*reproduced*);
2) completed.

1848
D 61. *The Fire at the Farm (Reminiscence of the Morvan)*
Etching, 105 × 198 mm.; H. 53.
Another attempt at an original etching, this one more important in format and extensiveness of work than its predecessors and certainly considered so by its author, who lavished much care on it. It is not irrelevant that when Daubigny began to aim at a personal and innovative approach, the number of states increased, whereas plates done for illustrations are virtually without states or have only unimportant modifications. This one has four states, though very few prints are known. Henriet knew only three, those in the possession of Daubigny himself, Geoffroy-Dechaume, and Burty, while Delteil was able to locate seven, of which four are now in Baltimore (constituting a complete collection of states) and one, a fourth state, is in the BrM. The fourth state owned by Curtis went to the BN.
1) With a black horse in flight in the middle and before considerable additional work (Baltimore, the only known proof of this state: *reproduced*).
2) With the black horse removed.
3) With figures on the right.
4) With trees at the left and in the background (BrM, BN, Baltimore: *reproduced*).

D 62. *The Mill, after a Drawing by Jan Pynas* (1st version)
Etching, 120 × 190 mm.; H. 54, cat. no. used also for D 63.
Not reproduced by Delteil.
This commission of October 30, 1848, from the Chalcographie makes it clear that the Bureau of Fine Arts, to which Charles Blanc had been appointed, was sympathetic toward artists considered "modern," though this first plate reproducing a drawing by Pynas owned by the Louvre was nonetheless refused, no doubt with the usual objection to artists who are a bit too modern, that their work is not sufficiently "finished." This explains why the piece has remained very rare, known virtually only in the prints of the first and second states in Baltimore.
1) With etching only (*reproduced*).
2) With an aquatint grain except in the sky and on the hill (*reproduced*).
3) Delteil mentions a third state that is entirely aquatinted (location unknown).
Henriet provides several details about this work:

The print is surrounded by a quintuple frame line. This state of etching and "*cravate*" combined has all the accent of a drawing. Nevertheless it did not satisfy the administration, and Daubigny began a new plate more in line with the views expressed by him. This is the well-known plate of the Chalcographie, of soft and insipid workmanship. The prints, slightly bistre-toned, without engraved lettering or titles, bear the dry embossed stamp of the Chalcographie [see D 63].

In accord with the liberal policy of the new Director of Fine Arts, Daubigny was permitted to make his own choice of the drawing to be reproduced. That he selected one by Jan Pynas (formerly attributed to Rembrandt) is taken by Fidell-Beaufort to indicate a great fa-

miliarity with the collection of Dutch drawings in the Louvre, since the artist is not well known. He was born in Haarlem in 1583 or 1584, visited Rome with Pieter Lastman, may have worked with Rembrandt for a while, and died in Amsterdam in 1631.

D 63. *The Mill, after a Drawing by Jan Pynas* (2nd version)
Etching, 126 × 190 mm.; H. 54, as above.
It is this version that is still sold at the Louvre Chalcographie (see D 62).
1) An early state before the sky and before the upper frame line, with the signature *Daubigny d'après Pinas* below the frame line at the left.
2) Completed (*reproduced*).

1849
D 64. *The Watering Place, after a Drawing by Claude Lorrain*
Etching with "*cravate*" and roulette, 215 × 295 mm.; H. 56.
For this second commission from the Louvre Chalcographie, obtained after 1848 thanks to Charles Blanc, our artist was paid four hundred francs on April 18, 1849. Two pre-lettering states:
1) etching only, unsigned (Baltimore);
2) with an aquatint tone, still unsigned (NYPL); then
3) completed with, below the frame line, at the left: *Claude Lorrain del.*; in the middle: *musée du Louvre*; and at the right: *Daubigny sculp.* (*reproduced*). Still being printed by the Chalcographie.

D 65. *The Valley of San Juan del Oro (Gathering Cinchona Bark)*
Etching, 270 × 392 mm.; H. 55.
It was probably through the connections of Steinheil with the botanist Decaisne that Daubigny was commissioned to do this illustration for a book on quinine and related substances.
1) Pre-lettering proofs (with wide margins on China paper according to Henriet) with engraved signature. Delteil mentions also "a slight variant of this composition engraved on wood and reversed" by Jean-Baptiste Carbonneau.
2) Printing in H.-A. Weddell, *Histoire naturelle des Quinquinas ou monographie du genre Cinchona*, Paris, V. Masson, 1849, folio (*reproduced*), whose title page also indicates 34 plates drawn by Riocreux and Steinheil. Below the frame line at the left: *J. Denis del. ad lin. A. Wedd*; at the right: *Daubigny sculp.*; title in the margin below: *Vallée de San Juan del Oro*; to the right of title: *N. Rémond imp.*; above: *Exploitation du Quinquina dans les forêts de Carabaya au Pérou.*

1850
D 66–78. *Album of Etchings*
In 1850 Daubigny felt the time was ripe for commercial exploitation of his own etchings, and this doubtless for two reasons. Since his successes in 1848 he had become a painter of note. With the backing of men in high positions in the Second Republic he would go from success to success, and engraving offered a means of expanding his public. Never having abandoned the etching needle, since 1845 he had begun preparing for this new step by

working more often on original etchings. At the same time, the situation of etching itself was improving; a taste was developing for artistic utilization of the process within the tradition of the great Dutch masters. At first still timid, the reaction against the industrialization of the image was to make its real impact only after 1855 and even more after 1861, when the Société des Aquafortistes was organized. But that movement, promoted by Cadart, could not have come about unless a large number of artists had already converted to pure etching, and in fact the start of the vogue in certain ateliers must date from a few years earlier. With the publication of his first album of etchings, Daubigny was one of the earliest, together with Charles Jacque, to exploit that vein, though this came to him very naturally since, like Jacque, he had remained an illustrator and had never given up engraving.

In 1851 he brought out two series of six etchings each. These were in a very personal style owing nothing to the Romantic approach to illustration which still to some degree marked his previous efforts. He himself seems to have taken full charge of the project, commercially as well as technically, and assigned the work on the first edition to the printer Beillet, whose shop was near his studio on the Quai de la Tournelle. Even if we lack precise figures, the number of reeditions and printings attests to the success of the venture. The printings were not limited and the prices relatively modest: one franc per print, five francs for the six, which shows that Daubigny was still working within the system of the print considered as a modest image of unlimited distribution. At the time, contrary to what has come about since, there was scarcely any difference in price between an original engraving and the ordinary printed image.

Delteil claimed to distinguish eight or nine different printings of the albums, and one does find numerous variants in the covers that tell us a good deal. However, we know almost nothing about how the enterprise was carried through and least of all about how the albums were distributed for sale. There were two issues with a total of twelve etchings but a single cover and no listing of the engravings. The first version of the cover bears the date of 1850, but it is probable that publication did not take place until the following year. In any case, the list of variants of the cover remains, for better or worse, our only source of information for printings and editions.

D 66. *Album cover with Wreath of Field Flowers*
Etching, 188 × 135 mm.; H. 60.
1) With the date *1850* and *ans* instead of *an* (year), and no address.
2) With *1851* but still no address.
3) With the address: *A. Beillet imp. quai de la Tournelle 35 Paris.*
4) With the same address and the simple title *Eaux-fortes par Daubigny.*
4-b) Without address but with title as above (BN: *reproduced*).
5) With the address: *Imp. par Aug. Delâtre Fᵇᵒᵘʳᵍ Poissonnière 145 Paris* (which puts it between 1856 and 1858).
6) Again with the address of Beillet,

printed over that of Delâtre.
7) With the name of Beillet but not his address.
8) Again with the address of Delâtre.
9) With the address: *Imp. Ch. Delâtre, rue Sᵗ-Jacques, 303, Paris* (thus, 1875).
10) Again with *A. Delâtre,* but this time with a new address, *Montmartre* (thus, after 1876).
This makes eleven editions of which two are before lettering and eight with printers' names, to which must be added the printings without lettering (NYPL), "proofs in which either the address or the name of the artist or, finally, the order number [its number in the set] was not inked, and this most often deliberately, which adds to the confusion and at times to the uncertainty as to the priority of the proofs" (Delteil). "Meanwhile proofs without lettering, though not before lettering, were printed with traces of erasure. In one of the numerous peregrinations of these plates Delâtre very cleverly printed a few proofs on Japanese paper whose luminous tone attenuates the fatigue of the plate and masks the heaviness of the blacks," writes Henriet, who advises also that "a very small artist's edition of the entire series was done, without printer's name, before the two albums were put out for sale." All of which proves their great success, something that must be taken into account in the history of etching between the failures of Théodore Chassériau and those of Manet, and which also explains why several other artists— Millet, Jongkind, Manet among them —would likewise attempt to launch their own albums.

D 67. *Sunrise*
Etching, 134 × 233 mm.; H. 61.
1) Before work on the terrain at the left and the trees and sky (BN).
2) With only working of the sky lacking.
3) Completed (BN, BrM, NYPL).
4) With the address of Beillet.
5) With that of Aug. Delâtre, Faubourg Poissonnière (*reproduced*).
RELATED WORK: Painting on the same subject, 1873.
PLATE in the Louvre Chalcographie.

D 68. *Tow Horses*
Etching, 80 × 157 mm.; H. 62.
1) Before considerable work on the terrain and below the horses (Baltimore), the plate being larger "with small grotesque figures in the lower margin; before the plate was given its definitive effect and the final work done with the needle on the man on horseback" (Henriet).
2) Before some work on the clouds, the plate still not reduced.
3) Completed (BN, Brussels).
4) With the address of Delâtre.
5) With that of Delâtre as in D 67 and in all subsequent references to Delâtre in this series (*reproduced*).
RELATED WORK: Preparatory drawing (?) shown by F. Keppel in the exhibition of graphic works by Daubigny, New York, April 18 to May 1, 1907.
PLATE in the Louvre Chalcographie.

D 69. *The Banks of the Cousin*
Etching, 147 × 117 mm.; H. 63.
1) With a herd of cows and two figures;

signed at the left (reproduced by Delteil).
2) With additional work on the terrain and in the trees.
3) With four cows effaced.
4) With the figures effaced.
5) With the number *3* above on the right (*reproduced*).
Some with A. Delâtre's address (BN). Others without the number *3*; on Japan paper (BN).
PLATE in the Louvre Chalcographie.

D 70. *The Little Birds*
Etching, 148 × 100 mm.; H. 65.
Two states before the address of A. Delâtre:
1) with a rabbit in the middle of the road (NYPL: proof from Burty).
2) with the rabbit effaced and two lines of a song of the time engraved in the lower margin: *Petits oiseaux le printemps vient de naître / oiseaux chantez le printemps et l'amour* (Brussels, BN: *reproduced*).
Some with A. Delâtre's address.
Others with his address effaced.
PLATE in the Louvre Chalcographie.

D 71. *Autumn (Souvenir of the Morvan)*
Etching, 115 × 199 mm.; H. 66.
As for some of the preceding prints, the history of this one is complicated. We have seen in D 69 and 70 that Daubigny did not hesitate to change a plate almost completely from one state to another, even removing figures and animals. This plate shows the most complete transformation: the man on the ground becomes a peasant with his mule, the group of trees at the right was entirely reworked.
Four states before the first printing with address:
1) with the man lying on the ground and drinking from the stream, before considerable work including use of the roulette; signed *Daubigny inv. et sculp. 1848* below the frame line at the left (Baltimore, BN: *reproduced*);
2) with the figure reflected in the water and cross-hatching on the terrain (reproduced by Delteil);
3) still with the figure but with work with the burnisher around him and also new work on the trees (BN);
4) greatly transformed, a peasant with mule and dog replacing the drinking wanderer, the trees at the right very much higher, etc. (BrM, BN: *reproduced*); then
5) with address of Beillet;
6) after the Beillet edition, publication in *L'Artiste,* July 1, 1852;
7) again reworked in the landscape, trees, and hill, but "these new areas were quite badly matched up in the acid-biting with the preceding work" (Henriet). The plate must have been quite worn down by then but was nonetheless still printed.
8) With the address of Delâtre;
9) additional printings with address removed.
RELATED WORK: The etching was doubtless done after a drawing made during the visit Daubigny paid in 1847 to the Morvan and Burgundy regions (Château-Chinon, Avallon) in quest of new subjects.
PLATE in the Louvre Chalcographie.

D 72. *The Donkey at the Watering Place*
Etching with aquatint, 95 × 153 mm.;

H. 64.
Two states before address:
1) with quite strong aquatint grain, the plate larger *(reproduced)*;
2) with the aquatint grain toned down and the plate reduced; then
3) with the address of Beillet;
4) with that of Delâtre.
RELATED WORKS: This is a first version of D 92, which reproduces the painting Daubigny exhibited in the Salon of 1859.
PLATE in the Louvre Chalcographie.

D 73. *The Satyr*
Soft-ground etching, 149 × 114 mm.; H. 67.
1) A single pre-address state, signed lower left, with the number *7* at both top and bottom right (BN).
2) With the address of Beillet (BN, NYPL).
3) With that of Delâtre *(reproduced)*.
PLATE in the Louvre Chalcographie.

D 74. *The Ferry (Souvenir of the Islands in the Seine at Bezons)*
Etching, 162 × 100 mm.; H. 68.
Two states before address:
1) with the mass of foliage in the upper left blank as well as the trousers of the figure;
2) with work with drypoint and roulette, the number *8* above at the right, and *1850* after the engraved signature; then
3) with the address of Beillet;
4) with that of Delâtre *(reproduced)*.
PLATE in the Louvre Chalcographie.

D 75. *The "Virgin Islands" at Bezons (The Fishing Place)*
Etching, 170 × 135 mm.; H. 69.
Two states before address:
1) etching only, before the number (BN);
2) completed, with the number *9* at the top at left and right and again at the bottom at the right (reproduced by Delteil); then
3) with the address of Beillet *(reproduced)*;
4) with that of Delâtre.
RELATED WORK: Painting on the same subject titled *Les Îles Vierges à Bezons* in the Salon of 1850 (now Musée Calvet, Avignon).
PLATE in the Louvre Chalcographie.

D 76. *Haulage Wagons (Souvenir of the Morvan)*
Etching with *"cravate,"* 90 × 150 mm.; H. 70.
Two states before address:
1) with trial needle marks in right margin and the number *10* above at the right (BN: *reproduced*);
2) completed, with margins cleaned up (BrM, BN); then
3) with the address of Beillet;
4) with that of Delâtre.
PLATE in the Louvre Chalcographie.

D 77. *The Ruins of the Château at Crémieu (Isère)*
Etching with *"cravate,"* 94 × 173 mm.; H. 71.
1) A single state before address, signed below at the left, numbered *11* above at the right (NYPL, BN: *reproduced*).
2) With the address of Delâtre.
RELATED WORK: Drawing in the Cabinet des Dessins, the Louvre.
PLATE in the Louvre Chalcographie

under the title of *Les Ruines* (a reused plate, already engraved on the reverse by another engraver).

D 78. *Stags at the Waterside (Souvenir of the Islands at Bezons)*
Etching with *"cravate,"* 115 × 154 mm.; H. 72.
Another example of a plate completely transformed before the edition with the printers' addresses. The first state was treated entirely in undetailed masses done with cloth overlay, anticipating the Impressionist experiments of Pissarro such as *L'Île Lacroix à Rouen,* while the fifth state presents a completely different aspect.
1) Entirely with cloth overlay (BN: *reproduced,* retouched with pencil by the artist to add the stags in the middle of the composition).
2) With two stags added and an indication of two clouds at upper right (BN: *reproduced*).
3) With the clouds more fully worked and new work in the lower left (BN).
4) With the *"cravate"* effect obliterated, the image reworked in lines; with the number *12* (as in all previous states).
5) With additional work on the trees and sky *(reproduced)*.
6) With the address of Beillet.
7) With that of Delâtre.
PLATE in the Louvre Chalcographie.

1851
D 79. *Child and Flowers*
Etching on steel, 147 × 107 mm.; H. 57.

D 80. *The Two Riverbanks*
Etching on steel, 192 × 103 mm.; H. 58.
Although these illustrations for the *Fables de Lachambeaudie* represent an interlude between work on his own albums, it was by no means a routine commission. For one thing they are still landscapes, the genre in which he specialized, and thus were well suited to his aspirations, which are effectively brought out here in *Child and Flowers*. For another, these *Fables* were celebrated in the republican and socialist circles, and Pierre Leroux wrote the preface for the second edition. Henriet gives a good commentary, explaining how *The Two Riverbanks* represents the "allegory of the positive as against the ideal." The first edition of the book was in 1839; the edition illustrated by Daubigny and published by Michel in 1851 was already the eighth.
1) Proofs before lettering (BN: *reproduced*).
2) Publication with lettering and addresses: *Michel et Cie Editeurs rue Saint-André des Arts, 27 Paris* and *Imprimerie Drouart, Paris, rue du Fouarre*.
3) A second edition of the book in 1853, with address: *Bry aîné éditeur, 27, rue Guénégaud.*
4) An edition of D 80 listed by Delteil with title in Spanish: *La Aurora de los minos,* and below: *Las dos riberas.*

D 81. *The Ferry at Bezons*
Etching, 98 × 164 mm.; H. 74.
Executed for the album of the second series of etchings.
The success of the first series of twelve etchings published in albums certainly encouraged Daubigny to pursue that

enterprise, and nine other original compositions were done for that purpose, our D 81–85, 88, 90, 91, and 96, plus perhaps D 97 (see our entry for that work). Of these one finds printings with the address of Delâtre, Faubourg Poissonnière, 145, Paris, others by him without his address (sometimes on Japan paper), still others with the address of Beillet overprinting his. Although some plates have a number, it is not known how the prints were exploited commercially, if they were sold under the same cover as the first series or separately, nor if they had as successful a sale as the first series which, we have seen, went through several editions.
Like the first twelve, these additional nine plates were turned over to the Louvre Chalcographie.
Of this plate, three states before the editions with printers' addresses:
1) etching only after an initial acid-biting, the ferryman without skullcap (Baltimore);
2) with additional work, the ferryman with black skullcap;
3) still more work, a tree added between the two groups at the left (BN: *reproduced*); then
4) with the address of Delâtre;
5) with *Imp. Beillet.*
PLATE in the Louvre Chalcographie.

D 82. *Stags in the Woods*
Etching, 160 × 110 mm.; H. 75.
Executed for the second series.
1) A single state, proofs with engraved signature but no address (BN); then
2) with the address of Delâtre;
3) with that of Beillet overprinting the end of that of Delâtre *(reproduced)*;
3-b) an additional printing with the addresses removed.
PLATE in the Louvre Chalcographie.

D 83. *Cows in the Marsh*
Etching, 125 × 224 mm.; H. 76.
Executed for the second series.
1) A single state, proofs before address, with engraved signature below the frame line at the left: *Daubigny inv. sculp.;* and at the right: *Daubigny* (BN);
2) the signature at the right removed; then
3) with the address of Delâtre;
4) with *Imp. A. Beillet;*
4-b) another printing with address removed *(reproduced)*.
PLATE in the Louvre Chalcographie.

D 84. *The Marsh (with Storks)*
Etching, 124 × 198 mm.; H. 77.
Executed for the second series.
1) A single state but numerous printings. One finds pre-lettering proofs with engraved signature *Daubigny inv. sculp.* at lower left and the title *Le Marais* in the center below (reproduced by Delteil).
1-b) Others with signature but not title.
2) With the address of Delâtre.
3) With *Imp. Beillet.*
4) With the engraved inscriptions obliterated, but this is the printing of 1874 (see below) for which unlettered proofs were done, and for this the signature was reengraved as *Daubigny invt et sculpt (reproduced)*.
5) Printing by Salmon as full-page plate accompanying the first of two articles by Henriet on the work of Daubigny,

277

Gazette des Beaux-Arts, vol. IX, March, 1874 (750 copies).
6) Proofs with title and signature done for the *Gazette* but without the address of Salmon.
RELATED WORK: A painting done in 1873 based on this etching.
PLATE in the Louvre Chalcographie without address or mention of the Chalcographie, having at the left *Daubigny Invt et Sculpt* and in the middle the title.

D 85. *The Heavy Shower*
Etching, 135 × 230 mm.; H. 78.
Executed for the second series.
Two states before address:
1) etching only "with a horizontal line in the sky indicating the artist's intention to cut down the height of the image" (Delteil) and with engraved signature below at the left (Baltimore, BN);
2) completed state "darkened *(engraissé)* by a second acid bath" (Henriet); then
3) with the address of Delâtre;
4) with Beillet's name *(reproduced)*;
5) some proofs with Beillet's name obliterated;
6) some with his name replaced by *A. Quantin Imprimeur;*
7) still others in which the last name is in turn scratched off.
PLATE in the Louvre Chalcographie.

D 86. Follows D 48 above.

1855
D 87. *The Thicket in the Dunes, after a painting by Jacob Ruysdael*
Etching, 327 × 392 mm.; H. 73.
In 1853, profiting from the fact that Charles Jacque had withdrawn from an order, Daubigny received another commission from the Chalcographie and was paid the four thousand francs budgeted for it. The task suited him perfectly since it involved engraving two paintings by Jacob Ruysdael, whom he considered, along with Claude Lorrain, as his ideal master.
The appropriations for the Chalcographie were paid out from the Civil List funds (from which members of the government, public servants, retired luminaries, and the like were supported) despite some protest, which became particularly pronounced when the law concerning artistic property was proposed in 1841, publishers being accused of despoiling the artists of reproduction rights and the government of conducting itself like an owner and publisher with money taken from the Civil List. Daubigny was well thought of by the new regime of the Second Empire because his style was not too eccentric, and it was the Count de Nieuwerkerke himself who awarded him the commission. Henriet, who was the count's secretary, reports the granting of the commission in 1853 and its completion in 1855 (followed by another on the Civil List of 1855 delivered in 1860, our D 93):

The Comte de Nieuwerkerke, Director-General of Museums, assigned Daubigny to translate the *Thicket* of Ruysdael, which no engraver had as yet taken on. Daubigny acquitted himself of this delicate task very honorably. He rendered the masterpiece of the Master

of Haarlem not as a clever manipulator of cross-hatchings but as a painter interpreting another painter and penetrating directly into the feeling of the model. He attained the power of effect of the original and at the same time expressed its austere melancholy. Following the example of the masters of the great periods of engraving, Daubigny executed his plate with a great simplicity of means. He made use of scarcely anything more than etching and drypoint. He made little or no use of the burin. . . . He rigorously ruled out the use of roulettes and other mechanical means. He made up for them by energetic and repeated [acid] baths; his work owes its frankness and vigor to those audacities in acid-biting, but the drawing was to some extent made heavier, and the plate lost by this a little of the spirit and finesse that distinguish the "first state" of pure etching so sought after by print lovers.

Four pre-lettering states:
1) etching only, with *Daubigny* engraved below the frame line at the right (BN, NYPL);
2) plate re-bitten *(reproduced)*;
3) additional work on the sky and the village at the left;
4) further work on the sky, the engraved signature effaced and replaced below the frame line at the left with *J. Ruisdaël pinxit* and at the right with *C. Daubigny sculp. 1855;* then
5) printing by the Chalcographie with the title. The first prints were done by A. Delâtre.

D 88. *The Beach at Villerville*
Etching, 94 × 198 mm.; H. 80.
Executed for the album of the second series.
1) A single state, with engraved signature, before addresses *(reproduced)*.
2) With the address of Delâtre.
3) With Beillet's name (NYPL, BN).
4) Later publication illustrating the Henriet article and first catalogue of Daubigny's engravings in the *Gazette des Beaux-Arts*, vol. IX, May 1, 1874, with the title *Plage de Villerville* below the print, *Daubigny int et sculpt* below the frame line at the left, and still lower the designations *Gazette des Beaux-Arts* and *Imp. A. Salmon, Paris.*
5) A printing of 1874 with the last two indications removed.
Delteil mentions false pre-lettering printings: "These falsified proofs are easily recognizable in that they do not have the engraved signature below the frame line at the left, signature that is to be found on the copies genuinely done before lettering."
There exists also an anonymous copy, reversed and lacking the boat, which measures 77 × 147 mm.
PLATE in the Louvre Chalcographie.

1857
D 89. *Springtime*
Etching, 119 × 244 mm.; H. 81.
This reproduces the painting Daubigny showed at the Salon of 1857 and which entered the national collections (the Louvre). The engraving was done for publication in *L'Artiste* and went through several extensive printings.
1) A single state, with a few proofs before all lettering, some on old paper, without signature or date (NYPL, BN).

2) Printings with *Daubigny eau-forte 1857* engraved below the frame line at the left (Baltimore: *reproduced*).
2-b) A printing intermediary between the second and third states identified by Delteil, with address but not title (BN).
3) Publication in *L'Artiste*, vol. II, September 6, 1857, without signature and date as above but with lettering, above: *L'Artiste, Salon de 1857;* under the frame line at left: *Daubigny del. et sc.;* and at right: *Montmartre Imp. Delâtre, r. Nicolet, 10;* and below: *Le Printemps.*
A proof approved for printing (Baltimore) gives valuable information concerning the 1857 edition for *L'Artiste:* "1,200 prints of which 25 on *Grand Chine* [full sheets of China paper] and 50 in quarter-columbier format on *Grand Chine*," which tells us that the review had a circulation of about a thousand copies.
4) Subsequently the plate was used again for the offprint of the review of the Salon by Théophile Gautier, *Expositions de Paris* (Paris, Éditions de L'Artiste, 1859), for which printing the mention *L'Artiste, Salon de 1857* and the title were removed.
5) Additional printings with, at the bottom, the name of the publisher: *Marchant, Editr Alliance des Arts, 140, rue de Rivoli.* The title is retained, but appears in a different typeface than was used for the *L'Artiste* printing.
6) A printing with this last address removed and the plate reduced from a height of 209 mm. to 172 mm.
The commentary in *L'Artiste* remarks significantly:

M. Daubigny is not only one of our leading landscapists, he also occupies a high rank among our engravers using etching. He himself has reproduced—and one can see with what a luminous and vivid needle—his landscape of *Le Printemps,* one of the canvases in the Salon where nature most freely breathes in all its freshness and its freedom. M. Daubigny has translated himself as a poet, or rather he has made, with respect to his painting, an original and new work.

D 90. *Dog Keeping Watch*
Etching, 84 × 149 mm.; H. 82.
Executed for the album of the second series.
Three pre-lettering states of the edition for *L'Artiste*, one not described by Delteil:
1) with etching only and on the same plate as D 91 (Baltimore, NYPL);
2) with additional work, the plates separated (BrM, BN);
2-b) printing for *L'Artiste* with the address of Delâtre but without the title (BN: *reproduced*); then
3) printing for *L'Artiste*, series 6, vol. III, 1847, with the name of the review at the top and, below at the left: *Ch. Daubigny invt;* and at the right: *Paris Imp Delâtre, Fbg Poissonnière, 145;* and below in the middle the title, *Le Guet du chien.*
Delteil lists three later printings:
4) without the address of Delâtre;
5) with the name of Beillet and the indication *L'Artiste* retained;
6) with the name of Beillet but not the name of the review.
PLATE in the Louvre Chalcographie

with *Ch. Daubigny inv^t* at lower left and title in the middle but no mention of the Chalcographie.

D 91. *Dawn (The Song of the Cock)*
Etching, 144 × 113 mm.; H. 83.
Executed for the album of the second series.
Two pre-lettering states:
1) with etching only and on the same plate as D 90 (Baltimore: *reproduced*);
2) with additional work and the plates separated; then
3) printing by Delâtre with engraved title: *corri coco* (BN);
4) another printing, with *Fg Poissonnière, 145* after *Imp. par Aug. Delâtre*;
5) printing with the address of Beillet;
6) printing in Édouard Lièvre, *Le Musée Universel*, vol. II (Paris, Goupil, 1868), with title *L'Aurore* and *Delâtre imp.* below and *Daubigny, 10* above.

1859
D 92. *Setting Sun*
Etching, 115 × 184 mm.; H. 84.
This reproduction of the painting exhibited by Daubigny in the Salon of 1859 was engraved for publication in the *Gazette des Beaux-Arts* on that occasion. It goes back to a subject the artist had already treated in aquatint (D 72).
1) A few pre-lettering proofs with engraved signature and date, *Daubigny, 1859* (NYPL, BrM, BN: *reproduced*).
2) Printing for the *Gazette des Beaux-Arts*, vol. II, no. 5, June 1, 1859, p. 295 (750–1000 copies).
3) Some prints without the address of Delâtre.
4) Some with the address of Salmon.
5) Later printing in *L'Album de la Gazette des Beaux-Arts*, 1867.
PLATE in possession of the *Gazette des Beaux-Arts*.

1860
D 93. *The Ray of Sunlight ("Le Coup de Soleil"), after a painting by Jacob Ruysdael*
Etching, 325 × 392 mm.; H. 79.
The First Class Medal awarded Daubigny in the Salon of 1853 won him the privilege of figuring on the list of artists entitled to receive commissions from the Chalcographie. The immediate result was our D 87. In 1855 he won another medal, this one Second Class, and was given another task by that government agency for the arts, again to reproduce a Ruysdael, a task that seemed to call for his talents. (Note that he also received a *"rappel de médaille de 1re classe,"* a first-class distinction, in 1857 and 1859, thus in each of the Salons, since they were held every two years at that time.) Ordered in 1855, the engraving was not completed and delivered to the Chalcographie until 1860, and the print was exhibited at the Salon of 1861 (as no. 3698).
1) A few proofs with etching only after an initial acid-biting.
There are two very distinct pre-lettering states:
2) before numerous cross-hatchings and with engraved signature *(reproduced)*;
2-b) much more densely cross-hatched (BN).
3) According to Henriet, "about ten

warm and coloristic proofs were printed by Delâtre before delivery of the plate to the Chalcographie. They are more appreciated by print lovers than the pre-lettering proofs of the Chalcographie [which are] colder and moreover marked with the stamp of that service" (one in BrM dedicated "*à mon ami Delâtre, Daubigny*").
4) Chalcographie edition with the title *Le Coup de soleil;* and below the frame line, at the left: *Ruisdaël pinxit;* in the middle: *Chalcographie impériale du Louvre;* and at the right: *Daubigny sculp^t.*
PLATE in the Louvre Chalcographie.

D 94. *The Machine for Threshing Grain*
Etching, 119 × 213 mm.; H. 85.
This was done for the review of Charles Labourieu, *L'Art au XIXe siècle*, which was the organ of the Société Libre des Beaux-Arts (founded October 18, 1830) and the Société du Progrès de l'Art Industriel (founded March 22, 1858) and accordingly interested in the relations between art and science. The magazine, a semimonthly selling at one franc per copy, had been in existence since 1858. In the issue in which Daubigny's print appeared in 1860, there was a long poem by Louis Goujon titled *L'Épi de blé* (The Ear of Grain) with a comment by the editor, Labourieu:

This piece of verse by our colleague of the Athénée des Arts, read in the second public meeting of this society, is the complement and corollary of our engraving on the same subject due to the eminent artist M. Daubigny who, like M. Louis Goujon, sees in agriculture, in work, in a word, the energetic and male expression of the truth of art; it is therefore with deliberate purpose that we publish today the poetical work of our colleague; other artists, other poets will also come to our support, we shall soon see.

1) A few pre-lettering proofs with engraved signature *(reproduced)*.
2) A few proofs with lettering but before the address.
3) Publication in the review, no. 8, 1860, with address: *Imp. Pierron, r. Montfaucon, 1, Paris.*

D 95. *The Large Sheepfold*
Etching, 184 × 342 mm.; H. 86.
In 1862 Daubigny, like all the somewhat well-known painter-engravers of the time (still anything but numerous), became involved in the enterprise of organizing and launching etchers promoted by the publisher Cadart. Thanks to Cadart, Daubigny was able to publish seven separate plates, and then an album of fifteen etchings titled *Voyage en bateau* (see D 99–115). As Janine Bailly-Herzberg has rightly noted in her study on the Société des Aquafortistes (vol. II, p. 63), it is entirely probable that the "collection of 22 etchings" listed in Cadart's catalogue of 1876 comprised in fact the three series of original etchings that Daubigny was selling in albums, thus the twelve of the two first series (see D 66) plus ten done later, specifically the nine of which Henriet speaks (see D 81) together with D 97, which to our mind seems to belong to that same project.

As for Daubigny's commitment to the Société des Aquafortistes, it was certainly decisive for the organization itself. In fact, this plate—the first by Daubigny to be published by Cadart—appeared in their very first album immediately following the etching by Bracquemond that inaugurated the publication. The plate, however, was not made with that purpose in mind since its first state is clearly dated 1860, a date at which Cadart does not seem to have as yet conceived his project. Consequently this large work, in a style that all the commentators have recognized to be new, more vigorous, and more rugged, owed nothing to the initiative of Cadart. On the other hand, the desire of artists such as Bracquemond, Daubigny, and Manet to have some outlet for such unconventional plates was unquestionably an incentive for the foundation of the society.
The new taste for realism and the dawning success of etching at the start of the 1860s induced certain artists to deal with the medium differently, no longer in the decorative spirit of the finely engraved miniature as inherited from the last great school of French etchers at the end of the eighteenth century, but instead as a picture true and proper, with strongly bitten lines, broad forms, and securely constructed composition. This treatment set the character of the large prints produced for the Société des Aquafortistes.
Of this plate there exist at least two and perhaps as many as five states before the printing for the Société:

1) a "very rare artist's proof, absolutely first proof, with several small sketches etched in the lower margin" was mentioned in the Hôtel Drouot sale catalogue of old prints of January 14–19, 1883, for which the expert was Clément (the Daubigny lots, nos. 778–86, consisted entirely of first proofs), but Delteil was unable to track it down;
1-b) with the signature engraved and the date *1860* (BrM, proof from Burty);
2) with the date removed and with effects reworked in drypoint;
2-b) "a definitive state before any lettering, of which proofs were printed on Japan paper and on old paper" (Henriet);
2-c) a printing on laid paper (*vergé*) with the signatures of artist and printer but neither the title nor the publisher's address *(reproduced)*;
3) printing for the Société des Aquafortistes, published in their first installment, September, 1862, as the second print, with lettering; below the frame line at the left: *Daubigny pinx^t & sculp^t;* at the right: *Imp. Delâtre, Rue des Feuillantines, 4, Paris;* in the middle: *Parc à moutons, le matin* and *Paris, Publié par A. Cadart & F. Chevalier, Éditeurs, Rue Richelieu, 66;* above the print, at the right, the number *2;*
4) printings (some on China paper) without the names of publisher and printer.
False pre-lettering states exist which, contrary to the true ones, do not even have the engraved signature below at the left.
RELATED WORKS: A preparatory drawing was shown by Keppel in New York in his Daubigny exhibition, April

18–May 1, 1907. There is a fusain drawing in the Bibliothèque Municipale, Fontainebleau, and a painting on the same subject was shown in the Salon of 1861 (now Rijksmuseum Hendrik Willem Mesdag, The Hague). Two paintings on the same subject, studies of 1861, are reproduced in Fidell-Beaufort and Bailly-Herzberg, 1975, pls. 71 and 73, and there was an engraving on wood by Julien Antoine Peulot in *Le Monde Illustré*, March 14, 1863.

D 96. *The Pig in an Orchard*
Etching, 102 × 158 mm.; H. 87.
Executed for the album of the second series.
1) A few proofs with etching only before additional work (Baltimore: *reproduced*).
2) With additional work but before the printer's name.
3) Edition with the name of Beillet.
The plate bears a legend engraved under the frame line in the middle: *Un cochon de propriétaire qui ne fera de bien qu'après sa mort*, which may be rendered as "a pig of a landlord of no use except dead." Henriet reports that it was the sculptor Jean-Louis Chenillion, a friend of Daubigny, who came up with this caption while watching the artist working at his plate directly from nature. Daubigny himself engraved the legend. It is found on all the printings but not, contrary to what Delteil states, on the plate in the Chalcographie, where it was canceled and replaced by the title *Le Porc* (The Pig). The Chalcographie authorization to print shows that the first title proposed there was *Le Porc dans un paysage* (The Pig in a Landscape).
PLATE in the Louvre Chalcographie.

D 97. *The Hen and Her Chicks*
Etching, 94 × 153 mm.; H. 88.
Two states before the address:
1) etching only, with a chicken on the fence and before various additions;
2) completed but without address; then
3) with the address of Beillet *(reproduced)*;
4) with that of Delâtre.
The fact that this plate was printed by Beillet and was given to the Louvre Chalcographie suggests that it too was composed for the album of the second series, but Henriet says nothing about that.

1861
D 98. *Moonrise*
Etching and drypoint, 94 × 168 mm.; H. 89.
Reproduction of the painting Daubigny exhibited in the Salon of 1861 (no. 794), engraved for publication in the *Gazette des Beaux-Arts* on that occasion.
Four or five states before the *Gazette* publication:
1) etching only (Baltimore, BrM, BN);
2) with new work on the terrain and trees, using drypoint as well (BN);
3) plate reduced from 165 × 235 mm. to 133 × 195 mm. (BN: *reproduced*);
4) with additional work on the sky "to bring out the effects," says Henriet, who also distinguishes additional states according to whether the drypoint does or does not show burr marks; then

5) printing for the *Gazette des Beaux-Arts* but published first in a brochure by Léon Lagrange, *La Peinture et la sculpture au Salon de 1861, avec un appendice sur la gravure, la lithographie et la photographie par Philippe Burty*, Paris, Gazette des Beaux-Arts, 1861; not published in the review itself until 1871 (vol. IV, pp. 446–47), and then without the indication *Salon de 1861*;
6) new printing with the address of the printer Salmon instead of that of Delâtre, which appears in the *Gazette* printing, and with the plate beveled down.

D 99–115. *Voyage en bateau (The Boat Trip)*
Robert Wickenden (1913, pp. 190–93) gives the best explanation of the "boat trips" made by Daubigny after 1857 which resulted in this album:

So many demands came from all sides for repetitions of this and similar subjects that Daubigny found it difficult to satisfy them. To paint these river scenes, which accorded so well with his temperament and tastes, Daubigny thought it would be well to have a floating studio which could be moved about at will to the best points of view; and to catch the fleeting effects of dawn and sunset he wished to be free from the restraints of meal-hours and hotels. With these objects in view, he went to Asnières to see his friend Baillet, who happened to have in stock a boat that had been built for use as a ferry. Accompanied by his son Karl, Daubigny looked over the boat, which was some twenty-eight feet long, six feet beam, flat-bottomed, and drew only about eighteen inches of water. Baillet agreed to complete it so that three or six rowers could be used, and a sail if needed. At the stern a cabin was to be placed large enough to work or sleep in, with lockers on each side for bedding, cooking utensils, provisions, and artists' materials.
Thus equipped, Daubigny made numerous voyages up and down the Oise, Seine, and Marne in the "Botin," as this curious-looking craft was christened by an impudent rustic. . . . Freed from all restraint, Daubigny did an enormous amount of work during the river-trips, tempered by amusing experiences that were recorded in a series of free etchings called "Le Voyage en Bateau," done at first for the amusement of his family and friends, and afterward published by Cadart. In one of the plates we see the artist at work in a ray of sunshine that enters the end of the cabin where he is seated, while nearer the spectator are the canvases, panels, working-utensils, and bedding. On the back of one of the canvases is seen the word "*Réalisme*," and the legend scratched on the margin of the earliest proofs was "*Le travail tient l'âme en joie.*"

Thus the story of the "Botin" came to be told and retold among the painters in Daubigny's circle, and Henriet likewise recounted it in his *Paysagiste aux champs* with a good lot of amusing anecdotes, such as the tale of how Daubigny, engrossed in his work and forgetting he was on a boat, stepped back to judge the effect of a painting. Which does not make it any less sur-

prising to find such rough sketches engraved and passed off as finished works and, what is more, published by Cadart at the end of 1862 and sold for twenty francs the lot of fifteen prints. An artist's joke? Or a significant piece of "realism" for once not deadly serious? All the critics have posed the question. For Beraldi, a "*plaisanterie*," something done for the fun of it; for Henriet, "a series of sketches without pretension, dashed off with a swift and summary engraving point and treated with the freedom appropriate to trifling jests"; for Bailly-Herzberg, however, "the proof of a finely observant mind open to creatures and things, and of a happy temperament inclined to good humor."
To begin with, these etchings represent a choice of subjects from among forty-seven quick sketches done in pencil and wash (formerly Le Garrec Coll., now in the Louvre), and there simply can be no doubt that those rough drawings were no more than jottings intended to enliven the tales of the voyages as recounted to family and friends. (Corot, appointed "Honorary Admiral," did not sail on the "Botin" but did take part in the convivial feastings at departures and returns, which seem to have been quite lively occasions.) Yet one cannot question the seriousness of a publication for which Cadart had to put out no small sum (there were fifteen plates, after all) and would certainly not have done so without the expectation of a good profit. If nothing else, this proves that the popularity of the name of Daubigny in a certain artistic milieu in 1862 carried sufficient weight among potential customers to justify the expense of publishing a series of vignettes of really scarcely more than domestic interest. But the literature of the time, which swathed everything to do with the lives of artists of even minimum celebrity in an aura of blissful admiration (to which Corot lent himself even more than Daubigny), leads us to think that that attitude alone can explain this astonishing series of etchings.
As a rule in this set there is a single state only of each plate, which is further evidence of the offhand way they were turned out. The first proofs, however, bear captions that were subsequently effaced. Henriet notes:

All the plates of the *Voyage en bateau* were acid-bitten straight off and did not give rise to different states. Born during convivial evenings spent around the hearth, these unpretentious whimsicalities were really meant only for the amusement of a small circle of friends, and the artist—so far was he from even dreaming that they might deserve to be made public—engraved in the lower margin of the plates legends that were rather decidedly familiar which the publishers obliterated before bringing them out.

This notwithstanding, D 106 and 107 do have distinct states.

D 99. *Title frontispiece for the Album "Voyage en bateau"*
Etching, 170 × 123 mm.; H. 90.
The title frontispiece carries the date 1862, but Henriet claims to have seen copies with the date 1861.

1) A proof before lettering (NYPL: *reproduced*).
2) Edition with title and below, at the left: *A. Cadart & F. Chevalier Éditeurs;* and at the right: *Imp. Delâtre, Paris* (*reproduced*).
3) New printing without the name of Chevalier.

D 100. *The Lunch Before Going Aboard at Asnières*
Etching, 103 × 155 mm.; H. 91.
1) Legend on first proofs: *Le Déjeuné du Départ à Anière* (Baltimore: *reproduced*).
2) A few proofs before the address of Delâtre.
3) Edition with, below at the left: *Daubigny;* and at the right: *Imp. Delâtre Paris.*
For thirteen of the fifteen published plates one finds proofs before the address of Delâtre, then the edition without legends and with *Daubigny* engraved below at the left and *Imp. Delâtre Paris* at the right. This can be taken for granted for the remainder of the set except for D 106 and 107.

D 101. *Moving into "Le Botin" (The Ship's Furnishings)*
Etching, 103 × 160 mm.; H. 92.
Legend on first proofs: *Emménagement au botin* (V & A, Baltimore: *reproduced*).

D 102. *Heritage of the Cart (The Children with the Cart)*
Etching, 102 × 160 mm.; H. 93.
Legend on first proofs: *héritage de la voiture* (Baltimore, BN: *reproduced*).

D 103. *The Cabin Boy Hauling the Tow-Rope (Hauling by Rope)*
Etching, 102 × 160 mm.; H. 94.
Legend on first proofs: *le mousse tirant au Cordeau* (Baltimore, BN: *reproduced*).

D 104. *Guzzling (Lunch on the Boat)*
Etching, 105 × 158 mm.; H. 95.
Legend on first proofs: *Avallant*, a play on words, meaning both "swallowing" and "going downstream" (Baltimore: *reproduced*).
The edition printing has some additional work on the water and cabin.

D 105. *Le Mot de Cambronne (The Slanging Match)*
Etching, 109 × 163 mm.; H. 96.
Legend on first proofs: *Le mot de Cambrone*, a euphemism roughly equivalent to "the four-letter word beginning with *s*" (V & A, Baltimore: *reproduced*).

D 106. *The Search for an Inn*
Etching, 105 × 158 mm.; H. 97.
The only one of these etchings to have been the object of different (and very rare) states (all in the Maryland Institute, Baltimore). Legend on first proofs: *La recherche d'une Auberge.*
1) Etching only (*reproduced*).
2) Oblique lines added to the sky.
3) Additional work on the rays of the lantern and, with drypoint, on the ground (*reproduced*).
4) Work with the roulette in the sky and on the ground (*reproduced*).
5) Additional work on the cabin of the boat and the boy's face, and new shadows on the ground (*reproduced*).
6) The same state but with the legend effaced, before the printer's address.

7) Definitive edition, with the address of Delâtre.

D 107. *Interior of an Inn (The Corridor of an Inn)*
Etching, 92 × 130 mm.; H. 98.
Legend on first proofs: *Intérieur d'une auberge.*
1) State without lantern (Baltimore: *reproduced*).
2) Completely reworked (*reproduced*).

D 108. *Night Voyage or Net Fishing* (1st version)
Etching, 105 × 155 mm.; not in H. "The varnish having split in several places, Daubigny canceled out his work and on the same plate, planed down, engraved the same subject a second time" (Delteil).
A single proof of a plate unknown to Henriet and which evidently was not included in the album comprising fifteen prints plus frontispiece (Baltimore: *reproduced*).

D 109. *Night Voyage or Net Fishing* (2nd version)
Etching, 100 × 158 mm.; H. 99.
1) Legend on first proofs: *Voyage de nuit* (Baltimore, V & A).
2) Before lettering (*reproduced*).

D 110. *The Cabin Boy Fishing (Line Fishing)*
Etching, 96 × 158 mm.; H. 100.
Legend on first proofs: *Le Mousse à la pêche!* (Baltimore: *reproduced*).

D 111. *The Studio on the Boat*
Etching, 102 × 135 mm.; H. 101.
The most interesting plate in the album is this one mentioned by Wickenden as having the word *réalisme* on the back of a canvas and the legend *Le travail tient l'âme en joie* (Work keeps the soul joyous).
Henriet mentions "a few very rare proofs printed on Japan paper which are very marvelous."
Third state (*reproduced*).

D 112. *The Steamboats (Watch Out for the Steamers)*
Etching, 110 × 155 mm.; H. 102.
Legend on first proofs: *Les bateaux à vapeurs* (V & A, Baltimore: *reproduced*).

D 113. *Bedding Down Aboard the "Botin" (Night on the Boat)*
Etching, 100 × 120 mm.; H. 103.
Legend on first proofs: *Coucher à bord du bottin* (Baltimore: *reproduced*).

D 114. *Rejoicing of the Fish at the Departure of the Cabin Boy (The Fish)*
Etching, 100 × 162 mm.; H. 104.
Legend on first proofs: *Réjouissance des poissons du départ du mousse* (V & A, Baltimore: *reproduced*).

D 115. *The Departure (The Return)*
Etching, 100 × 158 mm.; H. 105.
Legend on first proofs: *Le Départ* (Baltimore).
Third state (*reproduced*).

1862

D 116. *A Brook in the Valmondois*
Etching, 185 × 117 mm.; H. 106.
Done for the magazine *La Vie à la Campagne* (Country Life), whose first issue had appeared the year before,

published by Furne. Between 1861 and 1866 Daubigny supplied it with several illustrations (see Fidell-Beaufort, vol. II, p. 102).
Two pre-lettering states:
1) etching only (NYPL, BrM);
2) completed (BN: *reproduced*); then
3) printing in *La Vie à la Campagne*, vol. IV, 1862, p. 305, with *Imp. Sarazin, 8, r. Gît-le-Coeur, Paris* under the frame line at the right and with the title in the middle.
RELATED WORK: Painting entitled *Le Ru du Valmondois*, 1847, now in a private collection in New York.

1865

D 117. *The Vintage (Souvenir of the Morvan)*
Etching, 195 × 335 mm.; H. 107.
The second plate supplied to the Société des Aquafortistes (see D 95) and in the same style. Henriet identified it with the title "after a study painted in the Morvan region." The engraving was brought out in the ninth installment, May, 1865, of the third year of the Société (Bailly-Herzberg, 1972, vol. I, p. 146), with the number *161*, and was exhibited in the Salon of 1865.
Two pre-lettering states:
1) after a first acid-biting and before further work;
2) completed but without lettering though with *Daubigny 1865* engraved under the frame line at the left (NYPL, BN: *reproduced*); then
3) printing for the Société des Aquafortistes with, under the frame line at the left: *Daubigny sculp.;* and at the right: *Imp. Delâtre, Rue Sᵗ-Jacques, 303, Paris;* at the bottom: the title and *Paris, Publié par Cadart & Luquet Editeurs, 79, Rue Richelieu;* and at the top: the number *161.*
4) A few subsequent printings without signature or publishers' names, sometimes on China paper;
5) others without printer's name.
False pre-lettering state without the engraved signature present on genuine prints.
RELATED WORK: Painting in the Salon of 1863.
PLATE in the Louvre Chalcographie.

D 118. *The Ford*
Etching and drypoint, 252 × 337 mm.; H. 108.
Third contribution to the Société des Aquafortistes (see D 95, 117), published in their fifth selection, fourth year, 1866 (see Bailly-Herzberg, 1972, vol. I, p. 182), with the number *201*. It was exhibited in the Salon of the same year and again at the Exposition Universelle, the world's fair of 1867. Daubigny had already treated the subject in a glassplate print in 1862 (D 139) and used it also for an illustration engraved on wood by Étienne published in *Le Monde Illustré*, vol. XVII, August, 1865, p. 89, with the mention: "drawing by M. Daubigny after one of his pictures" (Fidell-Beaufort, vol. II, p. 97).
As with other plates by Daubigny for the Société des Aquafortistes, one finds two pre-lettering states:
1) before various additions and cross-hatching;
2) completed (NYPL, BN: *reproduced*); then

3) printing for the Société des Aquafortistes with, under the frame line at the left: *Daubigny sculp.*; and at the right: *Imp. Delâtre, Rue St-Jacques, 303, Paris*; at the bottom: the title and *Paris, Publié par Cadart & Luquet, Editeurs, 79, Rue Richelieu*; and at the top: the number *201*;

4) with the address of Sarazin replacing that of Delâtre;

5) without names of printer or publisher.

False pre-lettering state without the engraved signature present on genuine prints.

RELATED WORK: Painting entitled *Le Matin sur les bords de l'Oise* (Morning on the Banks of the Oise) shown in the Salon of 1865, now Musée des Beaux-Arts, Lille.

PLATE in the Louvre Chalcographie.

1866

D 119. *The "Botin" at Conflans (The Landscapist in the Boat)*
Etching and drypoint, 90 × 128 mm.; H. 109.

Done as an illustration for F. Henriet's *Le Paysagiste aux champs*, a modest but elegant book containing twelve etchings accompanied by an amusing text with anecdotes of the adventures of landscape artists working outdoors directly from nature, an approach Henriet had always championed. There are illustrations by Corot, Léopold Desbrosses, Jean-Alfred Desbrosses, Maxime Lalanne, Léon Lhermitte, Auguste Péquégnot, and A. Portier, and Chapter XVI is devoted to Daubigny and his nautical studio.

1) Artist's proofs on China paper *appliqué* or *volant* and on Japan paper, before lettering but with engraved signature below at the left (BN: *reproduced*).

2) Printing for *Le Paysagiste aux champs*, Paris, Achille Faure, 1866, with *Daubigny inv. et sc.* below at left and *Imp. Delâtre, Paris* at right.

3) An additional printing, according to Henriet, in which "the sky was slightly lowered in tone, which constitutes a second state of the plate."

1867

D 120. *Tree with Crows*
Etching, 183 × 280 mm.; H. 110.
This, perhaps the most celebrated of Daubigny's etchings, marks a change in style toward a realism which is more spare and, as Laran said, more oriented toward "luminous effect" and "an almost tragic beauty." It is also an engraving that Daubigny must have done purely for itself since—something rare indeed with him—it is unconnected with any project for publication. Further, it served as the basis for a painting he did in 1873. Thus we find ourselves here well within the new movement of the original art-print treated with the same dignity as a canvas, though Fidell-Beaufort (vol. I, p. 114) does suggest that the plate was intended for the Société des Aquafortistes and was not brought out by them because they disbanded in 1867.

1) A few proofs after the initial acid bath (Baltimore).

2) Definitive second state after obliteration of lines in the sky and after a second acid bath (BN: *reproduced*).

RELATED WORKS: Preparatory drawing (reproduced in Bailly-Herzberg and Fidell-Beaufort, 1975, p. 227) and another pen drawing reproduced as an autolithograph in V. Frond, *Panthéon des illustrations françaises au XIXe siècle* (Paris, 1869), printed in bistre and signed at the right *Daubigny 1867.*

PLATE in the Louvre Chalcographie.

1868

D 121. *The Orchard*
Etching, 185 × 120 mm.; H. 111.
This was Daubigny's contribution to the celebrated *Sonnets et eaux-fortes*, a volume assembled by the critic Philippe Burty as a kind of anthology of "modern" painter-engravers and including also Corot, Millet, Jongkind, Manet, Bracquemond, and others who had achieved celebrity by then (see Corot 9, Jongkind 16, Millet 20). Each etching accompanied a sonnet, and because of his proficiency in landscape Daubigny was assigned a rustic subject by Gabriel Marc, "Un pré vert au printemps; des fleurs au soleil" (A verdant meadow in spring; flowers in the sun).

Three states before book publication:
1) after an initial biting, neither signed nor dated (Baltimore);
2) with some additional work and signed *Daubigny 1868* at the right;
3) completed but with the signature now at the left *(reproduced)*; then
4) publication of that state in P. Burty, *Sonnets et eaux-fortes*, Paris, A. Lemerre, 1869 (350 copies on laid paper plus a few on China paper, *appliqué* or *volant*, in black or bistre, and two or three on vellum paper).

RELATED WORKS: Preparatory drawing in the Cabinet des Estampes, BN; also a painting on the same theme, done parallel with the etching, entitled *Le Printemps* (Spring) and shown in the Salon of the same year.

1874

D 122. *The Shepherd and the Shepherdess*
Etching, 251 × 195 mm.; H. 112.
After 1868 Daubigny was much in demand as a painter and for six years did no engraving. Then, between 1874 and 1877, he produced his six last plates, and these were increasingly close to the style of the Impressionists in their use of delicate and vibrating small strokes. All six were published, and this one was chosen by the review *L'Art* to illustrate an article by Henriet concerning the artist.

1) First state after initial acid etching but before considerable additional work (Bremen, Baltimore, BN; reproduced by Delteil).

2) With the arm of the shepherdess removed (BN).

3) Completed, pre-lettering proofs *(reproduced)*.

4) Printing for the de luxe copies of the review *L'Art*, vol. XXV, 1881, p. 84, and separately for the series *Maîtres anciens et modernes* published by the review in miscellanies (series 2, no. 2, 1874), with, below the frame line at the left: *Daubigny del. et sc.*; below this: the title and *L'Art* and *F. Liénard, Imp. Paris.*

5) Printing in *L'Art*, vol. LXIII, 1904, p. 560.

6) New printing without the name of the review and printer.

7) Another printing with the address *Imp. L. Fort, Paris.*

8) Yet another printing in 1921 to illustrate vol. XIII, devoted to Daubigny, of *Le Peintre-graveur illustré* by Loÿs Delteil, with three asterisks engraved below the frame line at the left; 60 prints on Japan paper, 420 on Holland.

1875

D 123. *Moonrise on the Banks of the Oise*
Etching, 97 × 152 mm.; H. 113.
Executed to decorate Henriet's catalogue of the artist's graphic work.
Two states before lettering:
1) with lines on the moon but before cross-hatching with drypoint in the sky and water (Baltimore, BN: *reproduced*);
2) completed; then
3) printing for Frédéric Henriet, *C. Daubigny et son oeuvre gravé*, Paris, A. Lévy, 1875.

D 124. *The Pré des Graves at Villerville (Calvados)*
Etching, 127 × 205 mm.; Beraldi 114.
The last four etchings of Daubigny were done for Cadart and his successors after the firm of Cadart & Luquet broke up in 1867. The publications of the Société des Aquafortistes were suspended and replaced by a new publication, *L'Illustration nouvelle*, which appeared from 1868 to 1881, thus even after the death of Cadart in 1875. Daubigny remained loyal to that review to the end, supplying it with his final four plates between 1875 and 1877.

Two pre-lettering states:
1) before considerable additional work;
2) completed (NYPL: *reproduced*); then
3) printing for *L'Illustration nouvelle*, vol. VIII, 1876.

False pre-lettering state without the engraved signature present on genuine prints.

RELATED WORKS: Painting of the same title in the Salon of 1859, now Musée des Beaux-Arts, Marseilles; lithograph by Vernier published by Goupil et Knoedler, October 1, 1870; wood engraving by Adrien Lavieille in *Le Magasin Pittoresque*, June, 1860.

1876

D 125. *The Seine at Port-Maurin (Eure)*
Etching, 127 × 224 mm.; Beraldi 115.
1) A single state, a few pre-lettering proofs with engraved signature *Daubigny 1876 (reproduced)*.

2) Printing for *L'Illustration nouvelle*, vol. VIII, 1876, with, below the frame line at the left: *Daubigny del. et sculp.*; at the right: *Vve A. Cadart, Edit. Imp. 56 Bd Haussmann, Paris*; in the middle the title: *La Seine à Port-Maurin*; and at the top the number *3*.

3) Printing for the first number of *Bords de l'Oise* of Alphonse Lambert, Paris, 1881.

False pre-lettering state without the engraved signature present on genuine prints.

1877

D 126. *Apple Trees at Auvers*
Etching, 143 × 242 mm.; Beraldi 116.
The most "Impressionist" of Daubigny's etchings, done at a time when Pissarro had already begun to engrave, though the latter relied instead on the drypoint process.
Three pre-lettering states:
1) with a second figure on the path and two birds in the sky, along with a different general treatment;
2) one figure eliminated as well as the sky (NYPL, BN);
3) the figure replaced by new needle lines, the sky reengraved *(reproduced)*; then
4) printing for *L'Illustration nouvelle*, vol. IX, 1877, with, below the frame line at the left: *Daubigny del. et sculp.*; at the right: *Vve A. Cadart, Edit. Imp. 56 Bd Haussmann, Paris*; in the middle the title: *Pommiers à Auvers*; and at the top the number *3*.
There are prints without the address of Cadart, and false pre-lettering state without the engraved signature present on genuine prints.
RELATED WORKS: Painting entitled *Le Printemps*; lithograph by Vernier published by Goupil et Knoedler, October 1, 1870; and a burin engraving by J. Fattorini for the Société des Artistes-Graveurs au Burin, 1902.

D 127. *Moonlight at Valmondois*
Etching, 134 × 217 mm.; Beraldi 117.
Two pre-lettering states:
1) before lines on the moon, with engraved signature and *1877* (Bremen);
2) completed; then
3) printing for *L'Illustration nouvelle*, vol. IX, 1877, with lettering;
4) printing for the *Gazette des Beaux-Arts*, 1878, pp. 346–47, without the number *409 (reproduced)*, to illustrate the obituary article on Daubigny, who died on February 19, 1878. The author, Alfred de Lostalot, explained that "this etching was drawn two months before the death of the artist. Daubigny intended to do some retouching: he wished to burnish it, that is, tone down the haystacks and the tree-covered mountainsides that bound the horizon: death did not leave him the time to do so."
RELATED WORKS: Painting of the same title; lithograph by Vernier published by Goupil et Knoedler, October 1, 1870.

LITHOGRAPHS

Not feeling himself competent in the medium, it was only exceptionally that Daubigny turned his hand to lithography, and never as a creative artist but only, it seems, when pressed by friends to render them that service. It is understandable, therefore, why Henriet made no attempt to compile a complete list of such works but merely cited a few examples. Prints of some were unearthed by Delteil, but it may well be that Daubigny did more in this medium than has been identified.

1844

D 128. *House for Rent at Argenteuil*
Lithograph, 185 × 303 mm.
A small publicity poster undoubtedly done on order and deposited at the Bibliothèque Royale in 1844 by the printer. The artist may have accepted the job because the view of the house was not unrelated to the landscape art in which he specialized. Several of his paintings do in fact have views of villas in gardens, and he even proposed to the French government to produce a series of plates illustrating the imperial palaces and gardens.
Signed below the frame line at the left: *Daubigny*; at the right: *Imp. d'Aubert & C. (reproduced)*.

1847

D 129. *View of a Phalanstery (Proposal for a French Village Organized According to the Societary Theory of Charles Fournier)*
Lithograph, 300 × 445 mm.
Again a subject related to landscape, which explains why once again Daubigny went beyond his usual métier of metal engraving. Here, however, he was also expressing his own social ideas and indulging in political action, since the lithograph was sold by the Fourierite bookshop that doubtless was responsible for commissioning it. Little is known of Daubigny's political ideas, but, like his friends, he does seem to have been a Catholic partisan of social reform and therefore very close to the ideas popularized by Hugues Félicité de Lamennais, and also much attracted by those of Charles Fourier. But attempts to compare the life in common of Daubigny and his painter friends in the 1830s with a phalanstery are simply patent exaggerations.
This imaginary view of an ideal Fourierite community is of immense documentary importance as an illustration of the social-reformist ideas of that movement and especially, as Fidell-Beaufort has pointed out, as visual proof of the major role accorded the Church.
Below the frame line, at the left: *Composé d'après les Théories de Ch. Fourier par H. Fugère*; in the middle: *Lith. Prod-homme rue du Temple, 89*; at the right: *Dessiné par Ch. Daubigny*; and, below, the legend: *(Voir le Nouveau-Monde Industriel, de Ch. Fourier.) Librairie Phalanstérienne Quai Voltaire, 25.*

D 130. *Pension de Mme. Dautel*
Lithograph, 227 × 188 mm.
Besides being not unrelated to landscape, this task was taken on because of family connections. The Madame Dautel who kept this boarding school for girls was a relative of Amélie Dautel, miniature-painter and wife of Pierre Daubigny, likewise a miniature-painter, who was a younger brother of Edme Daubigny and uncle of our artist.
Signed below at the left: *C. Daubigny*; at the right: *Imp. Lemercier à Paris*.
RELATED WORK: Drawing in the Cabinet des Dessins, the Louvre.

c. 1847

D 131. *Study of White Mullein (Bouillon-Blanc)*
Lithograph, 325 × 270 mm.
We have seen that, thanks to Louis Steinheil, Daubigny was given work illustrating various books on botany. He did several such lithographs, which are cited by Henriet, and Delteil was able to reproduce this one, of which Giacomelli owned a proof that went to the BN with the Curtis Donation *(reproduced)*. Surely however there must be others—"What else?" asks Henriet, "Studies of white mullein, thistle, etc."—and since we do not know what work these plates were intended for and since they were printed by Lemercier, the next step is obviously to look into that printer's vast production.
Signed at the lower right *C. Daubigny*.

AUTOLITHOGRAPHS

1873

D 132. *The Herd of Cows (Coming into the Village)*
Autolithograph (?), 164 × 257 mm.
It is open to question if Delteil was correct in including this in a catalogue of original prints (see our introduction) because it is by no means certain that Daubigny himself traced this drawing onto the block used for printing. Further, we do not know exactly what process was used for the *Album contemporain* for which the drawing was done, though the images were printed by a lithographer and the publisher's announcement boasted of a "New Process of Printing" (see Corot 34). Given the date of 1873, a time which saw the rise of the transfer process of Firmin Gillot, and the fact that without exception all the prints in the *Album contemporain* were reproduced in pure line without any halftones, it is possible that the "New Process" was a kind of zinc stereotypy. Although the publisher's announcement is by no means reticent in its own praise, it never speaks of direct participation on the part of the artists but only of their "patronage" and their "counsels," and in fact qualifies the prints as "copies." Thus only the drawing would have been "executed by the Author of the Picture himself," and the enterprise would have been like those of *L'Autographe au Salon* or the *Album Autographique*.

GLASSPLATE PRINTS (CLICHÉS-VERRE)

1862

The exact circumstances in which Daubigny did these eighteen glass plates are not known except that it was in response to a request from Cuvelier, who had installed himself in the Barbizon region (see our explanation and history of glass plates). Then too, through his friend Corot, Daubigny is likely to have been in contact with Constant Dutilleux, who settled in Paris after 1860 and regularly frequented Barbizon and its painter-denizens. Certainly Daubigny would have been aware of the glass plates produced by Corot, but, unlike the older artist, who turned out his plates over the years and a few at a time, he seems to have done all of his in a single period.

D 133. *Swamp with Ducks*
Glass plate, 109 × 183 mm.
In the margin, a rough scribble of a small boat with rower.

EARLY PRINTS in NYPL, Dresden, BN *(reproduced)*.
PRINTING for Le Garrec.
GLASS PLATE in Boston.

D 134. *Stags*
Glass plate, 152 × 186 mm.
EARLY PRINTS in NYPL, BN *(reproduced)*.
COUNTERPROOF in BN.
PRINTING for Le Garrec.
GLASS PLATE in Boston.

D 135. *Path Through the Grain Field*
Glass plate, 150 × 185 mm.
In margin, rough sketch of a man's head in profile and a wagon hitched to a horse, the numbers 1 to 8, etc.
EARLY PRINTS in NYPL, BN *(reproduced)*.
PRINTING for Le Garrec.
RELATED WORK: Etching D 89.

D 136. *The Bridge*
Glass plate, 150 × 187 mm.
EARLY PRINTS in NYPL, BN *(reproduced)*.
COUNTERPROOF in BN *(reproduced)*.
PRINTING for Le Garrec.

D 137. *The Brook in the Clearing*
Glass plate, 186 × 154 mm.
EARLY PRINTS in Dresden, Budapest Museum of Fine Arts, NYPL, BN *(reproduced)*.
PRINTING for Le Garrec.

D 138. *The Large Sheepfold*
Glass plate, 185 × 345 mm.
EARLY PRINTS in NYPL, BN *(reproduced)*.
ALTERATIONS: Prints made with a diagonal break in the plate.
PRINTING for Le Garrec.
GLASS PLATE in the Louvre.
RELATED WORKS: Painting in the Salon of 1861; etching of 1860 (D 95).

D 139. *The Ford*
Glass plate, 278 × 347 mm.
EARLY PRINTS in Dresden, NYPL, BN *(reproduced)*.
PRINTING for Le Garrec.
GLASS PLATE in the Cabinet des Estampes, BN.
RELATED WORK: Etching (D 118).

D 140. *The Return of the Flock*
Glass plate, 338 × 272 mm.
EARLY PRINTS in NYPL (signed on the terrain), BN (without signature: *reproduced*).
PRINTING for Le Garrec.

D 141. *The Goatherd Girl*
Glass plate, 342 × 272 mm.
EARLY PRINTS in NYPL, BN *(reproduced)*.
PRINTING for Le Garrec.

D 142. *The Hay Harvest*
Glass plate, 211 × 344 mm.
EARLY PRINTS in NYPL, BN *(reproduced)*.
REVERSED PRINT reproduced by Delteil.
PRINTING for Le Garrec.
RELATED WORK: "This composition was drawn on wood for *Le Monde Illustré*. That block, which we believe was not engraved, now belongs to M. Charles Yriarte" (Henriet).

D 143. *Donkey in the Field*
Glass plate, 156 × 190 mm.
EARLY PRINTS in Dresden, BN *(reproduced)*.
PRINTING for Le Garrec.

D 144. *Nightpiece*
Glass plate, 150 × 190 mm.
EARLY PRINTS in NYPL, BN *(reproduced)*.
PRINTING for Le Garrec.

D 145. *The Clump of Alders*
Glass plate, 151 × 185 mm.
EARLY PRINTS in NYPL, BN *(reproduced)*.
COUNTERPROOF in BN.
PRINTING for Le Garrec.

D 146. *Cows at the Watering Place*
Glass plate, by impasto, 164 × 199 mm.
EARLY PRINTS in NYPL, BN *(reproduced)*.
PRINTING for Le Garrec.

D 147. *The Hydraulic Machine*
Glass plate, 215 × 342 mm.
EARLY PRINTS in NYPL, BN *(reproduced)*.
COUNTERPROOFS in BN.
PRINTING for Le Garrec.
RELATED WORK: "This composition was drawn on wood by Daubigny for *Le Monde Illustré* [of October 18, 1868, with the title *Autumn: Banks of the Morvan*]. M. C. Yriarte, responsible at that time for the artistic direction of the magazine, has preserved the original block, and the plate published in vol. XXIII, no. 600, was engraved by M. Étienne by means of a photographic transfer onto another block" (Henriet). See also the etching D 83 from around 1850.

D 148. *Pollarded Willows (Souvenir of Bezons)*
Glass plate, 150 × 190 mm.
EARLY PRINT in NYPL *(reproduced)*.
No other printing, the plate having been destroyed.

D 149. *Cows in the Woods*
Glass plate, 150 × 190 mm.
EARLY PRINTS in NYPL, BN *(reproduced)*.
COUNTERPROOFS: Two of very different appearance of which one lacks the signature (BN).
PRINTING for Le Garrec.

D 150. *Two Horses at the Watering Place*
Glass plate, by impasto, 145 × 66 mm.
EARLY PRINT in BN from the Curtis Collection *(reproduced)*.
No other printing, the plate having been destroyed.

JULES DUPRÉ
(1811–1889)

As a graphic artist Jules Dupré realized no more than ten or so lithographs reproducing his own paintings. With perhaps two or three exceptions these were all for publication in *L'Artiste* in 1835 and 1836. Later he left that sort of reproduction work to specialized lithographers, but since he himself does not seem to have found any essential difference between his and others' graphic work, it is possible that he turned out more without signing them. Our Du 10 at least can be attributed to his own hand, though even that attribution, according to the inventory of the French holdings of the Bibliothèque Nationale, is "very doubtful." Less, however, than the "study using two pencils" that the same inventory attributes to him in an entry reading: "No. 9: Jules Dupré, no. 2, Étude aux deux crayons, camaïeu [monochrome], chez J. Bulla et F. Delarue et à Londres, à l'Anaglyphic Company, 1844."

Du 1. *Pastureland in the Limousin*
Lithograph, 138 × 216 mm.; Hédiard cat. no. 1; Aubrun cat. no. 1.
1) Pre-lettering proofs.
2) Printing for *L'Artiste*, series 1, vol. IX, 1835, p. 180, with *L'Artiste* above and *Jules Dupré, Lith. de Frey* below along with the title, *Pacages du Limousin (Salon de 1835) (reproduced)*.
3) Printing in *Souvenirs d'artistes* (collections of lithographs from the stock of the Imprimerie Bertauts) with, at the top: *Souvenirs d'artistes 127;* and at the bottom: *Jules Dupré del. et lith. Imp. Bertauts, Paris* and the title.
RELATED WORKS: Painting in the Salon of 1835 titled *Villageois dans la forêt* (Villagers in the Forest; A. 60, undated, whereabouts unknown); and a preparatory drawing of 1834 (A. 24, private coll.).

Du 2. *Mill in the Sologne*
Lithograph, 197 × 140 mm.; Hd. 2; A. 2.
1) Printing in *L'Artiste*, series 1, vol. X, 1835, p. 196, with *L'Artiste* at the top and *Jules Dupré* and *Lith. de Frey* at the bottom along with the title *Moulin de la Sologne (reproduced)*.
2) Printing in *Souvenirs d'artistes*, with *Souvenirs d'Artistes, 111* at the top and *Jules Dupré pinx. et lith.* and *Imp. Bertauts, Paris* at the bottom together with the title.
3) Printing for *L'École de Dessin*, vol. X, no. 118, 1887, pl. 703, unchanged from above except that *L'École de dessin* replaces *Souvenirs d'Artistes*.
RELATED WORKS: Painting titled *Le Moulin* (A. 79), now Musée de Peinture et de Sculpture, Grenoble; and especially another painting from around 1835 (A. 80), undated, present whereabouts unknown.

Du 3. *View from Normandy*
Lithograph, 138 × 208 mm.; Hd. 3; A. 4.
1) Printing in *L'Artiste*, series 1, vol. X, 1835, p. 220, with *L'Artiste* at the top and *Jules Dupré, Lith. de Frey* and the title, *Vue Prise en Normandie*, at the bottom *(reproduced)*.
2) Printing without frame line and slightly tinted, for the Galerie Durand-Ruel, with *Jules Dupré.* and *Imp. Lemercier* along with the title, *Normandie*, at the bottom, and *Galerie Durand-Ruel* at the top.
RELATED WORKS: Painting entitled *L'Abreuvoir* (The Watering Place) of 1836 (A. 76), now Musée Saint-Denis, Reims; and an undated drawing, *Une*

Ferme en Normandie (A Farm in Normandy; A. 40).

Du 4. *View from the Port of Plymouth (Devon)*
Lithograph, 204 × 228 mm.; Hd. 4; A. 5.
1) Printing for *L'Artiste*, series 1, vol. XI, 1836, p. 12, with *L'Artiste* at the top and *Jules Dupré del., Lith. de Frey* and the title, *Vue prise dans le port de Plimouth (Dewon)*, at the bottom *(reproduced)*.
2) Printing in *Souvenirs d'artistes* with that designation at the top left (plate 119) and *Jules Dupré pinx. et lith., Imp. Bertauts. Paris* and the title at the bottom.

Du 5. *View from England*
Lithograph, 129 × 207 mm.; Hd. 5; A. 6.
1) Pre-lettering proof.
2) Printing for *L'Artiste*, series 1, vol. XI, 1836, p. 132, with *L'Artiste* at the top and, at the bottom: *Jules Dupré* at the left; *L. de Benard et frey* at the right; the title *Vue prise en Angleterre* in the center; *Salon de 1836* below it *(reproduced)*.
2-b) Printing with name of another printer: *Imp. d'Aubert et de Junca, Gal. Colbert* (a third state, according to Hédiard).
3) Printing for *Souvenirs d'artistes* with that heading at upper left (plate 136) and, at the bottom: *Jules Dupré pinx. et lith., Imp. Bertauts, Paris* and the title.
RELATED WORK: Painting of the same title (A. 44 bis) of around 1835 (private coll.).

Du 6. *Banks of the Somme (Picardy)*
Lithograph, 138 × 213 mm.; Hd. 6; A. 7.
1) Printing for *L'Artiste*, series 1, vol. XII, 1836, p. 120, with *L'Artiste* at the top and, at the bottom: *Jules Dupré, Lith. de Benard et Frey* and the title *(reproduced)*.
2) Printing for *Souvenirs d'artistes* with that heading at upper left (plate 99) and, at the bottom: *Jules Dupré del. et lith., Imp. Bertauts, Paris* and the title.
RELATED WORKS: Undated painting, *Le Passage de la rivière* (Crossing of the River), whereabouts unknown (A. 53); and a preparatory drawing (A. 33).

Du 7. *View from Alençon*
Lithograph, 136 × 190 mm.; Hd. 7; A. 3.
1) Printing for *L'Artiste*, series 2, vol. IV, 1839, p. 112, with *L'Artiste* at the top and, at the bottom: *J.Dupré del., Im. de Lemercier, Bénard & C.* and the title, *Vue prise à Alençon (Dépt de l'Orne) (reproduced)*.
2) Tinted and without frame line, published in *Galerie Durand-Ruel* with that name at the top and, at the bottom: *J. Dupré del., Imp. Lemercier*, and the slightly changed title, *Près d'Alençon*.

Du 8. *Banks of the Somme* (study)
Lithograph, 137 × 214 mm.; Hd. 8; A. 8.
This plate remained unpublished. Hédiard's supposition that the two unpublished works were originally intended for *L'Artiste* is plausible. It should be noted that this one represents, reversed, the same subject as Du 6 and was perhaps a discarded or unfinished trial for that lithograph.

Marie-Madeleine Aubrun dates it around 1836. A single print is known, once in the possession of Hédiard, then of Curtis, now of the BN *(reproduced)*.

Du 9. *Landscape* (not reproduced)
Lithograph, 173 × 133 mm.; Hd. 9; not in A.
This unpublished work has been lost and we, like Delteil, have been unable to find any prints. Thus we can only copy the description given by Hédiard:

The banks of a calm watercourse which extends to the depth of the perspective and, closed in by a grassy and wooded point of land, makes a bend toward the left in its nearest stretch. In the foreground the swarded bank with a cow in the middle, grazing; a little farther, at the foot of a cluster of large tall trees, a man leaning on a long pole watches over a herd. At the left, in front of the point of land, people in a boat. Height 173, width 133.—[surrounded by a] Frame line. — Initials below at the left: *J. D.*—representing the same site but more extended, and with minor changes, was engraved for *L'Artiste* by Le Petit under this title: *Un Pâturage* [A Pasturage].

Du 10. *Landscape with Three Horses*
Lithograph, 123 × 187 mm.; not in Hd. or A.
This unsigned and unpublished lithograph is found among the work of Dupré in the BN *(reproduced* as Du 9 in this edition). Its manner as well as the fact that it was purchased by Curtis as coming from the Giacomelli Collection make the attribution probable. It would therefore be the third unpublished lithograph. Its format leads one to think that, like the others, it was intended for *L'Artiste* but was never finished. The explanation given by Hédiard for the preceding piece can serve here too: "Dupré . . . may not have been fully satisfied and so replaced it by one from among the other pieces. Several things are incomplete in it, half brought out."

JOHAN BARTHOLD JONGKIND
(1819–1891)

Almost all of the etchings of Jongkind are connected with the publications of Cadart: to be exact, seventeen of his total of twenty-two. Only those catalogued here as J 9 and 17 remained unpublished; J 16 was done for Burty's *Sonnets et eaux-fortes*, published by Lemerre; and two, listed by Delteil as *A* and *B*, are lost.
For Jongkind's etchings we generally have a pre-lettering proof and one or more printings by Cadart, who usually also turned out false pre-lettering prints. Of J 15, 18, 19, and 20 there is also a later printing brought out by the dealer Charles Delorière with his name replacing that of Cadart, and of J 8, 10, 11, 12, 14, 15, 19, and 20 a printing in bistre ("a little heavy," according to

Delteil) was done in London by the printer Goulding when the plates were in the possession of the Dutch engraver Charles Storm van 'sGravesande. Besides the twenty-two etchings Jongkind realized, other projects for engraving are known. An ink drawing in the Grenoble Musée de Peinture et de Sculpture (Hefting cat. no. 250) is annotated *"Eau-forte pour Burty"*; a pencil drawing (Hg. 574, private coll.) is a study for the cover of a projected *"Cahier de huit eaux-fortes, paysages de Nevers, 1871"*; and another project is mentioned in a letter to the publisher Poulet-Malassis dated April 28, 1862: "If that work could be acceptable, I shall propose to you to do two albums of Dutch views, of which you could be the sole publisher, and if I should be paid for my work it would never be in my interests that you should lose thereby." [Translator's note: The French of Jongkind, who came to Paris only in 1846 from his native Holland, was often very inaccurate, particularly as regards tenses and punctuation, and we have tried to preserve some of its savor.]
Apart from work done at the urging of Cadart and its occasional sequels, Jongkind seems to have shown no particular interest in etching. He persisted in referring to it as "drawing," and of some of his work he once said to the critic L. de Fourcaud, "Those are pieces of trash from the time when they were trying to make an engraver out of me."

1862
J 1. *Title page of the Album of Six Etchings*
Etching, 127 × 207 mm.; Hefting cat. no. 253.
The first etching by Jongkind and his first collaboration with the publisher Cadart. The album was announced, together with those of Manet and Legros and five etchings by Millet, on the back of the cover of a portfolio brought out by the Société des Aquafortistes in 1862, with its price given as twelve francs. On March 17, 1862, Jongkind wrote to Burty that "there has appeared an album of six drawings, Views of Holland, with title engraved in etching by Jongkind, 9 Rue de Chevreuse, and from the printer Delâtre, 265 Rue Saint-Jacques, price twenty francs the album, by this means a few albums have been procured from me or at Delâtre's." Burty wrote a long review in the *Gazette des Beaux-Arts* of March 23, 1862. On April 28, Jongkind wrote to Poulet-Malassis: "I will tell you that up to the present I have not yet got my expenses back on my etchings although I have certainly had praise—so-called— the Printer has done 150 copies and I have taken back the plates." He then proposed to do two other albums for that publisher.
Besides the announcement of the album in 1862, Bailly-Herzberg has found among the advertisements of Cadart one of 1874 for "a collection of eight original etchings" by Jongkind (which is not known); one of 1876 with the same announcement, asking the price of thirty francs for the collection; one of 1878 announcing a "collection of ten original etchings, with lettering: 30 francs, pre-lettering: 60 francs."

1) Pre-lettering with only signature and date (reversed) (BN: *reproduced*).
2) Cadart edition.
3) Printing for Sagot, just before or after World War II, by the printer Lacourière, in one hundred copies, numbered in pencil on the back. Twenty-five were made on old, greenish paper and seventy-five on Holland paper. Some of the prints carry the dry embossed stamp of Sagot. This applies also to J 2–7, that is, the entire album.
The copper plates of the album (J 1–7) are in the Sagot–Le Garrec Collection.
RELATED WORKS: ("1 BIS") A cover (brought to notice by Delteil) without image and with handwritten text; 115 × 185 mm. (*reproduced*); also the preparatory drawing of the illustrated title.

J 2. *The Canal*
Etching, 160 × 203 mm.; Hg. 254.
1) Before printer's address, with *N⁰ 1* reversed in upper right corner and signature and date reversed in lower right (*reproduced*).
2) Cadart edition with *Imp. A. Delâtre Rue Sᵗ Jacques 265 Paris* below the frame line at the right.
3) Printing for Sagot.

J 3. *Houses Along the Canal Bank*
Etching, 169 × 210 mm.; Hg. 255.
1) Before address, with *N⁰ 2* reversed in upper right corner and signature and date reversed in lower right (*reproduced*).
2) Cadart edition with the address of Delâtre (as above) below the frame line at the right.
3) Printing for Sagot.
RELATED WORK: Preparatory drawing mentioned by Hefting but not described.

J 4. *The Nurse*
Etching, 166 × 207 mm.; Hg. 256.
1) Before address, with signature and date reversed in lower right corner (*reproduced*).
2) Cadart edition with the address of Delâtre (as above).
3) Printing for Sagot.
RELATED WORKS: Drawing on the same subject, 120 × 140 mm. (Hg. 251, private coll.); painting of the same name of 1862 (Hg. 231, private coll.).

J 5. *The Towpath*
Etching, 167 × 209 mm.; Hg. 257.
1) Before signature and date.
2) Before printer's address but with, in the lower right corner, *Jongkind 1862* reversed (*reproduced*).
3) Cadart edition with the address of Delâtre (as above).
4) Printing for Sagot.
RELATED WORK: Painting of 1859 on the same subject (Hg. 196, Rijksmuseum Twenthe, Enschede, the Netherlands).

J 6. *The Moored Boat*
Etching, 167 × 205 mm.; Hg. 258.
1) Before printer's address but with signature and date reversed in lower right corner (*reproduced*).
2) Before address but with a scratch across the sky at the left.
3) Cadart edition with the address of

Delâtre (as above) and the scratch removed.
4) Printing for Sagot.

J 7. *The Two Sailboats*
Etching, 167 × 207 mm.; Hg. 259.
1) Before printer's address but with signature and date reversed in lower right corner (*reproduced*).
2) Cadart edition with the address of Delâtre (as above).
3) Printing for Sagot.

J 8. *View of the Town of Maassluis, Holland*
Etching, 223 × 312 mm.; Hg. 252.
1) Before lettering, with an interruption in the frame line on the left.
2) With the frame line completed.
3) Printing for the second selection of the first year of the Société des Aquafortistes, October, 1862 (see Bailly-Herzberg, 1972, vol. I, p. 57), with, below the frame line, the address of Cadart and Chevalier, the title *Vue de la Ville de Maaslins (Hollande)*, and the address of Delâtre. The title, signature, and date are engraved in the lower left corner (*reproduced*).
4) Later printing with the lower right corner of the plate rounded.
—Edition in *L'Eau-forte depuis 10 ans,* 1872.
—Edition in *L'Eau-forte depuis 12 ans,* 1874.
Printing by Goulding, London.
False pre-lettering state with the lower right corner of the plate rounded.
RELATED WORKS: Three paintings on this subject, one from 1862, the others from 1864 (Hg. 232, 284, 285, all in private colls.).

J 9. *The Old Port of Rotterdam*
Etching, 230 × 370 mm.
One of the two unpublished etchings, with very rare proofs (BN, formerly Curtis Coll.: *reproduced*).

1863
J 10. *Entrance to the Port of Honfleur*
Etching, 221 × 306 mm.; Hg. 283.
1) Before lettering (*reproduced*).
2) Before lettering, the image slightly reduced at the bottom.
3) Printing for the fifth selection of the second year of the Société des Aquafortistes, January, 1864, with title, addresses of Cadart & Luquet and of Delâtre (see Bailly-Herzberg, 1972, vol. I, p. 97).
—Edition in *L'Eau-forte depuis 10 ans,* 1872.
Printing by Goulding, London.
False pre-lettering state.
RELATED WORKS: Painting of September 18, 1864 (Hg. 312, the Louvre); and another dated 1864 (Hg. 297, Art Institute of Chicago).

1864
J 11. *Exit from the Port of Honfleur*
Etching, 227 × 303 mm.; Hg. 319.
"Last year in etchings I did for the Aquafortistes the Entrance to the port of Honfleur and this year the exit. I am waiting for the proofs and will be very happy to offer you and to have you accept one of each of these drawings" (Jongkind to Burty, January 5, 1865).
1) Pre-lettering, the corners of the plate sharp.

2) Pre-lettering, the corners of the plate rounded.
3) Printing for the fifth selection of the third year of the Société des Aquafortistes, January, 1865 (Bailly-Herzberg, 1972, vol. I, p. 141), with title, the number *143,* the addresses of Cadart & Luquet and of Delâtre (*reproduced*).
4) Later printing without number in upper right corner and often without the addresses.
—Edition in *L'Eau-forte depuis 10 ans,* 1872.
Printing by Goulding, London.
False pre-lettering state.
RELATED WORKS: A watercolor and sepia drawing with image reversed, 1864 (Hg. 318, the Louvre); painting dated 1864 (Hg. 295, private coll.); pencil drawing from same viewing point but not identical, not reversed, dated September 23, 1865 (Hg. 365, the Louvre).

1865
J 12. *Wooden Jetty in the Port of Honfleur*
Etching, 225 × 306 mm.; Hg. 368.
"I have just done etchings for the Aquafortistes, I offer you the proof. I first did for the Société des Aquafortistes, 1. Dutch Skater, 2. Entrance into the Port of Honfleur, 3. Exit from the Port of Honfleur, and today the 4th, the wooden jetty in the port of Honfleur thus I offer you the proof" (Jongkind to Burty, December 16, 1865).
1) Before lettering and number (*reproduced*).
2) Edition for the fifth selection of the fourth year of the Société des Aquafortistes, January, 1866 (Bailly-Herzberg, 1972, vol. I, p. 182), with title, the addresses of Cadart & Luquet and of Delâtre, and the number *202.*
3) Later printing with address and number removed but with title.
Printing by Goulding, London.
False pre-lettering state, without a horizontal line parallel to the frame line in the right margin.

1867
J 13. *View of the Port at Honfleur with the Railroad Dock*
Etching, 255 × 327 mm.; Hg. 411.
"As I promised you, I offer you with this the fifth drawing in etching that I have done for the Société des Aquafortistes, depicting railroad port at Honfleur" (Jongkind to Burty, April 15, 1867).
1) Before lettering and number. A proof previous to this first state with, on the back, a drawing of the etching traced in pencil, doubtless in preparation for a transfer, is in the BN (formerly Curtis Coll.: *reproduced*).
2) Printing for the sixth selection of the fifth year of the Société des Aquafortistes, February, 1867, with the number *267* (Bailly-Herzberg, vol. I, p. 225) and the address of Cadart & Luquet, etc.
—Edition in *L'Eau-forte depuis 10 ans,* 1872.
False pre-lettering state.
RELATED WORKS: Three paintings on this subject (Hg. 338, 388, 389, all

in private colls.); pencil drawing dated 1866 (Hg. 410, Rijksmuseum, Amsterdam).

J 14. *Windmills in Holland*
Etching, 137 × 189 mm.; Hg. 444.
This etching was not commissioned by Cadart but by Philip Hamerton, through the intermediary of Guy Delâtre, on December 6, 1867, as an illustration for Hamerton's book on etching (see Bailly-Herzberg, 1972, vol. II, p. 122). However, it was republished by Cadart's widow in *L'Illustration nouvelle*, the series that continued the activity of the Société des Aquafortistes after its demise in 1868.
1) Before lettering and number (Baltimore).
2) Before lettering, with a vertical scratch beside the figure at the left *(reproduced)*.
2-b) Printing in Philip Gilbert Hamerton, *Etching and Etchers*, London, Macmillan, 1868, p. 224.
3) Printing for *L'Illustration nouvelle*, vol. XII, 1880, with the number *536*, the title, and the address of Cadart's widow.
Printing by Goulding, London.
False pre-lettering state.

1868
J 15. *Setting Sun, Port of Antwerp*
Etching, 151 × 233 mm.; Hg. 492.
1) Before lettering and number (BN: *reproduced*).
2) Printing for *L'Illustration nouvelle*, vol. I, 1868, with the number *14* in upper right, the address of Cadart & Luce, the title, and, in lower left: *Imp. Delâtre, Paris*.
3) Later printing with *14* removed.
4) Later printing with address of new publisher, Charles Delorière, 15 rue de Seine, Paris.
Printing by Goulding, London.
False pre-lettering state.

J 16. *Batavia*
Etching, 123 × 192 mm.; Hg. 491.
Done at the request of Burty for the book of sonnets and etchings he edited, to accompany the sonnet of the same title by Robert Luzarche (see Corot 9, Daubigny 121, Millet 20).
1) Proofs before printer's address.
2) Published in *Sonnets et eaux-fortes*, Paris, Lemerre, 1869, in an edition of 350 copies on laid paper *(reproduced)*, 2 or 3 on vellum, a few on *appliqué* or *volant* China paper. *Imp. Salmon* is above the frame line at the right.
RELATED WORK: Preparatory drawing (BN, formerly Curtis Coll.).

1873
J 17. *The Bridge over the Canal*
Etching, 144 × 231 mm.
The second unpublished etching.
1) First state before lines in sky at right (Baltimore).
2) With lines filling the blank above house at right (BN: *reproduced*).
3) Final state, with cross-hatching on roof of second house at right, on tree at right, and in the water (BN).

J 18. *Demolition of the Rue des Francs-Bourgeois Saint-Marcel*
Etching, 148 × 236 mm.; Hg. 665.

1) Before lettering and number, with the frame line incomplete at the right-hand corners *(reproduced)*.
2) Before lettering and number, with frame line completed.
3) Printing for *L'Illustration nouvelle*, vol. V, 1873, with number *222* and address of A. Cadart.
4) Printing with address of Charles Delorière, without title and number.
False pre-lettering state.
RELATED WORKS: Painting dated April 19, 1868 (Hg. 469, Gemeentemuseum, The Hague); painting signed and dated 1873 (Hg. 599, private coll.); watercolor dated April 17, 1868 (Hg. 475, the Louvre).

J 19. *Canal in Holland near Rotterdam (Winter)*
Etching, 148 × 228 mm.; Hg. 666.
1) Before lettering and number, with incomplete frame line; "a large spot resulting from a biting on the bare copper and resembling a tinting with India ink covers the mass of the two large windmills as well as the cluster of trees and the adjoining terrain" (Delteil) (BN, two proofs: *reproduced*).
2) Before lettering and number, with spot removed from ground but not from windmills and trees.
3) Completed but before lettering and number, the frame line complete, the spot removed.
4) Printing for *L'Illustration nouvelle*, vol. VII, 1875, with title, engraved signature, number *293*, and address of Cadart.
5) Printing with address of Delorière.
6) Later printings, with ten or so scratches on the plate at the left.
Printing by Goulding, London.

1878
J 20. *Leaving the Maison Cochin, Faubourg Saint-Jacques (Evening)*
Etching, 143 × 233 mm.; Hg. 709.
1) Before lettering and number, proofs with trials of etching needle in lower margin.
2) Without the needle marks in the margin.
3) Printing for *L'Illustration nouvelle*, vol. XI, 1879, with title, engraved signature, number *484*, and address of Cadart's widow.
4) With address of C. Delorière *(reproduced)*.
Printing by Goulding, London.
False pre-lettering state.
RELATED WORKS: Painting titled *Funeral of the Poor, Leaving the Hôpital Cochin, Rue du Faubourg Saint-Jacques* (Hg. 671, private coll.), signed and dated November 3, 1876 (the etching, curiously enough, is dated November 3, 1878); watercolor of the same date (Hg. 680, private coll.).

Besides these twenty etchings the critic L. de Fourcaud, a friend of Jongkind, recalled having seen two others which no one has been able to track down. Delteil gave De Fourcaud's descriptions of these works, under the letters *A* and *B*, in the appendix to his catalogue:
A. "On one there was to be seen a Dutch site along the Meuse, with a sailboat standing out in front; at the right and in the rear, low vegetation, and a large windmill in the middle plane. The lapping of the water around

the boat was rendered by nibblings. Mere lines silhouetted some clouds in the sky. Besides all this, here and there were hatchings done in pencil" (L. de Fourcaud).
B. "A street in a Paris faubourg enlivened by two or three small figures of street sweepers. This looked like a simplified repetition of the painting *The Snow Sweepers*. It was extremely incomplete in execution. I do not believe that these plates were completed and consequently put into circulation. This is all that Jongkind said of them to me: 'Those are pieces of trash from the time when they were trying to make an engraver out of me. I began with those stupidities and I didn't go on with them very much'" (L. de Fourcaud).

JEAN-FRANÇOIS MILLET (1814–1875)

ETCHINGS

Before 1848 (1847?)
We have no information whatsoever about the circumstances in which Millet made his first and very modest attempts at etching, but it can be supposed that they were done in imitation of his friend Charles Jacque, the engraver and painter who was his neighbor on the Rue de Rochechouart, where he had taken lodgings in 1845 (see M 5), and with whom he left Paris in June of 1849 to settle in Barbizon. In any case, those first efforts were so unpretentious that the earliest cataloguers simply ignored them, and in fact the only time they ever turned up on the market was when Alfred Lebrun sold his collection to Keppel in 1886, a collection which, intact, finally went to the Art Institute of Chicago, where the only prints of these first experiments are still found. In addition to the prints, Lebrun sold to Keppel the copper plates for nos. 3, 4, 8, 9, 10, 11, 12, 13, 15, 18, and 19, from which reprintings have been made and of which one can find prints done after holes had been bored through the plates.

M 1. *The Small Boat*
Etching, 60 × 52 mm.; Lebrun cat. no. 1.
The only two proofs known, one in blue, the other in black, "printed by Millet with oil paint" (Lebrun), are in the Art Institute of Chicago *(reproduced)*.
PHOTOGRAVURE for the catalogue published by Keppel in 1887 with, at lower left: *Photogravure Co., N. Y.* (reproduced by Delteil).
RELATED WORK: A woodcut attributed to Millet in the Feuerdent Collection (see M 29 BIS).

M 2. Plate with three subjects: *Woman Hanging Up Washing, Small Digger Resting, Seated Peasant*
Etching using roulette, 91 × 150 mm.; L. 2, 3, 7.

In the Lebrun Collection (now in Chicago) there was a cut-up proof of this of which the two most important pieces had been preserved—those with the woman hanging up washing (62 × 83 mm.) and the man resting on a spade (42 × 68 mm.; both *reproduced*)—along with an intact print with all three subjects (L. 7), of which the NYPL has another copy *(reproduced)*.
Lebrun stated that ten proofs of the plate had been printed on old laid paper and that, like the first etching (M 1), the one he owned had been printed by Millet with paint rather than printer's ink.

M 3. *Man Leaning on Spade*
Etching, 85 × 67 mm.; L. 4.
Four proofs known: NYPL, Chicago, Baltimore (Garrett Coll.), BN *(reproduced)*.

M 4. *The Two Cows*
Etching, 91 × 151 mm.; L. 5.
First composition with different states:
1) before signature (Chicago);
2) with *J. F. Millet* at lower right (Chicago);
3) before work with roulette but with the addition at the right of a peasant woman bending down (Chicago);
4) with roulette work (Chicago, NYPL, BN: *reproduced*).
Later edition with corners cut off.
This plate was printed in a good number of copies, and the first three states were run off by Millet himself. One proof in the BN, two in NYPL, four in Chicago: in dark brown (1st state), very lightly inked (2nd), in bistre (3rd), in black (4th).

M 5. *Sheep Grazing*
Drypoint, 46 × 118 mm.; L. 6.
This plate engraved in 1850 is from the hand of Millet. Etchings by Jeanron, Subercaze, etc. [but] bearing the signature of Charles Jacque are still today falsely attributed to that master, who in any case recalls perfectly well having seen J. F. Millet engraving the essay in drypoint in question. . . . The signature of Charles Jacque was added only as a joke and not to assure the sale of the engraving, which was done one evening on a table corner in the printer Auguste Delâtre's place.

(Lebrun)

Here we find ourselves in one of those circles in which, thanks to Jeanron and Jacque, the taste for the art-etching was relaunched. The plate does in fact have the signature of Jacque in the upper left and the mention *Jackson invenit et fecit* in the lower left. Delteil thought it might date from 1849 and thus before the departure for Barbizon, though Millet subsequently did a good deal of work in Paris, in the studio of Narcisse Diaz on Rue Frochot and in that of the engraver Lavieille on Rue de Navarin in 1850. Thus Lebrun's proposal of 1850 is probable, though it should be noted (and we owe this information to the painstaking research of Bailly-Herzberg, 1972, vol. I, p. 9, n. 8) that Delâtre in 1847 had installed himself at 38, Rue de Rochechouart, which made him a close neighbor of Charles Jacque and Millet, who were then living at 42 bis on the same street,

whereas before 1846 and after 1848 the printer had his shop on the Rue St.-Jacques. One therefore wonders if the engravings may not have been products of convivial evenings with a neighbor and if this would not provide a clue to more precise dating.
The plate was canceled by five vertical lines, which proves that Millet did not consider it satisfactory. One proof in NYPL *(reproduced)*, three in Chicago, of which one is canceled.

M 6. *Plate with Sketches* or *Woman Knitting*
Etching, 192 × 118 mm.; L. 8.
Sketches dashed off on the back of a plate bearing the address of the metal planer Juery, 27, Rue de la Huchette, Paris. Lebrun was able to decipher on one proof a reversed signature at the right, *Diaz delineavit*, but this would mean only that this plate was executed in the same spirit of amusement as our M 5.
Ten proofs printed, according to Lebrun, of which only two are now known (BN, Chicago: *reproduced*).

M 7. *Woman Knitting*
Drypoint, 107 × 75 mm.; L. 8.
Lebrun considered this a separate printing of the motif on the preceding plate, but since there are no proofs of it in his collection, now in Chicago, and since Delteil affirmed that its authenticity was doubted by no less than Millet's son-in-law Heymann, one is left wondering just what its origin was. Heymann and Giacomelli each knew one proof, but where those are now is not known. Our reproduction derives from the photograph published by Delteil. Note that like M 6 it was engraved on the back of a plate with the planer's address.

M 8. *Kelp Gatherers*
Etching using roulette, 99 × 122 mm.; L. 9.
Only ten proofs, according to Lebrun (NYPL, Chicago: *reproduced*). The plate was bought by Keppel and withdrawn and pierced, and there exist printings from it in that state.

1855–56

After the first attempts, which we date before 1848 (with the possible exception of M 5), the history of Millet as etcher becomes easy to follow.
Five rather more worked-out plates were begun during the winter of 1855–56 in response to the urging of Sensier, who saw in engraving a financial resource for his friend as well as a means of spreading his reputation. His letters to Millet (in the Cabinet des Dessins, the Louvre) have much to say about that spurt of activity, which seems to have gone on into 1857 and involved our nos. 9 through 13. This was confirmed by Lebrun, who noted that the printing of the five plates was the same: "For numbers 10 to 14 [Delteil's 9 to 13] the first printing was done on hand-made paper, *appliqué* China paper [half-columbier], the other proofs were always printed on *vergé*, China, or Japan paper."
Nos. 14, 15, and 16 were considered failures by Millet and their plates destroyed. The next four were commis-

sioned for the *Gazette des Beaux-Arts* (1861), the Société des Aquafortistes (1862), the Société des Dix (1863), and the volume *Sonnets et eaux-fortes* (1869). Sensier informs us when this series was begun:

It was in 1855, after having finished his picture for the International Exhibition, that Millet engraved in etching five rustic subjects that he put out immediately for sale. Two others had also been engraved by him [our M 14, 15], but he was dissatisfied with the biting and did not publish them. Some time earlier he had made trials on copper and zinc which were of too little importance to be shown [M 1–8].

This is confirmed by the American painter Edward Wheelwright, who in his reminiscences of Millet and Barbizon (*Atlantic Monthly*, September, 1876, pp. 257–76) mentioned that Millet completed four or five plates between October, 1855, and June, 1856. By July of 1857 the etchings had been printed, as trial proofs at least, since Sensier proposed to show them to Charles Le Blanc (letter of July 4, 1857). But the project of an edition seems to have been dropped; the plates were bundled up and put away and even forgotten until the day Millet again took up the idea of a publication and had Sensier get in touch with Delâtre. On February 8, 1858, Sensier wrote to the artist:

Now to speak about Delâtre. I wrote to him and the letter finally reached him. He came and I spoke to him about what you have in mind. He promptly asked for an advance for the paper. I advanced him ten francs. He wanted to take the plates with him but I put off handing them over. This morning he again sent for the plates, and I sent word that one was lacking. (This was only a pretext, because I can tell you that I was able to find all five. They were tied up in such a way that the smallest had disappeared beneath the others.) So Delâtre attacks again!! I shall bring him the plates on Friday, the day chosen by him, but he will have still other excuses for delaying, and it is hard and awkward to play the suspicious game. What to do? Really, I shall more or less have to put my trust in God when I have exhausted all the ways of holding onto them, with the thought that perhaps you are not likely to do better than I. So it is Friday that he will get at the printing.

The grounds for Sensier's distrust of Delâtre are not very clear, unless it was that he did not wish to let the plates out of his hands. It seems as if Sensier was holding out to be present in person at the printing while Delâtre was just as eager to do his job without anyone looking over his shoulder. The printer, after all, was beginning to be well established and had built up quite a clientele of artists. In fact, in the same letter Sensier remarked: "Delâtre is basking in opulence. He is director of the workshops of the printers Gide and Baudry with a salary of 1,800 francs plus four hours for himself every day and four presses." On March 4 Sensier wrote to Millet: "I am in possession of the proofs of Delâtre that I had him print Tuesday and Wednesday. Delâtre printed one collection of them on old paper which he would like you to give him to present as a gift to M. About who is sponsoring his attempt to be taken on at the Chalcographie of the Louvre. He requests this [as compensation] for the proofs for [copyright] deposit, the errands he ran, and the [formalities of] deposit he has done. What to answer? I am deciding nothing. As soon as the lot is dry I will bring some to Papeleu and I'll keep the accounts with double entries." Millet replied in August: "I would have it on my conscience if I hindered the good fortune of Delâtre, if all that is needed to help him win it is the few proofs on old paper he spoke with you about. Let him take them and do with them as he wants."

There were other printings of those plates, by Charles Meryon in 1860 and by "a printer in the Latin Quarter" in 1867. On November 21, 1860, Sensier wrote to Millet: "Diaz has at least forty prints of your *Diggers* and *Gleaners*. The other subjects should be printed but I decidedly object to Delâtre. Meryon who has a press proposes to run them off for you entirely free of charge. He is a man who is serious and honest to the very highest degree and who prints his proofs very well. Do you agree to this operation?" To which Millet replied on December 4: "Because decidedly M. Meryon is so very virtuous, let him do the printing of the etchings, we won't be let down." And Sensier later in the same month: "As for Meryon, he is someone with his head forever in the clouds *(un verre fumeux)*, a fakir who lives on tea and currants, who will require nothing more than a smile from Your Excellency and a proof of your *Diggers* with these words from your hand: 'Millet to Meryon.' He will be truly satisfied. And there you are, promoted to prince. M. Niel is certain that M. Meryon will be truly delighted. Shall we print?"

Some years later, on October 24, 1867, Sensier wrote:

I have seen Mantz again several times. . . . He again begged me to try to get for him your *Diggers* and your *Gleaners*. Six months ago you did authorize me to have them printed for him. . . . The day before yesterday it was fine weather, I was in the mood; I went off to the Latin Quarter and there, at a printer's who is not Delâtre, I had printed in my presence a few proofs which are good (from ten o'clock to noon). I have two of them for you, four for Mantz, and I took the liberty of offering myself one to put up in my office so as to sound out visitors; then a last one for Robert's salon.

The series of five plates was sold by Cadart (for the relations between Millet and that publisher, see M 18), who announced the album on the back of the title page of the first year of publication, 1862, of the Société des Aquafortistes.

M 9. *Woman Sewing*
Etching, 105 × 74 mm.; L. 10.
1) First state printed by Millet himself, before additional work on the background (Chicago), of a "very different effect from that of the Delâtre printing" (Keppel).

2) Definitive printing (Chicago, BN).
3) With plate beveled down, the vise mark in the lower right effaced (NYPL, Baltimore: Garrett Coll., BN: *reproduced*).

M 10. *Woman Churning*
Etching, 179 × 119 mm.; L. 11.
1) First state, doubtless printed by Millet himself, before considerable work (Yale, BN: *reproduced*).
2) Second state, completed, but still without address (Chicago, NYPL).
3) Printing by Delatre, with address below at the right: *Impᵉ par Aug. Delâtre Rue Sᵗ Jacque 171* (BN, Chicago, Baltimore).

M 11. *Peasant Returning from the Manure Heap*
Etching, 163 × 133 mm.; L. 12.
1) Signed lower right, before address and further work (Yale, NYPL, BN, Chicago: 3 proofs).
2) Completed; with address at the bottom: *Paris, Imp. par Aug. Delâtre Rue Sᵗ Jacque 171*.
3) Printing with plate beveled down, still with address of Delâtre (*reproduced*).
4) Printing with address of Delâtre removed (NYPL, BN, Baltimore: Garrett Coll.).
RELATED WORKS: Drawing of 1853–54 plus ten or so sketches "of which the most important are in the Louvre and Boston" (*Jean-François Millet*, exhibition catalogue, Paris, 1975–76, no. 126).

M 12. *The Gleaners*
Etching, 190 × 252 mm.; L. 13.
1) Printing (by Millet?) without address (BN, Yale, Chicago: 2 proofs).
2) With address below at the right: *Paris Imp. par Aug. Delâtre Rue Sᵗ Jacque 171* (NYPL, Baltimore: Garrett Coll., Chicago: 3 proofs, BN: *reproduced*).
Misleading copy (by Belin-Dollet?) with *Delâtre* instead of *Aug. Delâtre* (see L. Delteil in *L'Estampe et l'affiche*, May, 1899).
RELATED WORKS: Painting of 1857 and numerous studies (*Millet*, exhib. cat., 1975–76, nos. 65, 99–106, 127).

M 13. *The Diggers*
Etching, 237 × 337 mm.; L. 14.
1) First state with signature engraved in upper right (Yale, Chicago, BN).
2) "The sky completely effaced and the signature removed" (Lebrun), but no example of this state was known to Delteil, who, according to Keppel, affirmed that only a single proof was printed (Chicago).
3) The sky reengraved, still without signature and address (Chicago, NYPL).
4) With *Paris Imp. par Aug. Delâtre Rue Sᵗ Jacque 171* at lower right (Baltimore: Garrett Coll., Chicago: 2 proofs, NYPL, BN: *reproduced*).
RELATED WORKS: Painting of 1866 and numerous drawings (*Millet*, exhib. cat., 1975–76, nos. 115–24, 128).

M 14. *The Vigil*
Etching, 151 × 110 mm.; L. 15.
This and the next etching were done at the same time as the five plates of 1855–56 but were not published. According to Lebrun the plate was too heavily bitten—in fact, even eaten through by the acid at some points. A very few

proofs were printed, and Millet had the zinc plate destroyed.
Of this plate Burty (*Gazette des Beaux-Arts*, 1861) explained: "Either because the varnish was badly prepared or because the acid was too violent, the metal was attacked so deeply that in printing it gave only a heavy image and was canceled after a few trial proofs."
1) Printing before the edges of the plate were beveled (Chicago, BN: *reproduced*).
2) With corners rounded off and edges beveled (Chicago, NYPL, BN).
According to Keppel there exists a forgery whose effect is somber and heavy.

M 15. *Woman Carding*
Etching, 256 × 177 mm.; L. 16.
The story of this plate is much like that of the preceding, and Lebrun said of it: "Etching only and without retouching. This fine piece should never have been brought out. Millet found it too deeply bitten, and he did not wish to publish it. Inadvertently he had left the plate in the bath an entire night."
Note that in his *Gazette des Beaux-Arts* article of 1861 Burty identified this as the first plate done by Millet, M 14 as the second, and both as preceding the series of five, which is contrary to the order adopted by Lebrun and followed by Delteil. However, the fact that these two were unsuccessful experiments does rather suggest that they may have been done before the ones that came out better: "M. Millet was far from satisfied with this essay which nonetheless is very attractive. . . . He then engraved on a zinc plaque two seated women [our M 14]" (Burty).
A single state (Baltimore: 3 proofs, Chicago: 2, NYPL: 3, BN: 2, *reproduced*).
COUNTERPROOF (NYPL: *reproduced*).
RELATED WORKS: Preparatory sketch (Chicago); several sketches, drawings, and a painting of 1863 (*Millet*, exhib. cat., 1975–76, nos. 129, 162).

M 16. *The Goosegirl*
Drypoint, 145 × 122 mm.; L. 17.
Like the two preceding, this plate was destroyed. According to Lebrun, only a few proofs on China paper and old laid paper were run off (Chicago: 2 proofs, NYPL, BN: *reproduced*).

1861
M 17. *Gruel (Woman Feeding Her Child)*
Etching, 158 × 130 mm.; L. 18.
Produced at the request of Burty to illustrate his *Gazette des Beaux-Arts* article of 1861. Of it he wrote: "This is the free and slightly relaxed reproduction of a painting that M. J.-F. Millet had sent to the exhibition of this year. . . . It would be desirable for M. J.-F. Millet to reproduce all of his compositions by this means and on his own. His talent is too personal not to lose something in a reproduction by someone else, however skillful it might supposedly be."
Delteil reprints a long text published by Maurice Tourneux in the *Revue rétrospective* in 1892 ("Notes sur quelques artistes contemporains") in which Burty tells how on June 10, 1861, Millet came by and asked him to ac-

company him to Bracquemond's studio where the plate was to be acid-bitten:

The copper plate was really quite eaten. It was bitten well the first time. The ground was coated again and it was bitten once more. Finally Millet insisted on himself putting two touches of pure acid on the heads of the woman and her child. The instant the brush touched them Bracquemond quickly splashed drops of water on them. We went to Delâtre's. A worker ran off proofs for us. At the third Millet used the drypoint to close up a large high-light on the woman's neck, put a few lines on the shadow of the bonnet, a few points on the wrist holding the infant. We had nineteen in all printed, of which two were retouched. Bracquemond is going to add the signature. Only three have the sketch at the bottom, the printer effacing or bringing them out at will. I myself burnished them on the plate.

1) Before the signature and with the sketches, three proofs according to Burty, four according to Lebrun (Chicago, Yale).
2) Before the signature, without the sketches (Chicago: 2, NYPL).
3) With the signature by Bracquemond (Chicago, BN).
4) Printing with lettering, at lower left: *Gazette des Beaux Arts;* at lower right: *Imp^e A Delâtre Paris (reproduced).*
5) Reprinting for Roger Marx, *Études sur l'école française,* Paris, 1903.
6) Reprinting for André Marty, *L'Imprimerie et les procédés de gravure au XXe siècle,* Paris, 1906.
RELATED WORKS: Painting of 1861 and preparatory drawing in Boston (*Millet,* exhib. cat., 1975–76, nos. 130, 157).

1862

M 18. *The Large Shepherdess*
Etching, 317 × 236 mm.; L. 19.
The relations between Cadart and Millet are still unclear. Millet does seem to have been invited to do a plate for Cadart's association of print collectors, and Lebrun reports that "this fine piece was to have been published by the Société des Aquafortistes (Cadart). But the publisher having asked Millet to give up the plate, the artist dropped the idea of belonging to the Société." However, the discussions concerning Cadart found in the correspondence of Sensier and Millet seem not to refer to this particular plate. On July 31, 1862, Sensier wrote:

Cadart, the publisher of the Société des Aquafortistes, has been to see me again, saying that you were authorizing him to have a certain number of your etchings printed by Delâtre for which he was to take care of the selling. You did say something about this to me some time ago, but I no longer recall very well what you decided. Here are his propositions: 1) the copper plates to be turned over to Delâtre to have ten copies of each plate printed; 2) deposit them with him for sale; 3) he will take over the expenses which would be deducted from the selling price; 4) the price would be fixed at 30 francs for the collection and 33 percent remittance to his profit. If all that is acceptable to you, write to me so I can have the

printing done before leaving for Barbizon which, I think, will not be later than August 10.

Then on August 3: "I have received no reply on the subject of Cadart and Delâtre. What to do? I shall be gone in three days." But their letters had crossed, and that same day Millet had written: "Here is what is to be done with Cadart: if he wishes to have my etchings, let him buy them and take whatever number of copies of them he wishes. Except that I do not know at what price to sell them to him. In any case, I give you carte blanche in and for everything; do whatever you think good to do, or do not do it if you think it better. . . . If you do not have the time to arrange something with Cadart, it can't be helped."
A single state (Baltimore, Yale, Chicago: 2 proofs, NYPL: 2, BN: 2, *reproduced*).
RELATED WORKS: Four preparatory drawings of which one is lost, one each is in Boston and Chicago, and the fourth is a sketch known only from an old photograph; painting of 1868–72 in Chicago (*Millet,* exhib. cat., 1975–76, no. 131).

1863

M 19. *Going to Work*
Etching, 385 × 310 mm.; L. 20.
In 1863 the demand for etchings by Millet began to catch on, witness this letter of May 16 from Sensier: "I have been seeing people again: two young enthusiasts. They want your etchings. I told you so, your name is going up."
On October 3 an elderly lady wished to purchase two engravings at a hundred francs each, an enormous sum for a print. Print lovers were beginning to become known, and Sensier was selling them "collections": "I shall not have proofs printed until two hundred francs are sent you for seven collections." This was on July 8, and six days later we find: "M. Chassaing turned up only this morning for the etchings. He is going to arrange to take two or three collections of them, more if he can. M. Moureau, two, and when I have the stake of 200 francs I shall go and have the printing done by Delâtre in my presence. I will have the results in the next days."
Sensier then got the idea of setting up a society of print lovers, the Société des Dix, to commission from Millet a plate of which the ten members would enjoy co-ownership. The artist set to work in November of the same year and asked Sensier for one thousand francs to guarantee himself the free time to carry through this task, which meant the drawings ordered from him as well as "my etching, and in connection with that I am in the process of cleaning up my composition." On November 3 Sensier wrote: "Push ahead with the etching. I am counting a lot on it, a lot. I should like really everyone to want it and to have it exhibited as a criterion of your talent." Six days later: "Let me know when the etching is done. . . . The Dix are counting on seeing your etching turn up by the end of the month. For the one for the Twenty [a new society] we shall see if it might not be a good thing to think of a scene with

a large group of laborers: 'The Return of the Last Wagon of the Harvest,' 'Interior View of Farm,' etc., etc. Whatever you might like on that rustic tune."
Millet wrote on November 16: "Today I am beginning to trace my composition for the etching onto my plate." The trial proofs of details that were preserved, and which are reproduced here, show with what care Millet approached this work. On November 23 he finished the plate: "I may have to have some things bitten again. Does Delâtre know how to revarnish a plate? If he does it, let him try to have on hand everything needed for this. I shall also have some spots to be removed, and we may perhaps need the help of an engraver who is really clever in his profession." That same day Sensier wrote: "I've alerted Delâtre!" and six days later: "Would you believe that Delâtre has sent me absolutely nothing, neither Friday nor yesterday evening nor today. I am going to go there again tomorrow." Finally on December 2: "Delâtre sent the proofs yesterday evening. . . . I had written to M. Burty to come by and pay up."
There followed the lengthy altercation between Sensier and Burty which is so revealing of the evolution of a public for graphic works (see our introduction).
On December 15: "I shall also turn over to M. Rousseau, Sr., the first ten copies of the first state of your etching so that you can yourself write on each this indication: *1st state, M. Jules Niel, November 1863. J.-F. Millet.* The nine others are: Théodore Rousseau, Henri Tardif, Charles Forget, Théodore Sensier, Michel Chassaing, Philippe Burty, Moureau, Charles Tillot, and myself. Please write the Christian names just as I indicate them, in pencil, in whatever place you wish. . . . Do this at home alone. The numbers for the proofs are of no interest since they are all from the same day."
Finally on December 26: "Burty finds, like you, that the second state is too heavy and too oily. He complains a good deal about this printing or rather about the new mania of Delâtre to push all his prints to blackness and heaviness. He will come with me to Delâtre's when we print the 3rd or 4th states. His advice seems good to me."
1) Before signature and address (Chicago: 2 proofs).
2) Signed *J. F. Millet* at lower left (Chicago, Yale).
2-b) With address of Delâtre but not that of Moureaux (Chicago: *reproduced*).
3) With addresses, below at the left: *Se vend chez Moureaux Rue Fontaine St Georges 26;* and at the right: *Imp. A. Delâtre Paris,* printed on laid paper, China paper, and wove paper (Chicago, BN).
4) With the addresses removed (NYPL, BN: *reproduced*).
5) Printing with three points at lower right.
6) Second state, with a few added lines prolonging the clouds.
7) With the three points removed.
Copy by Belin-Dollet measuring 460 × 380 mm., thus much enlarged, with only *Millet* as signature. Keppel states that this plate was much exploited after Millet died, that there were numerous

printings with the three points, and that the plate became very tired and worn.

RELATED WORKS: Seven preparatory drawings (*Millet,* exhib. cat., 1975–76, nos. 70, 135, 171) and an oil painting of 1850 in the Glasgow Art Gallery and Museum.

M 19 BIS, TER, QUATER. *Going to Work,* trial details.
The seven preparatory drawings (three in the Louvre, one in the Musée Bonnat, Bayonne, one in Chicago, one in the former Beurdeley Collection, one in a private collection in Japan) are good evidence that this was the most carefully worked-out plate of its author, who, as we see, even executed a number of trial runs of details to test the effect. Delteil reproduced one of the two detail prints he had seen in the Beurdeley Collection (both now Davison Art Center, Wesleyan University, Middletown, Connecticut), and the Art Institute of Chicago has three other such fragments printed by Millet and given by him to Sensier:

19 BIS. Head and shoulders of the man, 65 × 60 mm. (motif); 205 × 128 mm. (sheet) *(reproduced)*;
19 TER. Head and shoulders of the woman, 82 × 68 mm. (motif); 200 × 138 mm. (sheet) *(reproduced)*;
19 QUATER. Left arm of the woman carrying the basket, 114 × 52 mm. (motif); 143 × 105 mm. (sheet) *(reproduced)*.
In addition there are:
19 QUINTER. Details printed on the same sheet, including the woman's head, her arm, the landscape in the right background with a horse and house (Wesleyan University: *reproduced*); and
19 QUINTER. Details of woman's head, man's head, landscape in left background with a wagon, two trials of printing of the central part of the background between the two figures, and the stones in the foreground (Wesleyan University: *reproduced*).

1860–69
M 20. *Auvergnat Woman Spinning*
Etching, 199 × 129 mm.; L. 21.
Millet turned his hand to etching one last time when invited by Burty to contribute to the volume of *Sonnets et eaux-fortes* he was preparing (see also Corot 9, Daubigny 121, and Jongkind 16).
The affair was not exactly smooth sailing. To start with, Millet came up with an image that had nothing at all to do with the sonnet Burty had selected for him to illustrate. Instead of going ahead with his drawing of young girls watching a flight of wild geese, he went back to a reminiscence of his trips to Vichy, where Mme. Millet had gone for the cure. On November 8, 1868, Millet wrote to Sensier: "I have had a letter from M. Albert Mérat in which he sends me a sonnet already printed. He thinks that I have done or am supposed to do the etching on the same subject. I am going to tell him that that is not the case and to explain to him what I am doing. His letter is perfectly pleasant. I am working at my etching and, at the present moment, the copper plate is half incised. If my migraine does not interfere too

much you will find it at Martinmas [November 11]." Then on November 11: "I am leaving today at two o'clock to go to Paris to have my etching bitten. If I do not see you this evening I shall see you tomorrow before going to Burty's."
Then there was a new altercation with Burty because Millet refused the condition that the plate was to be canceled after the edition (see our introduction). Millet was disappointed. On January 15, 1869: "I have received the book of *Sonnets.* My etching is really pretty sad." And nine days later: "I have given my consent to the destruction of the plate despite my desire to hold on to it. . . . Between us, I find this destruction of plates absolutely and wholly brutal and barbarous. I am not well enough up in commercial manipulations to understand what is achieved thereby, but I do know that even if Rembrandt and Ostade had each made one of those plates they would have been destroyed. Enough said."
1–4) The first four states distinguished by Delteil (but not by Lebrun) have only very minor differences of no interest and which could all have come from variations in printing: the right eye of the woman not well defined, five marks in the upper left, dribbles of acid on the right margin, an asterisk in the lower right. All four versions of the trial proofs are in Chicago (the second: *reproduced*).
5) Definitive state published in *Sonnets et eaux-fortes,* Paris, Alphonse Lemerre, 1869. Two or three copies on vellum, a few on *appliqué* or *volant* China paper, 350 on *vergé.*
RELATED WORKS: Pastel in the John G. Johnson Collection, Philadelphia Museum of Art, and two preparatory drawings in a private collection (*Millet,* exhib. cat., 1975–76, nos. 136, 214).

LITHOGRAPHS

1848
M 21. *But Where Is He?*
Lithograph, 170 × 145 mm.; L. 22.
In 1848 Millet was virtually poverty-stricken. "He got a job doing the cover illustration for a drawing-room ballad, *Où donc est-il?* Such was the title of that musical composition. Millet went stoutly to work at that task, whose fee was set at 30 francs, and he sent the lithograph stone to the publisher. The latter paid him with insolence only, and in reply to the poor artist's protests he slammed the door on him." So Sensier (1881, p. 110), but Keppel's version is less romantic: After having seen the first proof the publisher ordered that the stone be wiped off, and when the artist came to ask for his pay he slammed the door so violently that he broke Millet's thumb. But contrary to what Keppel thought (he knew only one proof) there exist:
1) a pre-lettering printing of which two proofs are known (NYPL, BN: *reproduced*);
2) a printing with lettering of which three or four proofs are known (Chicago, BN).
RELATED WORK: Delteil mentions a lithograph reproduction by Eugène Delâtre.

M 21 BIS. *Portrait of Chateaubriand*
Lithograph; dimensions unknown.
Burty mentioned another lithograph Millet is supposed to have done around the same time for another ballad, this one supporting the Legitimist Bourbonist claim. On the cover was a portrait of the writer and statesman Chateaubriand which, Burty said, "was miserably copied in Belgium." Neither he nor the other cataloguers ever saw this work, which is considered lost.

1851
M 22. *The Sower*
Lithograph, 191 × 156 mm.; L. 23.
According to Lebrun, this lithograph was intended for the periodical *L'Artiste,* which did not publish it, and it was only in 1889 that a few proofs were printed. It was in fact in 1850 that Millet began to work on the theme of the sower, of which a second painted version (now in the Provident National Bank, Philadelphia) was shown in the Salon of that year to anything but unanimous approval. Thus it seems perfectly likely that he would have attempted to make his canvas known through a reproduction in *L'Artiste.*
1) Only a single proof seems to have been printed in 1851, and this, given by Millet to Sensier, passed after the latter's death to Lebrun.
2) Printing of 1889 produced by Bertauts in about twenty-five copies which were signed and numbered by Millet's son-in-law Heymann and which have trial lithographic crayon marks in the lower margin (NYPL: *reproduced*).
3) Later printing without the crayon marks.

M 24. *In the Forest* or *Tall Timber*
Lithograph, 630 × 500 mm.; not in L.
The contribution of Millet to this lithograph, done about 1851, is minimal. It is by his friend Karl Bodmer, another of the denizens of Barbizon, and Millet helped him out merely by drawing the figure.
1) A few pre-lettering proofs.
2) With lettering, below at the left: *Karl Bodmer pinx. et lith.,* and at the right: *Imp. Bertauts r. Cadet 11 Paris* (Chicago, NYPL: *reproduced*).

M 25–26. *The Pioneers*
Lithographs, 360 × 530 mm.; not in L.

M 25. *Rescue of the Daughters of Daniel Boone and James Callaway*

M 25 BIS. *Capture of the Daughters of Boone and Callaway*

M 26. *Simon Butler, the American Mazeppa*

M 26 BIS. *The Leap of Major McColloch*

These four lithographs were likewise the product of collaboration between Bodmer and Millet. Delteil catalogued only two (M 25, 26), but the proofs of M 25, 26, and 26 BIS in the Avery Collection, NYPL, have an annotation made by Bodmer for the purchaser, Lucas, stating that Millet had done the figures in all four. On the other hand, the catalogue of the Millet exhibition in Paris, 1975–76, where the preparatory drawings for M 25, 25 BIS, and 26 BIS were shown, commented (p. 179) that "the drawings show that Millet was the author of the entire compositions and not of the figures alone; however, he probably did not himself draw them on the stone: the lithograph of the *Sower* that he did on the stone in 1851 is technically clumsy compared with the Bodmer series," an opinion with which we agree unreservedly. Note that we have no drawing for *Capture of the Daughters* (M 25 BIS), whereas there exists a drawing in this series (*Millet*, exhib. cat., 1975–76, no. 140) of which no lithographic rendering is known.

In 1851 the publisher Goupil ordered this series of prints from Bodmer with a view to publication in the United States, which was in fact carried through in the following year. Millet collaborated on them in July of 1851: "I am making drawings of savages. . . . I don't know if the deal will go through, because it has to be done in conditions that somewhat put me off. First of all, the drawings in question must be highly worked out *(ficelés)* because it's for engraving. But that's not all: they must also be in a style as finicky and plastered-down *(pommadé)* as possible" (letter to Sensier, in Moreau-Nélaton, p. 96). The publisher did in fact find that what the two of them came up with was, as Millet put it, "unfortunately an object of art, and that was what above all had to be avoided with utmost care; because this publication is being done strictly for the Americans so what is needed is something utterly pretty-pretty. I am giving myself a devil of a time to do what I can never do."

1) Pre-lettering printings (NYPL: *reproduced*).

2) Printing with, at the top in the middle: *Annals of the United States Illustrated—The Pioneers* and the number in the series; below at the left: *Composed & Drawn on stone by K. Bodmer;* in the middle: *Entered according to act of Congress in the year 1852 by W. Schauss . . . New York . . .* plus a legend of several lines in English and French; at the right: *Printed by Lemercier Paris;* lower: *Goupil & Cº Paris - London - Berlin - New York.*

RELATED WORKS: Drawings by Millet (of the entire composition and not figures only) for M 25 (Yale), 26 (Musée Thomas-Henry, Cherbourg), 26 BIS (lost but listed in Marmontel sale, January 25, 1883), and others of which no printing was made (see the very detailed catalogue entries, *Millet,* exhib. cat., 1975–76, nos. 137–40).

1858

M 23. *Olivier de Serres*
Lithograph, 98 × 78 mm.; L. 24.
Sensier himself ordered this lithograph from Millet to serve as the frontispiece for a small book he had written, under the pen name of Reisnes, on the celebrated sixteenth-century agricultural expert. On August 2, 1858, Millet wrote to him: "Have you had proofs printed of Olivier de Serres and did it come out well enough to make use of? I should like very much to have one."

1) With only *Olivier de Serres/ Seigneur de Pradel/ Né en 1539, mort le 2 Juillet 1619* (Chicago).

2) With *du* instead of *de Pradel (repro-*

duced), published in *Olivier de Serres, agronome du XVIᵉ siècle, sa vie, ses travaux, ses écrits, par Reisnes . . . Avec un portrait par J.-F. Millet,* Privas, Typographie de Roure fils, 1858, octavo, 63 pp.
Millet did his portrait after the one on vellum that Daniel de Serres did of his father, which, Delteil remarks, explains the somewhat "naïf" look of Millet's work, he having "conformed to the spirit of the model."

GLASSPLATE PRINTS (CLICHÉS-VERRE)

Apparently it was Cuvelier who induced Millet to draw on glass, and this at Barbizon in the same circumstances as Rousseau, to whom our artist wrote on December 31, 1861: "You must have seen Eugène Cuvelier: he had me look at some very beautiful photographs made in his home locality and others in the forest." It must have been shortly thereafter, in 1862, that he produced his two *clichés-verre,* since Sensier wrote to him on January 2, 1863, "If you have an extra copy of your two photographs drawn on glass, bring them to me in Paris. My brother in Tours was so very much impressed with mine that I gave them to him to round out his collection of Millet. So here I am without those two engravings and that is a double loss for me."
Eugène Cuvelier settled definitively in Thomery in 1865, having married the daughter of the innkeeper Ganne, but though he was then in the vicinity of Barbizon he did not succeed in getting Millet to follow up this first trial.
Lebrun described the two pieces after two proofs that were "retouched in the shadows by the master" in 1863.

1862

M27. *The Maternal Precaution*
Glass plate, 285 × 225 mm.; L. 25.
EARLY PRINTS in Baltimore, Chicago, NYPL, BN *(reproduced).*
COUNTERPROOFS.
PRINTING for Le Garrec.
Copy in watercolor by Belin-Dollet signed *J. M. F.*
RELATED WORKS: Painting of 1855–57 (the Louvre) and numerous studies (*Millet,* exhib. cat., 1975–76, nos. 107–14).
GLASS PLATE in the Louvre.

M 28. *Woman Emptying a Bucket*
Glass plate, 285 × 225 mm.; L. 26.
EARLY PRINTS in Baltimore, Chicago, NYPL, BN *(reproduced).*
COUNTERPROOFS.
PRINTING for Le Garrec.
GLASS PLATE in the BN.
RELATED WORKS: Pastel (the Louvre) and ink drawing (private coll., Paris) (*Millet,* exhib. cat., 1975–76, nos. 32, 132, 175).

WOOD ENGRAVINGS

Millet produced three or four engravings on wood in which he did all the work from drawing to engraving to printing. These appear to have been

connected with projects for book illustration conceived in collaboration with Chassaing, and comprise three fairly rough efforts and one more worked-out piece (M 31), the last done when he was thinking of illustrating Theocritus. It should be kept in mind that at that date an engraving on a block of wood split with the grain ("side-grain") and executed in such an "artistic" spirit was entirely exceptional. It was scarcely before the end of the century that that technique came back into favor with artists.

Before 1863

M 29. *Plate with Sketches*
Side-grain woodcut, 144 × 95 mm.; L. 27, 28, 31.
Lebrun catalogued this group of very rough sketches on a single block as three numbers corresponding to partial printings:
L. 27. Peasant seated at the foot of a tree, the wood not cut away around the figure, signed *Millet* and printed by the artist himself, 67 × 67 mm.; another printing together with the drawing of a man sowing (Chicago: *reproduced*);
L. 28. Head of a woman wearing a kerchief: "This is one of the first attempts at engraving on wood by J.-F. Millet, printed by himself," 25 × 25 mm. (motif), 32 × 43 mm. (sheet) (Chicago: *reproduced*), and another printing with these two motifs printed together on a sheet 154 × 143 mm. (Chicago: *reproduced*);
L. 31. With all the sketches: "We know only a single proof, printed purely as a curiosity."
The plate with the three sketches was engraved on the back of M 32, and two printings are known:
1) with the peasant and the woman's head very visible (Chicago: *reproduced*);
2) a later printing with those two figures almost unreadable and the block broken in several places.

M 29 BIS. *Sailboat*
Side-grain woodcut, 80 × 100 mm.; not in L. or Delteil.
This was attributed to Millet in the catalogue of the Feuerdent sale, March 23, 1934 (no. 75-c), which seems to us trustworthy evidence. In any case the attribution to Millet of this trial essay does not seem improbable if one considers the plate with three sketches and also M 30. Its subject is much like that of Millet's very first essay in etching (M 1). The only known print is in the BN *(reproduced).*

M 30. *The Small Seated Shepherdess*
Side-grain woodcut, 51 × 54 mm. (motif), 128 × 100 mm. (sheet); L. 29.
A single proof of this essay, printed by Millet himself, according to Lebrun, is known. It is printed in blue, and has on the back the figure of a peasant sketched in black lead (Chicago: *reproduced*).
PHOTOGRAVURE done for Keppel's translation of the Lebrun catalogue, 1887.

1863

M 31. *Man Digging with Spade*
Side-grain woodcut, 141 × 106 mm.; L. 30.

From July to October of 1863 Chassaing sent Millet books of Theocritus, Burns, Shakespeare, and Dante with a view to his illustrating them. On October 14 the artist wrote to him: "It appears that my poor woodcuts are giving you a lot of trouble, as Sensier tells me. Try to have only a few proofs printed by hand by Delâtre or Bracquemond. You will no doubt have talked it over with Sensier and come to some decision." Then on November 8, to Sensier:

M. Chassaing arrived here Thursday morning and remained till the next evening, Friday, then went off by the seven o'clock carriage. We have made a printing of my essay in engraving on wood, the Small Digger that you know, and our printing is very good. The first time I have something to send you I will slip in a few proofs for you. M. Chassaing thinks that the best thing for Theocritus would be to be able to present to a publisher an idyll entirely printed and illustrated, just as it would be in a fascicle of the work, and he thinks that a publisher would not resist that and would wish to continue the work.

Delteil describes and reproduces two very different states:
1) the background not cut away, with cutting trials, and only the figure fully cut out (Chicago: 3 proofs. BN: reproduced);
2) completed, with background cut away.
The fact is, there are several essays that differ much according to the degree of inking and the progress of the work. Other states of the block in the course of engraving are found in Paris and San Francisco (Achenbach Foundation for the Graphic Arts, California Palace of the Legion of Honor). Lebrun indicated that among the proofs printed by Millet was one retouched in black pencil and with a furrow marked in the terrain.

REPRODUCTION WOODCUTS

Besides the four woodcuts that Millet did himself, he composed drawings for blocks to be engraved by others. Delteil included three of these in his catalogue, no doubt convinced that Millet himself did the drawing on the block.

M 32. *Woman Emptying a Bucket*
Side-grain woodcut engraved by the artist's brother, the sculptor Pierre Millet, 144 × 95 mm.; L. 32.
A trial proof (formerly Gerbeau Coll.) was printed without the background and "with a substance other than printer's ink," according to Delteil (BN: reproduced).
RELATED WORKS: Glass plate of 1862 (M 28).

M 33. *The Large Seated Shepherdess*
Side-grain woodcut engraved by the artist's brother, the painter Jean-Baptiste Millet, 270 × 220 mm.; L. 33.

1) State before the sky, on the first proof of which, according to Lebrun, Millet added in pencil the sky and a plowman with two oxen (Chicago).
2) With the sky (Baltimore: proof on Japan paper, Chicago, NYPL, BN: reproduced).
COPY in etching by Belin-Dollet signed *J.-F. Millet* below at right.

1874
M 34. *Digger Resting*
Side-grain woodcut engraved by Pierre Millet, 188 × 131 mm.; L. 34.
1) Trial printing, apparently by hand, without frame line (BN: reproduced).
2) Printing of 1874 signed *J. F. Millet* below at left (Chicago, NYPL, BN: reproduced).
3) Later printing, block altered.

Besides these three, Millet drew other compositions on wood that were engraved by Adrien Lavieille but not included by Delteil in his catalogue, though Lebrun cited them and Burty insisted that they really were drawn on the wood itself by Millet, at least the four blocks for the *Four Hours of the Day*. Millet also drew specially ten other figures that Lavieille engraved for *L'Illustration*, but it is not known if he did these directly on the block or merely had them transferred.
If Lebrun thought that "it is perhaps advisable to add the few engravings in which Adrien Lavieille rendered the thought of the master with relative fidelity," Burty had another opinion:

This is how M. Lavieille has modified to the point of perceptible alteration the spirit of the drawings that M. Millet had himself done on wood. We have described minutely the series of the *Four Hours of the Day* in volume IV of the *Gazette* and, sensing at a certain point an alteration of the type, we attributed it to uncertainness in the original drawing. This was not the case, though, and M. Millet, who shares our feeling about the dangerous propensity into which modern illustration is slipping through abuse of the tool, wished on the contrary to be reproduced in facsimile, that is, with an utter simplicity. This moreover is what M. Lavieille had done previously, though still with some timidity, in the series of six pieces published by the periodical *L'Illustration*.

THÉODORE ROUSSEAU (1812–1867)

The connection of Théodore Rousseau with engraving was at most exceptional: three isolated tries at etching in 1836, 1842, and 1849, a final one published in 1861 but likewise without any follow-up, and two attempts at glassplate prints no doubt done in 1862 when Millet did his.

ETCHINGS

1836
R 1. *Edge of the Forest at Clairbois*
Etching, 113 × 222 mm.
Given such an early date, it is difficult to ascertain what occasion led Rousseau to make this attempt, but he was no doubt urged to it by Edmond Hédouin and Célestin Nanteuil, to whom he gave the only two known proofs.
Hédouin wrote on his proof (which went to Lebrun, then Beurdeley, then Curtis, and finally the BN: reproduced):

Théodore Rousseau. Edge of the forest at Clairbois, engraved in etching by him in 1836. First state given to E. Hédouin by him in 1836. A similar state had been retouched in black and white pencils. This proof had been given to Célestin Nanteuil at the same time. I have never seen other than these two proofs and think that the plate was never finished.

1842
R 2. *A Site in the Berry Region*
Etching, 72 × 175 mm.
Rousseau spent the latter half of 1842 in the Indre, at Fay. But it is not known when he did this etching, which was never published and is known only in very rare proofs (BN: reproduced).

1849
R 3. *View of the Plateau of Bellecroix*
Etching, 138 × 205 mm.
Few proofs are known of this unpublished etching. The one in the BN (reproduced) belonged to the engraver Jules Michelin, and one cannot help wondering if it owed something to him, as did those of Corot. It was colored by the artist himself.

1861
R 4. *Oak Tree Growing Among Rocks*
Etching, 126 × 168 mm.
This is the only etching by Rousseau to be published. It reproduced, for the readers of the *Gazette des Beaux-Arts*, the celebrated painting shown in the Salon of 1861.
1) Before lettering and signature (BN).
2) With *Th. Rousseau Mai 1861* engraved below the frame line at the right (BN: reproduced).
3) With, in addition, below the frame line at the left: *Gazette des Beaux-Arts* in engraving, and in the middle: *Imprimerie Delâtre Paris.* Published as a full-page plate in *Gazette des Beaux-Arts*, August 1, 1861, p. 136.
In his *Souvenirs sur Théodore Rousseau* (Paris, 1872, p. 258 with note 1; p. 259 with note 1), A. Sensier recounts the genesis of this etching and tells how, after the attacks that the painting had aroused in the Salon of 1861,

. . . this public injustice made him [Rousseau] persevere in the opinion that he had of his work and, precisely because of this dumb sheeplike reaction, he set about drawing on copper an etching of that picture which he offered to the *Gazette des Beaux-Arts.* It is dated May, 1861. That etching is superb, done all at one go, without retouchings. It has only two states, before and after this mention: *Th. Rousseau mai 1861.* The plate, loaned out by the *Gazette*, has been lost. The proofs of the first printing are very rare. It was Bracquemond who, after Rousseau had done his work with the needle, took care of the biting of the plate. Rousseau was a novice in the craft of the etcher; his engraving astounded the artists and had a great success in the studios and among the young school who did not know him in such a firm and thoroughly knowledgeable guise. He had however already ventured on that kind of work in two plates, one in 1842, *A View of the Berry Region*, the other of 1849, *A View of the Plateau of Bellecroix*, which are of a very dissimilar distinction and effect; the first is entirely Rembrandtesque, the second, [with its] effect of clear and calm full sunlight, gives an idea of Rousseau in his romantic and nervous compositions. . . . Those two engravings are very rare and have not been brought out. There exist only a few trial proofs of them; of the first I know two only.

RELATED WORKS: Painting exhibited in the Salon of 1861; drawing in graphite (*Théodore Rousseau*, exhib. cat., Paris, 1967–68, no. 79).

GLASSPLATE PRINTS (CLICHÉS-VERRE)

1862

We are not informed about the conditions under which these two attempts were done, but it can be presumed that, like those of Millet (M 27, 28), they were produced at the request of Cuvelier in Barbizon in 1862, though Osbert Barnard has pointed out that Rousseau had already spent some time in Arras with Cuvelier in 1855. It should be noted, as evidence, that around 1862 Rousseau did a drawing in black chalk on wood as preparation for a painting on the subject of the first of these plates (*T. Rousseau*, exhib. cat., 1967–68, no. 82).

R 5. *The Cherry Tree at La Plante-à-Biau*
Glass plate, 217 × 275 mm.
EARLY PRINTS (BN: *reproduced*).
COUNTERPROOF.
PRINTING for Le Garrec.
GLASS PLATE in the BN.

R 6. *The Plain of La Plante-à-Biau*
Glass plate, 256 × 287 mm.
EARLY PRINTS (BN: *reproduced*).
COUNTERPROOF.
PRINTING for Le Garrec.
GLASS PLATE in the Louvre.

PHOTOGRAPHIC CREDITS

Baltimore, Museum of Art: Daubigny 10, 12, 55, 60, 61, 62, 89, 91, 96, 100, 101, 104, 105, 106, 107, 108, 110, 112, 113, 114, 115.
Chicago, Art Institute: Millet 1, 2, 6, 8, 19, 19 BIS, 19 TER, 19 QUATER, 29, 30.
Middletown, Conn., Davison Art Center, Wesleyan University: 19 QUINTER, 19 QUINTER.
New York, Print Room, Public Library: Daubigny 99, 148; Millet 2, 5, 15, 22, 24, 25, 25 BIS, 26, 26 BIS.
All the other photographs were supplied by the photographic service of the Bibliothèque Nationale, Paris.

ACKNOWLEDGMENTS

Grateful acknowledgment is due all those who made it possible for us to carry through this work, in particular my colleagues abroad: Jay Fisher of Baltimore, Harold Joachim and Anselmo Carini of Chicago, Elizabeth Ross of the New York Public Library, Anthony Griffiths of the British Museum, and Professors Robert L. Herbert of Yale University and Richard S. Field of Wesleyan University. My thanks as well to the Parisian art dealers Paule Cailac, André Jammes, Paul Prouté, and Jean-Claude Romand who gave me free access to their archives; to Mr Méjanès and the personnel of the Chalcographie of the Louvre, and to Mlle. Michaud of the Bibliothèque Thiers. I have a special debt to Madeleine Fidell-Beaufort and Janine Bailly-Herzberg, whose studies on Daubigny and Corot, as well as their good counsel, provided me with a starting point.